RAPE IN
AMERICA

A Reference Handbook

RAPE IN
AMERICA

A Reference Handbook

Rob Hall

**CONTEMPORARY
WORLD ISSUES**

ABC-CLIO

Santa Barbara, California
Denver, Colorado
Oxford, England

Library of Congress Cataloging-in-Publication Data

Hall, Rob.
    Rape in America : a reference handbook / Rob Hall.
       p. cm. — (Contemporary world issues)
    Includes bibliographical references and index.
    1. Rape—United States. I. Title. II. Series.
    HV6561.H337   1995   364.1′532′0973—dc20   95-12102

ISBN 0-87436-730-1

00 99 98 97 96   10 9 8 7 6 5 4 3 2

ABC-CLIO, Inc.
130 Cremona Drive, P.O. Box 1911
Santa Barbara, California 93116-1911

This book is printed on acid-free paper ∞ .

Manufactured in the United States of America

*This book is dedicated to all victims of sexual
assault and to the women and men who
struggle on a daily basis in the war
against sexual violence.*

Contents

Preface

Rape in America: A Reference Handbook is intended to be a complete resource, offering a wide variety of current information under the general heading of sexual assault. The book provides a balanced overview of the historical and current social context of rape in the United States as well as major law enforcement, judicial and correctional system, and psychotherapy trends in dealing with both the rapist and the victim. It examines the legal definition of the term *rape*, identifies the nature of sexual assault through an examination of common rape myths, provides a description of the types and motivations of rapists, and offers statistical profiles of both offender and victim. The book identifies the pros and cons of the major response options to sexual assault, and it discusses the legal, medical, and psychological procedures and ramifications of rape. It also provides a directory of major providers of services for victims and offenders and an annotated bibliography of other print and nonprint resources for further research.

Because it brings together such a wide variety of current information, this book may prove helpful to an equally wide variety of readers—students; scholars; researchers; journalists and other writers; administrators and victim advocates of

women's shelters and rape crisis centers; rape prevention instructors; legislators and other policy makers; law enforcement
officials; and interested laypersons, particularly women who
have been, or fear becoming, victims of sexual assault. Through
the clear presentation of solidly researched information, this
book seeks to dispel common erroneous beliefs regarding sexual
assault.

About the Terms Used in This Book

It is impossible to identify a universal legal definition of the term
rape, as legal definitions vary from state to state. For example, in
Connecticut laws concerning "sexual assault" define the term
sexual assault as either sexual intercourse or sexual contact; sexual
intercourse includes vaginal and anal intercourse, fellatio, and
cunnilingus. Penetration, however slight, is required for fellatio
and vaginal and anal intercourse. This category includes penetration of the vagina or anus by an object manipulated by the assailant. Sexual contact involves any contact by the assailant of the
"intimate parts" (defined as the genital area, groin, anus, inner
thighs, buttocks, or breasts) of the victim. While Alaska's statutes
identify degrees of sexual assault and use in their definitions the
terms *sexual penetration* and *sexual contact*, Virginia's laws concerning criminal sexual assault define rape as penetration by the
penis of the vagina. Other Virginia laws address forcible sodomy
and sexual battery. Oklahoma laws are similar to those of Virginia in that they address forcible sodomy (referred to as "the detestable and abominable crime against nature") and sexual
battery. Oklahoma's definition of rape, however, includes anal
penetration.

On a national level, the *Uniform Crime Report* bases its statistics on reported cases of actual or attempted forced sexual intercourse (both termed *forcible rape*). On both the state and the
national levels, the offense is dependent upon a lack of consent
on the part of the victim or on an inability of the victim to give
legal consent as a result of mental incapacitation due to retardation, mental illness, alcohol, or drugs.

Whether to use the term *rape* or the term *sexual assault* is not
a question of frivolous semantics or legal nit-picking. The choice
of term has practical considerations. Many crisis programs in recent years have changed their name from "rape crisis center" to
"sexual assault crisis center," or some derivative thereof, in an
attempt to more accurately reflect their function and the clientele

they serve. Because for so many years the legal definition of rape specifically required penetration by the penis of the vagina, many state legislatures (as well as authors of professional literature) have replaced the term *rape* with *sexual assault* in an attempt to better define the offense and to make its description more gender neutral. (Bohmer and Parrot 1993; Lynch 1994) Indeed, many find the term *forcible rape* to be an oxymoron. Hospital emergency departments do not perform "rape exams," but rather "forensic gynecological examinations." The examiner is there as a person of science; his or her job is to collect evidence objectively to find the truth, whatever it may be. *Rape* is a legal, not medical, term; to use the term *rape* on an examination form would be inappropriate and considered pejorative to the accused. (Fines 1994; Lynch 1994)

The choice of term also has emotional significance. Because of the stigma that has long been attached to rape (see chapter 3), many advocates and counselors who work with victims prefer the term *sexual assault,* feeling that term to be both more technically accurate and less traumatic for the victim. In fact, many advocates and counselors refer to their clients as rape or sexual assault "survivors," rather than "victims," as a means of stressing the recovery process over the victimization.

The terms used in this book have been chosen carefully, with an attempt to balance technical accuracy with emotional impact and reality. A blend of the more commonly used generic definition and the legal definition of the term *rape* will be used; it will be understood to include all forms of sexual assault and will be used interchangeably with the term *sexual assault* unless otherwise noted. This definition will include, but will not necessarily be limited to, actual or attempted vaginal or anal intercourse, fellatio, cunnilingus, and penetration by a foreign object or digit, performed against the will of the victim and regardless of the victim's response to the attack. It shall be considered rape if any of the above actions are attempted or performed when the victim does not have the ability to consent due to mental or physical incapacitation. *Sexual offender* will be understood to include any individual who commits or attempts to commit sexual assault, regardless of legal ramifications or lack of ramifications of that action.

In most cases the term *victim* will be used to refer to the target of the assault. While recognizing and applauding the positive motivation and potential healing power of the use of the term *survivor*, it is believed that the former more readily reflects the criminal nature of the offense. Until such time that rape is universally recognized as being "one of the cruelest forms of criminal violence" (Abarbanel and Richman 1990), it is important in a work such as this that the criminality of rape be emphasized.

Because the vast majority of sexual assaults are by men against women, the feminine pronoun is most often used in this book in referring to victims of sexual assault, while the masculine pronoun is most often used to refer to assailants. This is not meant to imply that there are not male victims of sexual assault. Just under 8 percent of the men surveyed in the 1991 National Crime Survey reported having been sexually assaulted. There have been known cases of men being raped by women, though most frequently in society men (heterosexual and homosexual) have been raped by other men (heterosexual and homosexual) as an expression of dominance. The incidence of rape in the prison system is believed to be much higher than in the general population, but the "closed" nature of prison society prevents any accurate measure or estimate (see chapter 2). Numerous studies have estimated that between one in five and one in seven boys are sexually assaulted by age 18, most frequently by heterosexual men. A more accurate estimate may never be made, since sexual assault of males is even more underreported than that of females. Given that the majority of rapes are perpetrated by men against women and that the use of the masculine pronoun ("he") or combination of feminine and masculine pronouns ("she/he") to refer to victims would be both unwieldy and confusing, the feminine pronoun will denote victims and the male pronoun will denote assailants unless otherwise noted.

References

Abarbanel, G., and G. Richman. 1990. "The Rape Victim." In *Crisis Intervention Book 2: The Practitioner's Sourcebook for Brief Therapy,* edited by H. J. Parad and L. G. Parad. Milwaukee, WI: Family Service America.

Bohmer, C., and A. Parrot. 1993. *Sexual Assault on Campus: The Problem and the Solution.* New York: Lexington Books.

Fines, P. U. (assistant commonwealth's attorney). 1994. Telephone conversation with the author, 8 July.

Ibid., 5 August 1994.

Lynch, V. (forensic nurse). 1994. Telephone conversation with the author, 14 April.

Acknowledgments

Rape in America is the product of nearly two years of continuous research. My work in that time has brought me in contact with hundreds of individuals, from famous researchers and authors to nearly anonymous victim advocates. With only two or three exceptions, each one of them was passionately committed to the fight against sexual violence, with little regard for personal glory or gain. In fact, several of the more famous individuals declined to be profiled in the biography chapter.

I am in awe of the women and men who work in the trenches of sexual assault victim services and law enforcement. The risk of burnout is tremendous. As Bonnie Palecek said in a letter to me, "Please don't say I worked for anything 'tirelessly.' This work makes everyone tired. . . ." And yet they continue to battle the ignorance and evil that give rise to the sexual victimization of hundreds of thousands of women, children, and men each year, all in the unlikely hope that someday there will be no need for such services. Perhaps, as Ms. Palecek said, ". . . the only 'accomplishment' one can achieve is to continue to engage in the struggle."

Thanks go to Becky Bradway, Virginia Lynch, Pat Groot, Laura Slaughter, Helenmarie Zachritz, Bridgett Reeder, and Phil

Fines for freely giving of their knowledge and experience time and time again, and especially to Ann LaFrance, who offered insight and friendship. I thank my editor, Suzanne Chance, who patiently listened and quietly offered reassurance each time I was going ballistic over some writer's glitch. My thanks to my production editor, Amy B. Catala, who had a kind word when there needed to be one. I thank my mother, Edith Hall, who came across half the country to help me when I needed it. And finally I thank my mate, Leslie, without whose love, support, understanding, encouragement, and brilliance this book would never have been written.

Introduction 1

The Cycle of Rape Victimization

It is quite possible that the cycle of rape victimization begins for some in childhood. Studies have noted correlations of early childhood rape and sexual abuse with both sexual offenders and victims. A. N. Groth and H. J. Birnbaum (1979) found a third of 250 career sex offenders had experienced sexual trauma as children. Nearly half of those traumatized had been sexually assaulted. J. I. Warren, R. R. Hazelwood, and R. Reboussin (1991) found that three-quarters of the 41 serial rapists studied had experienced some type of sexual abuse as children.

Studies have also indicated that a significant percentage of victims of child sexual abuse later became victims of sexual assault as adults. A recent study done in Tulsa of 980 adult women found 13 percent had been molested as children and later raped as adults. The study found that these victims were most likely to be minority women living in poverty. (Novacek et al. 1993)

Findings from studies of sexual assault victims such as those cited above may be better understood by considering the following context. Children are relatively powerless. Sexual abuse of a child can reinforce

1

that sense of powerlessness and establish a programmed response of passivity to sexual aggression. ("I can't do anything to stop it, so to keep from being hurt worse I won't fight back.") While a child raised in a nonabusive environment learns the sanctity of personal physical boundaries, the abused child routinely has those boundaries violated. Repeated violation can result in desensitization—a stripping away of the personal power that would ordinarily alert the victim that personal boundaries are being violated. Such desensitization can leave the sexually abused child vulnerable to revictimization as an adult. As is noted elsewhere in this chapter and in chapter 2, rapists select victims on the basis of their vulnerability. For the sexually abused child/adult rape victim, as with anyone, danger must be recognized before it can be avoided. The adult who was sexually abused as a child may not recognize a sexual predator until it is too late. (Fredrickson 1994; LaFrance 1994)

A study recently conducted by J. White and J. A. Humphrey (1993) at the University of North Carolina at Greensboro may illustrate the increased vulnerability suggested above. White found that women who had been sexually assaulted as adolescents were nearly two and one-half times more likely to be victims of sexual assault their freshman year of college (the year most typically college women are raped) than were women who had not been molested as children.

Sexual abuse of children can also create a deep-seated anger that manifests itself later in life. It is in the manifestation of this anger that socialization plays a key role. Males in society are generally socialized to express anger outwardly through violent means, verbally and/or physically. The desensitization process may also severely degenerate an understanding of and respect for personal physical boundaries in others. It is not uncommon for sexually abused children to attempt to abuse other children. Conversely, women are generally socialized to contain anger, to remain "polite" and "ladylike," and to respond to aggression passively. Anger generated by sexual abuse is often turned by the female victim on herself; internalized in the form of destructive self-blame, guilt, and shame. Coupled with desensitization, anger and shame as a result of childhood sexual abuse ultimately can contribute to the development of both the sexual offender and the victim of sexual assault. (Frederickson 1994; LaFrance 1994)

Alcohol use has been linked as a possible precursor, catalyst, and/or result of sexual assault of both children and adults. Alcohol abuse is a common denominator among convicted rapists, and alcohol use by both assailant and victim is frequently found in cases of date rape (see chapter 5). A study of rape victims in Tulsa found that 23 percent of the victims increased their use of alcohol or drugs as a result of the assault. (Novacek et al. 1993) A longitudinal study of over 4,000 women recently completed by the National Crime Victims Research and Treatment Center at the Medical University of South Carolina in Charleston illustrates such a cycle. The study gathered information from the women about a number of topics, including any personal history of sexual assault or alcohol and drug use. Follow-up interviews were conducted one and two years later. The study identified a group of women who had no history of alcoholism and who were assaulted within the two-year follow-up period. Of this group, approximately 9 percent developed alcohol dependence. The study also found that women who initially reported alcohol dependence were more likely to be assaulted over the following two years than were women who abstained from alcohol and drugs. (Kilpatrick et al. 1994) The cycle continues: sexual assault results in rape trauma syndrome, which in turn increases the victim's risk of alcohol/drug abuse, which in turn increases the victim's risk of revictimization by another assault.

Pornography

Another possible contributor to the cycle of rape victimization is pornography. There has been an ongoing controversy over the relationship of pornography to rape for well over two decades, with no conclusive end in sight. Those who consider pornography to be the "undiluted essence of anti-female propaganda" (Brownmiller 1975) feel that such devaluing of women condones and actively encourages sexual violence against women. As Robin Morgan (1980) states, "pornography is the theory, and rape the practice." While numerous studies have found that convicted rapists regularly viewed pornography, most offender treatment experts believe that the use of pornography is correlational, not causal. (Bradway 1993; Groth and Birnbaum 1979) While pornography may serve a rapist's pre-existing disposition to view such materials, it is uncertain what role it plays in the facilitation and perpetuation of the rape cycle. Some studies have indicated that repeated exposure to sexually violent pornography desensitizes men toward women in general, and rape victims specifically. (Attorney General's Commission on Pornography

1986; Donnerstein 1989) Many experts believe that books and films that objectify and depersonalize women in sexually violent scenarios help the rapist rationalize his offense, because they appear to legitimize abusive sexual activity by men against women. (Freeman-Longo 1989) More conclusive statements will not be possible without much further study, if then. As with analysis of the effectiveness of different treatment programs for sex offenders, the impact of pornography on sexual assault may vary with the form the pornography takes and with the individual viewer.

Problems with Sexual Assault Studies

A major problem with studies of sexual assault in general, and of rapists in particular, lies in who is being studied. There is no picture of a "typical" rapist other than general demographics. The studies that have been done have utilized a select group of the rapist population—those rapists that got caught. This limited focus may not only invalidate general assumptions about a rapist's motivations, but it may also call into question the validity of findings of treatment efficacy. Rapists in prison are generally rapists who have raped extensively and have been caught with enough evidence to warrant a long sentence of incarceration. The studies of Dr. A. Nicholas Groth, a noted pioneer in research of sexual offenders (1979), were of over 500 hard-core rapists, over a 15-year period. A major study of 41 serial rapists by Dr. Janet Warren et al. (1991) was of men who, as a group, had committed 837 rapes, over 400 attempted rapes, and over 5,000 "nuisance" sex offenses. Dr. G. Richard Kishur (former program director for the Resident Sexual Offender Treatment Program with the Oklahoma Department of Corrections—a program recognized nationally and internationally in the early 1990s as one of the most progressive programs of its day) (1994) worked with sexual offenders who had received at least a 15-year sentence for their crimes; offenders who received less than 15 years did not have the option of entering the treatment program. (The *National Corrections Reporting Program, 1988* (1992) states that the median maximum sentence length, excluding "life without parole," "life plus added years," "life," and "death," for rape was 96 months in state prison, and 66 months in federal prison.) All the inmates in Kishur's program voluntarily elected to receive treatment and could discontinue treatment at any time they chose. Dr. Fred S. Berlin (head of the Sexual Disorders Clinic of the National

Institute for the Study, Prevention, and Treatment of Sexual Trauma at Johns Hopkins in Maryland) works with a highly motivated group of offenders who have acknowledged their guilt and have requested treatment. There are probably many rapists who have not built up such a dossier of reported assaults and incriminating evidence with law enforcement agencies or who have simply been saavy enough not to get caught. Such rapists are not reflected in the work of sexual assault researchers.

Another major problem with studies of treatment efficacy is the lack of a control group. Without the presence of a control group, it is impossible for researchers to identify anything as conclusive. The difficulty of establishing such a group is both logistical and ethical. The establishment of a true control would require two separate groups of sex offenders with equal desire for treatment (a precondition of most treatment programs). To deny treatment to a rapist who is genuinely desirous of treatment is ethically questionable. To deny him treatment in order to put him in a control group to see what he will do after he is released from prison is even more questionable, for the researchers would be gambling with the safety (and possibly lives) of innocent members of the community.

In addition to the difficulties noted above, there remains considerable controversy over the efficacy of treatment options currently being used, particularly as regards the physical versus psychological basis for rape (see chapter 2). Proponents of physical or chemical castration (also referred to as pharmacotherapy) assert that a significant proportion of the reasons a rapist rapes is due to biological anomalies, and the urge to rape can be corrected or, at the very least, controlled by adjustments to the offender's physical being. For many who work with victims of sexual assault, this sounds too nearly an absolution of the sex offender on grounds of biologically motivated (and thus beyond his control) behavior and supportive of the "I couldn't stop myself" rationale in date rape situations. Studies of programs utilizing such drugs as Depo-Provero and Lupron, however, have indicated some success of chemical castration, particularly the work of Dr. Fred Berlin at Johns Hopkins. Proponents of such programs attribute their success to the fact that the drugs depress/suppress the production of testosterone—thus lending weight to the belief in biological influence on sexual assault. Yet, the depression/suppression of testosterone does not explain why prepubescent male children have been able to obtain and maintain an erection and successfully rape other children (in some cases with ejaculation).

The only thing that is clear about the treatment of offenders is that there is no one effective "cure." Studies and surveys over the decades have often contradicted others' findings, while follow-up studies by the same researcher or institution have on occasion contradicted the findings of their previous study. The wide diversity within the rapist population makes it seemingly impossible for any treatment method developed to date to be touted as "the" answer. Behavior therapy seeks to control and redirect the offender's impulses, but it addresses the action rather than the cause of the behavior. Various forms of psychotherapy are only useful if the offender does, in fact, genuinely want to change. The results of physical castration may be a correlational reflection of the offender's motivation to change rather than a causal result of the removal of the testicles. Chemical castration is temporary, expensive, and prone to side effects, which reverse with the cessation of its administration. Ultimately, the most effective treatments are likely to be those that utilize a wide variety of treatment methods, with the recognition that there will still be offenders for whom no type or amount of treatment will work. (Types of treatment and the difficulty of determining treatment efficacy are discussed further in chapter 2.) In the final analysis, the only means by which society is guaranteed safety from convicted rapists is not treatment, but containment through incarceration or institutionalization.

Studies and crime statistics indicate that rapists tend to be young men, most often in their twenties. (See chapter 2 for more specific figures.) The number of convictions and the level of observed aggressiveness decrease significantly after age 45. (Federal Bureau of Investigation 1992; Groth and Birnbaum 1979) Unfortunately for society, the average length of incarceration falls far short of the time needed for rapists to age into the "less aggressive" age group.

A Contemporary View of Sexual Assault

One approach to exploring a society's view of a subject is to examine common myths regarding that subject. A 1994 survey of over 120 rape crisis centers around the country indicated that it is important for a reference work on rape to identify and debunk common myths about rape and sexual assault. (Hall 1994) While much of the information contained in the following section is presented in greater detail in chapters 2 and 5, an examination of the following common "rape myths" provides insight with regard to the nature of sexual assault, the perpetrators, and the victims.

Myth: Sexual assault has nothing to do with sex (or) sexual assault is a crime of sexual passion.

Rape is a form of sexual assault and is an act of aggression. It is a crime of violence that uses sexuality as a weapon. The rapist uses sex to express anger, to control, degrade, humiliate, and hurt the victim. Sexual assault is a sexual act (including forced intercourse, sodomy, cunnilingus, fellatio, and penetration by a digit or foreign object) done against the will of the victim. Rape is a sexual behavior done primarily to satisfy nonsexual desires.

Myth: Rapes usually occur at night in alleys, parks, and the like.

A high percentage of rapes occur in the victim's home, or at the home of someone the victim trusted; the next most common place of assault is in a car.

Myth: Rape usually involves a black assailant and a white victim.

Numerous studies have shown rape to be primarily intraracial, not interracial; victims and assailants are most frequently of the same race.

Myth: If a woman leads a man on, or allows him to spend a great deal of money on her, or changes her mind after having commenced foreplay, the man has a right to sex.

Sexual assault is a forced sexual act (including intercourse, sodomy, cunnilingus, fellatio, and penetration by a digit or foreign object) done against the will, or without the consent, of the victim. Without consent it is a crime, regardless of the previous actions of the victim or the assailant.

Myth: If there was no semen present, there was no rape.

While this argument was presented in court for many years, recent studies belie such statements. Studies of convicted rapists have found that between 34 percent and 58 percent experienced sexual dysfunction in the form of impotence, premature ejaculation, or retarded ejaculation, thus accounting for a lack of semen present. Additionally, in cases in which the assault was interrupted by external factors or brought to a halt by victim resistance prior to the rapist having an orgasm, there would not be semen present.

Myth: The sexual assailant is most often a stranger.

In all dynamics the sexual assailant is most frequently someone known to the victim. The most common estimate is that approximately 80 percent of all sexual assailants are known to the victim.

Myth: A rapist is a psychopath and looks like one.

Rapists come from all walks of life, frequently have families, and include clergy, policemen, teachers, and others who are generally respected as "model citizens." Most often the rapist is someone known to, and trusted by, the victim.

Myth: The rapist is most frequently a "sex starved" pervert.

The majority of convicted rapists had regular sexual outlets (via spouse, significant other, or lover) at the time of their offenses. They did not rape out of sexual frustration, but for the emotional gratification they received from the act of sexual violence.

Myth: A rapist is a man who cannot control his sexual desires.

Rape is most often a premeditated crime. It is an act of aggression and sexual violence, not an expression of sexual desire.

Myth: A husband cannot be found guilty of raping his wife.

As of the fall of 1993, all 50 states had removed the automatic "spousal exemption" from their laws on rape and sexual assault. A husband in the United States can be tried for the rape of his wife.

Myth: The victim was "asking for it" by the manner in which she was dressed, by flirting, or by where she was walking or spending time (such as a bar or the assailant's dwelling).

Rape is an act of violence that hurts the victim physically and psychologically, often for many years after the assault. No one asks to be hurt, and no one has the right to force another person to engage in sex, regardless of circumstances or the victim's prior actions. The attitude that the victim "asked for it" takes the responsibility for the attack away from the assailant, shifting it to the victim. Ironically, those who suggest victim complicity in a rape generally do not apply the same standards to victims of other violent crimes. Generally speaking, no one blames the victim of a mugging for wearing a watch, carrying a wallet or purse, or having an armful of groceries.

Myth: Rape only happens to certain kinds of women.

Rape happens to women of all ages, from babies a few months old to women in their nineties. Victims of sexual assault come from all races and socioeconomic, ethnic, and religious groups.

Myth: No one would rape an "unattractive" woman; rape only happens to young, "sexy" women.

Victims are chosen on the basis of their vulnerability, not their physical appearance. Rape victims are of all physical types, appearances, and ages.

✓**Myth:** No woman can be raped against her will; it is physically impossible to rape a woman who does not want to be raped.

Rape is most frequently committed through the use of force or threat of force. Rape is not sex; it is a physical assault. Any individual, male or female, can be physically overcome by a larger and stronger assailant. Any individual, male or female, can have their life threatened by a weapon.

✓**Myth:** A male cannot be raped.

The rape of males is believed to be even more underreported than that of females. (It is currently believed that between 50 percent and 90 percent of all rapes of females go unreported.) Numerous studies have indicated that between one in five and one in seven males have been sexually abused (including rape) by their eighteenth birthday. While both male children and male adults have been raped by females, they are more frequently raped by other heterosexual males. Male children are more likely to be assaulted by heterosexual men than by women or homosexual men. Very young males are most likely to be assaulted by family members or caretakers, young teenagers by authority figures, and young adult males by peers or older adults.

✓**Myth:** Women enjoy being raped.

Rape is not an act of "rough sex." Rape by its very nature is an unwanted act of violence against both the body and mind of the victim. It violates and destroys the victim's normal perception of and assumptions about her world; highly valued beliefs of trust and safety are shattered. The psychological damage of rape lasts long after the physical damage has healed. There is nothing enjoyable about such violation. The male who suggests that a woman should "just lie back and enjoy it" if rape is unavoidable has not considered the analogy of his being overpowered (by physical means or threat) and sodomized, and the amount of enjoyment he would derive from that act of violence upon himself.

✗**Myth:** Women frequently have an orgasm while being raped.

While it is theoretically possible for a woman or a man to experience an orgasm while being raped, it is a very rare occurrence. An orgasm under those conditions is a physiological response; a result of fear/adrenaline and direct stimulation through cunnilingus, fellatio, or manual stimulation. It is not an indication of sexual arousal. There have been cases noted in which heterosexual males who were being raped by other males had a physical orgasm as a result of the assailant masturbating them. There have also been cases in which males who were being raped by women (most commonly male children raped by older women) got and maintained an erection in a stressful and fearful situation. In such cases the ensuing orgasm was a physiological response rather than a result of sexual arousal. The difference between having an orgasm as a physiological response and being sexually aroused is crucial. Rape victims frequently experience a great deal of guilt and self-blame as a result of the rape; having had such a physiological response could exacerbate those feelings and cause the victim to erroneously question her own sexual inclination.

For most of the history of America rape has been a hidden crime, rarely acknowledged in private, and never talked about in polite society. Thanks to the feminist movement and organized "rape speakouts" the taboo began to be lifted in the early 1970s. Since then, the prevalence of the rape of adult females has gradually been brought to light (though the rape of children and males remains deeply shrouded), and significant legal and social changes have occurred. Victim shield laws have been written and passed in an attempt to encourage rape victims to prosecute their assailants, as well as to protect victims from a second victimization by character assassination (see chapter 2). States have eliminated the "utmost physical resistance" requirement from sexual assault laws; that requirement had demanded that a rape victim fight and continue to fight her attacker until she is physically unable to continue, lest she be judged to have "consented" to the rape. While numerous conditions remain, there is no longer an automatic legal immunity for husbands who rape their wives. Federal funding is now tied to the required reporting of sexual assaults that take place on college campuses, thereby preventing administrations from covering up or burying sexual assaults for purposes of image preservation. Colleges are now required by the Ramstad Amendment to develop and publicize a campus sexual assault policy (see chapter 3).

The number of rapes being reported to police grows each year. Although some may view this trend as a sign of an increasingly violent society, more likely it signifies a greater willingness on the part of sexual assault victims to publicize the offense. Law enforcement officials are gradually becoming more sensitized and are developing special sex crime units as well as special training programs for street-level officers dealing with sexual assault cases. According to the 1994 survey of over 120 rape crisis centers around the country, the majority of the centers felt that the sensitivity of local law enforcement officials, and the center's relationship with those officials, had significantly improved from five years earlier. (Hall 1994)

Another positive step is the recognition of, and provision of services for, male victims of rape. Within the group of rape crisis centers that responded to the survey cited above, virtually all the centers offered crisis counseling to male victims, and 56 percent had male advocates/peer counselors on staff. Rape crisis centers continue to develop and network through coalitions, as they seek to educate and serve more and more of the population.

Despite recent progress, there are still many problems. Sexual assault remains the most underreported crime. Not all law enforcement departments have embraced a new awareness of and sensitivity to sexual assault issues and investigative procedures; the "good ole' boy" mentality still thrives in some departments, and sexual assault victims often pay the price (see Law Enforcement System in chapter 2). Of the reported rape cases that do result in arrest, trial, and conviction, the vast majority of the convictions resulted from a guilty plea, suggesting that most of the cases brought to trial were very solid from the beginning (see Judicial System in chapter 2). While states may maintain a special victim's compensation fund that is supposed to pay for sexual assault examinations, in many cases the funds are exhausted before the end of the fiscal year, potentially leaving the victims open to collection proceedings. Some funding amounts for sexual assault examinations are far below the actual cost of the examinations, resulting in an even greater economic impact of sexual assault, as well as the potential for additional trauma for the victim (see New Mexico Coalition of Sexual Assault Programs in chapter 6). For funding for sexual assault examinations some states require the victim only to *report* the assault to the police, while others require a *commitment to prosecute*, potentially forcing the victim to choose between needed medical attention and keeping her victimization confidential.

While institutions of higher learning have received federal mandates, many are still floundering in their attempts to develop and institute policies that actively protect the rights of victims and that provide a clear academic due process for the investigation and prosecution of sexual assault on campus. Sexual assault on campus is a major problem in the United States, and sexual assault education aimed at prevention is still in its infancy at many (if not most) institutions.

There are more rape crisis centers, but many are in dire need of funding. In 1994, 21 percent of the centers surveyed reported their financial situation as "poor" or "shakey." An additional 27 percent reported their financial status as "fair." Only 9 percent reported their financial situation as "excellent." (Hall 1994) Many centers receive little or no state funding and are dependent upon locally administered sources, such as United Way, for survival. Such funds can vary in amount from year to year, depending on donations, funding priorities, and politics. The vast majority of survey respondents identified "funding stability" as their center's greatest need. Lack of funding translates directly into lack of needed staff. In recent years numerous rape crisis centers have merged with domestic violence service centers in order to financially survive. Other crisis centers have had to discontinue counseling of rape victims by trained therapists on staff, and now they can only offer short-term peer counseling by advocates and referrals to professionals in private practice. Many of the state coalitions operate with a volunteer staff or, at best, a skeleton paid staff.

Unity among crisis centers and coalitions is a problem on both the state and national levels. In several states political differences keep individual crisis centers from joining the state coalition. This divisiveness limits networking and support possibilities, and it diminishes the political clout of sexual assault services on the state level. National organizations suffer from the same sort of communication and organizational problems; one such organization has even had difficulty publishing a membership directory that accurately places members in the correct state.

Conclusion

Until the public is better educated about the realities of rape:

> Rape myths, which still abound in contemporary society and are often a major obstacle the prosecution faces in obtaining a conviction from a jury in acquaintance rape trials, will be perpetuated

> Lack of funding for the training of police and prosecutors will continue

> Rape crisis centers will go on suffering from a lack of funding (for staff and services) that severely limits their effectiveness

The tide of battle in the war against rape by strangers, acquaintances, friends, family, lovers, and mates will not be
turned

Without further education, all of the above will continue to
facilitate the cycle of rape victimization.

References

Attorney General's Commission on Pornography. 1986. *Final Report.*
Washington, DC: U.S. Department of Justice.

Bradway, B. 1993. "Pornography." In *Sexual Violence: Facts and Statistics.*
Springfield, IL: Coalition Against Sexual Assault.

Brownmiller, S. 1975. *Against Our Will: Men, Women, and Rape.* New York:
Simon & Schuster.

Bureau of Justice Statistics. 1992. *National Corrections Reporting Program,
1988.* Washington, DC: U.S. Department of Justice.

Davis, A. J. 1970. "Sexual Assaults in the Philadelphia Prison System." In
The Sexual Scene, edited by J. Gagnon and W. Simon. Chicago:
Transaction/Aldine.

Donnerstein, E. "Testing Theories: Social Science Research." In
Rosenberg, J. 1989. *Fuel on the Fire.* Brandon, VT: Safer Society Press.

Federal Bureau of Investigation. 1992. *Uniform Crime Report 1991.*
Washington, DC: U.S. Department of Justice.

Fredrickson, J. (psychotherapist). 1994. Conversation with the author.
Oklahoma City, OK, 5 August.

Freeman-Longo, R. "Opinions of Sex-Offender Treatment Specialists." In
Rosenberg, J. 1989. *Fuel on the Fire.* Brandon, VT: Safer Society Press.

Groth, A. N., and H. J. Birnbaum. 1979. *Men Who Rape: The Psychology of
the Offender.* New York: Plenum Publishing.

Hall, R. 1994. A survey of rape crisis centers in the United States.
Unpublished data.

Kilpatrick, D. G., et al. 1994. "Violent Assault and Alcohol Dependence
among Women: Results of a Longitudinal Study." Paper presented at the
annual meeting of the Research Society on Alcoholism, June, in Maui,
HI. In *Science News* 146 (1), 2 July.

Kishur, G. R. 1994. Interview with the author. Oklahoma City, OK, 12
July.

LaFrance, A. (psychotherapist). 1994. Telephone conversation with the
author, 25 July.

Ibid., 27 July.

Lynch, V. (forensic nurse). 1994. Telephone conversation with the author, 14 April.

Morgan. R. 1980. "Theory and Practice: Pornography and Rape." In *Take Back the Night*, edited by L. Lederer. New York: William Morrow.

Novacek, J., R. Raskin, D. Bahlinger, L. Firth, and S. Rybicki. 1993. *Rape: Tulsa Women Speak Out*. Tulsa, OK: Tulsa Institute of Behavioral Sciences.

Warren, J. I., R. R. Hazelwood, and R. Reboussin. 1991. "Serial Rape: The Offender and His Rape Career." In *Rape and Sexual Assault III*, edited by A. Burgess. New York: Garland Publishing.

White, J., and J. A. Humphrey. 1993. "Sexual Revictimization: A Longitudinal Perspective." Paper presented at symposium, 101st annual convention of the American Psychological Association, 20–24 August, in Toronto, Canada.

Procedures, Trends, and Developments

2

A ny addressment of the problem of rape and sexual assault in the United States must consider the various agencies that react to, and deal with, this form of criminal behavior. These agencies include, but are not limited to, the law enforcement, judicial, and correctional systems. This chapter deals with the part each plays in the war against sexual violence.

Law Enforcement System

According to the 1991 *Uniform Crime Report* for the United States (Federal Bureau of Investigation 1992), there were 92,398 forcible rapes known to law enforcement officials in 1991. This number includes assaults or attempts to commit rape by force or threat of force. It does not include statutory rape without force and other sex offenses, nor does it include reports of rapes deemed "unfounded" by law enforcement officials. Additionally, the number does not include actual rape figures from Illinois, and the figures from Iowa are estimated. It also does not include cases of male rape, reflecting known rapes of females only. (Federal Bureau of Investigation 1992) As is discussed in chapter 5, this number represents only a small percentage of the rapes that occur each year (Figure 2-1). Numerous large-scale studies conducted between 1979 and 1990 have resulted in rape prevalence estimates in the range of 15 to 25 percent of the female population. (Koss 1992)

A case is considered "cleared" by law enforcement officials when it is no longer being actively investigated as an unsolved crime. A case is cleared when a suspect is arrested or when the investigation is discontinued due to a lack of cooperation from the victim. In 1991 law enforcement officials cleared 52 percent of the reported rapes by arrest, a drop of 1 percent from the previous year. (Federal Bureau of Investigation 1992) In both the "over 18" and "under 18" categories, white males composed 55 percent of all males arrested for rape, while black males composed 44 percent of the total arrests. (Federal Bureau of Investigation 1992) Percentages were much closer in city arrests: 51 percent of those under 18 arrested were white, and 48 percent were black. Slightly more suspects in the "over 18" category were black (50 percent), compared to a lower percentage of whites (49 percent). (Federal Bureau of Investigation 1992) The greatest percentage of those males arrested for rape were between 20 and 24 years old (19.8 percent), followed by those 15 to 19 years old (18.8 percent), and those 25 to 29 years old (18.1 percent). Breaking the above groupings into separate age brackets, arrest figures for 18-year-olds topped the list, followed by those for 19-year-olds. There were 81 males under 10 years old arrested for rape in 1991 (Figure 2-2). A total of 386 females were charged with forcible rape in 1991, accounting for 1.3 percent of the total number of rapes. Females 18 and over accounted for 77 percent of those charged, with the largest percentage being those between 25 and 29 years of age (18 percent). (Federal Bureau of Investigation 1992)

Unfounded Rate

A certain percentage of all reported crimes each year are determined to be false or without sufficient evidence to support the claim of the offense. This percentage is termed the "unfounded" rate. Much to the chagrin of rape crisis workers, the national unfounded rate for forcible rape is higher than that of any other Crime Index offense. In 1991, 8 percent of forcible rape complaints were determined to be unfounded. The average for all Crime Index crimes was 2 percent. (Federal Bureau of Investigation 1992) In a related study, three non-police researchers reviewed 222 police files on reported rapes in a major metropolitan area, and they rated 28 percent of the cases "doubtful" as to whether a rape actually had occurred. The primary bases for this rating were inconsistencies in the victim's account of the assault and/or doubts raised by the described circumstances of the assault regarding the complainant's alleged lack of consent. The study found that the reports rated "doubtful" by the outside reviewers were more likely not to have ended in arrest (due to a lack of sufficient evidence) than were the reports the reviewers rated as being more legitimate. (Novacek et al. 1993)

Attitudes toward the Victim

The attitudes displayed by police officers toward victims of rape through the years has been a reflection of the evidentiary requirements of the court coupled with societal myths and attitudes about rape. A study of police in the Philadelphia area in the late 1970s found that male police officers were more likely to question the credibility of "extremely obese women" and "women who (had) seen psychiatrists" (and therefore classify the report as "unfounded"). (McCahill et al. 1979) This clearly reflected the societal myths that no one would rape an "unattractive" woman (rape being an act of sex) and that women with any history of therapy would be more likely to falsely claim rape than actually to have been a victim. A report published in 1980 found that police were influenced—either positively or negatively—by apparent physical evidence of an assault, the amount of time elapsed between the incident and the report of it, the consistency of the victim's story, and the social relationship between the victim and the assailant. (Feldman-Summers and Palmer 1980) The report was prepared in a time prior to the widespread implementation and acceptance of "victim shield" laws and before the abolishment of "evidence of earnest resistance" (i.e., proof of physical resistance) laws and corroboration requirements. The Federal Rule of Evidence 412—the federal "victim shield" law— was promulgated by the Supreme Court in 1978, yet a study conducted in the early 1990s found that the more a victim pleaded and physically resisted the assault, as opposed to giving her coerced consent, the more likely her report would be judged legitimate. (Novacek et al. 1993)

With the gradual revision of state statutes, and the accompanying changes in courtroom procedure, has come the development and refinement of police officer recruit training curriculum in many parts of the country. Most major metropolitan departments have developed special sex crimes units, whose members receive specialized training in dealing with victims of sex crimes. Some jurisdictions, however, have not changed dramatically from the late 1970s and early 1980s. Jeanne Boylan (1993), on a national television talk show, noted that new officers and sex crime investigators may be generally more sensitive, but members of the old regime are now in positions of power, significantly curtailing change. In a recent survey, over 120 rape crisis centers rated their relationship with local law enforcement agencies on a scale of 1 to 10, with "1" being extremely adversarial and "10" being extremely cooperative. Ratings ranged from "1" in a southern county and "3" in a major West Coast metropolitan area to "10" in several small towns in rural areas around the country. The mean rating was 7.2 and the median was 8.0, with a standard deviation of 2.312. A comparison with ratings given local district attorneys' offices found that 35 percent of the centers felt that the police were more cooperative than the local district attorney's office, 37 percent found them to be less cooperative than the district attorney's office, and 28 percent rated the two agencies equally. (Hall 1994)

Investigative Procedure

Due to a number of department-specific variables, the actual investigative procedure followed by the responding law enforcement agency may differ slightly from the one outlined below. Major metropolitan police departments may have specialized sex crime units that will assume the investigation following the initial contact by a uniformed officer; in smaller departments the case may be handled by the same detective that investigates burglaries and car thefts. Larger departments may have the personnel to handle several aspects of the investigation simultaneously (interviewing the victim and canvassing the area for other witnesses, for example), while smaller agencies may be restricted to pursuing information one step at a time. The investigation of a rape that is reported within hours of the assault may be handled differently than one that is reported a week later. While the size of the agency, the training its officers have received in dealing with sexual assault cases, and the specifics of the crime itself may necessitate some variation in sequence, the major processes and emphasis will generally remain the same. (National Institute of Law Enforcement and Criminal Justice 1978)

The main priorities of the first officer on the scene are to establish if the victim is still in danger (the presence of a violent perpetrator) and to tend to the immediate medical needs of the victim. The following questions must be addressed immediately: Is there evidence of serious physical injury? Is an Emergency Medical Service team required? What is the mental and emotional condition of the victim? Is there someone who needs to be contacted? If the circumstances permit, the officer conducts an initial interview, in which he seeks to establish the identity or physical description of the assailant, the vehicle he was driving, etc. The length and depth of the initial interview is determined by the condition of the victim and/or the procedural function of the officer within his or her police department. Depending on the circumstances of the assault and the victim's condition, the officer may forego the initial interview and immediately transport the victim to an appropriate medical facility for a full rape examination (see chapter 5 for hospital procedures).

If the location of the assault is accessible (the victim's home or vehicle, for example), the officer secures, or has secured, the crime scene for processing by other police personnel. Access to the area is strictly limited to authorized personnel, in order that evidence is preserved intact until it is collected. If the victim is present, the officer asks her what items the assailant may have touched with any part of his body (a glass, a towel, a knife, etc.).

The crime scene is processed to obtain evidence needed to identify and/or prosecute the assailant. Typical evidence might include bedding and clothing that possibly contain traces of the suspect (clothing fibers, hair follicles, bodily fluids, etc.), items handled by the suspect, items left at the scene (such as buttons, parts of clothing, etc.), footprints, or tire tracks. The clothes the victim was wearing at the time of the attack are also collected and sent, along with the other evidence, to a crime lab for forensic analysis.

The area is canvassed for witnesses. Officers identify any potential witnesses, acquiring their names, addresses, phone numbers, and where and how they can be reached. At this time, pertinent statements are taken. Witnesses are asked for any relevant descriptions (of the suspect, the suspect's vehicle, weapon, etc.) as well as their relationship (if any) to the victim and/or the suspect. Depending on the circumstances of the case, there may be several follow-up interviews with the witnesses.

At some point the victim is interviewed extensively, possibly many times. Depending on the circumstances and the department's procedural guidelines, the first extensive interview may be conducted by the responding officer at the time of the initial report, or it may be conducted by detectives at a later time. This interview must further establish the particulars of the crime, in much greater detail than in the initial interview. The interviewer must establish the specific circumstances of the crime: the identity of the assailant (by name or description), what transpired, and the location and time of the alleged crime.

Historically, the majority of rapes of adult victims reported to law enforcement officials have been "stranger rapes"—rapes committed by assailants unknown to the victim (see chapter 5). The number of reported acquaintance rapes, however, increases each year, narrowing the gap between the figures. The majority of reported cases of child rape have traditionally involved rapists known to the victim. (Carlton 1994) In cases of "stranger" rapes, it is very likely that the assailant has committed other rapes and has established a unique pattern of assault. For this reason, the interviewer seeks information that will allow a profile of the offender to be created. This is a complex process, the success of which can hinge on detailed information acquired from the victim. For purposes of identification, the interviewer needs to know specifically everything that happened leading up to, during, and following the attack. A common complaint of rape victims has been that they were repeatedly asked the same questions or asked questions that they felt questioned the validity of their report. Although the officer's probing is not meant to be antagonistic or to display disbelief, attempts to draw out and clarify details may give that impression. For example, the investigator may ask the victim several times to repeat every word she remembers her attacker saying, as they may be typical of that rapist. The victim may be asked why she responded to the attack in a particular manner, not to question whether a rape took place, but rather to establish what method the rapist used to gain and maintain control of the victim. The victim may be asked specific questions about any sexual dysfunction the rapist experienced, as research has indicated that approximately one-third of the rapists studied experience some type of sexual dysfunction during the attack (see chapter 5). (Groth and Burgess 1977) Key words and specific actions may link the attacker to other rapes and help establish a pattern that will ultimately result in his arrest. (Hazelwood 1993)

Follow-up interviews may require the victim to go back over the details of the attack, as other details may be remembered with the passage of time. If the attacker was a stranger, the victim may be asked to view mug shots or to work with a sketch artist. If the police locate and arrest a suspect, the victim may be asked to view a line-up. To avoid any challenge in court that the victim was influenced by seeing the suspect prior to the line-up, the police will often take pains to ensure that the victim does not have the opportunity to see the offender prior to the line-up. As a further protection, many departments now photograph all members of a line-up prior to the victim viewing them, as evidence that the selection of non-suspects for the line-up did not serve to bias the witness (i.e., that all members of the line-up sufficiently resembled the actual suspect). The victim's viewing of the line-up is done through a one-way mirror so that the suspect is unable to see her. In some instances the victim may be asked to view a photo line-up rather than a "live" one. A victim's inability to identify her attacker, either as a result of the trauma or because of the circumstances of the attack, does not automatically mean that the suspect will not be prosecuted. Other types of evidence will be considered in making that determination. Once the general facts of the attack have been established and a suspect has been sufficiently identified, the case is presented to the District Attorney's Office for consideration. The decision of whether or not to prosecute the suspect is made by the district attorney, not by the police.

The Judicial System

The number of rape suspects prosecuted in federal district court has shown a gradual increase over the years. In 1985 U.S. attorneys prosecuted in federal district court 60 percent of the suspects arrested for rape in their jurisdiction. By 1988 the number had risen to 61.5 percent, and in 1989 they prosecuted 68 percent of those arrested (a total of 151 cases tried). (Bureau of Justice Statistics 1992b) Of the 68 percent prosecuted in 1989, 86 percent were convicted. This figure represents 58.5 percent of those suspects initially arrested for rape.

State courts have generally prosecuted a greater percentage of arrested suspects, but obtained convictions of a smaller percentage. (Bureau of Justice Statistics 1992b) Information voluntarily supplied by eight states (Alaska, California, Kentucky, Minnesota, Missouri, New York, Oregon, and Pennsylvania) indicate that in 1988 states' attorneys prosecuted 77 percent of those arrested for rape. (Bureau of Justice Statistics 1991) Convictions were obtained in 62 percent of those cases (based on information supplied by the same eight states plus six others:

Alabama, Delaware, Nebraska, Utah, Vermont, and Virginia). Those convictions represented 48 percent of those suspects initially arrested for rape (Figure 2-3).

There were 116 rape convictions in U.S. District Court in 1988. (Bureau of Justice Statistics 1992b) On the state level in 1988, there were approximately 15,562 rape convictions nationally. Approximately 64 percent of the convicted rapists were white, and 33 percent were black. Approximately 72 percent of the rapists were between 20 and 39 years of age, equally divided between the 20 to 29 and the 30 to 39 age groups. (Bureau of Justice Statistics 1992b) It is of significant note that of those convicted 5 percent were found guilty by the bench, and 18 percent were convicted by a jury. The remaining 77 percent of rape convictions resulted from a guilty plea. (Bureau of Justice Statistics 1992b) These figures may suggest that only the most "solid" cases end up being prosecuted.

Rape victim advocates frequently complain that prosecutors are reluctant to prosecute "tough" cases, i.e., cases in which there is not an overabundance of evidence of the assailant's guilt. The fact that in 77 percent of rape convictions the prosecutor, by virtue of the defendant's guilty plea, did not have to convince a judge or jury lends credence to such complaints.

In a recent survey, over 120 rape crisis centers rated their relationship with local district attorneys' offices on a scale of 1 to 10, with "1" being extremely adversarial and "10" being extremely cooperative. Ratings ranged from "3" in a major West Coast metropolitan area to "10" in several small towns in rural areas around the country. The mean rating was 7.4 and the median was 8.0, with a standard deviation of 2.022. A comparison with ratings given local law enforcement agencies (see Attitudes toward the Victim above) found that 35 percent of the centers felt the local district attorney's office was less cooperative than the local police department, 37 percent found them to be more cooperative than the police, and 28 percent rated the two agencies equally. (Hall 1994)

The percentage of convicted rapists sentenced to incarceration by a federal district court has fluctuated over the years. In 1985, 80 percent of those convicted were sentenced to incarceration. The figure rose to 87.4 percent in 1987, dropped slightly to 83.6 percent in 1988, and dropped even further to 77.7 percent in 1989. This 77.7 percent represented 45 percent of those suspects initially arrested for rape. (Bureau of Justice Statistics 1992b)

In 1988, 87 percent of those convicted of rape on the state level were sentenced to incarceration. This represented 42 percent of those suspects initially arrested for rape. Of those sentenced to incarceration, 69 percent were incarcerated in state prisons, 18 percent in city or county jails (Figure 2-3). (Bureau of Justice Statistics 1992b)

Sentence lengths for both jail and prison are identified here as either "mean" maximum sentence length in months, or "median" maximum sentence length in months. The mean length is calculated by adding the lengths of the different sentences (with the exceptions noted below) and dividing by the number of sentences. The mean length may not be the length of a typical sentence because very large or very small individual sentence lengths can have a considerable effect on the mean calculation. The median sentence length may be more representative of a typical sentence length, since the median is less affected by extreme values. It is calculated by sorting the individual sentence lengths from smallest to largest and then selecting the sentence length that is in the middle position. For example, if there are nine sentence lengths, there will be four sentence lengths that are less than the median sentence and four that are greater than the median length.

Contradictions in source materials make it impossible to determine the mean or median sentence received by rapists in state court. The Bureau of Justice Statistics' *Sourcebook of Criminal Justice Statistics* (1992b) states that the mean prison sentence (excluding "life in prison" and "death") in 1988 was 183 months. The *National Corrections Reporting Program (NCRP), 1988* (1992), also published by the Bureau of Justice Statistics, states that the mean maximum sentence length (excluding "life without parole," "life plus added years," "life," and "death") in state prison for the crime of rape was 117 months, a difference of five and one-half years. The *NCRP, 1988* goes on to state that the median maximum sentence length (with the above exclusions) in state prison for rape was 96 months. The same source states that the mean maximum sentence length (excluding sentences of "life") in federal prison for rape was 126 months, and that the median maximum sentence (including "life") was 66 months. The mean maximum sentence length in state prison for other sexual assaults (excluding "life without parole," "life plus added years," "life," and "death") was 75 months. The median sentence was 60 months. Sentence length should not be confused with actual time served. While efforts are under way in various state legislatures to establish "truth in sentencing" (where a ten-year sentence means that the prisoner actually spends a full ten years incarcerated), in the vast majority of cases the offender is released from incarceration prior to the completion of his full sentence. Such early release may occur if the prisoner is paroled due to good behavior exhibited in prison, time credit earned by working various jobs while incarcerated, indicated rehabilitation through therapy, extenuating circumstances, prison overcrowding, or combinations of any of the above. Depending on the state and institution, it is not uncommon for a convicted rapist to serve four or five years (or less) of a ten-year sentence. (See Correctional System: Actual Time Served below.)

Judicial System Procedures

Post-Arrest

Following the arrest, identification, and formal charging of the accused rapist, the victim meets with the assigned prosecutor to prepare for the case to go to trial. At this meeting the prosecutor again goes over the details of the attack, paying particular attention to areas of testimony that could weaken the prosecution of the defendant. The prosecutor may be quite zealous in questioning the victim at this stage, as it is of extreme importance that no information be withheld from the prosecutor. The introduction in court by the defense attorney of information withheld by the victim can severely weaken the prosecution's case. The victim serves as a witness to a crime against the state. Accordingly, evidence of withheld information serves to impeach the witness's credibility before the court. (Fairstein 1993)

The victim is under no obligation to speak with the accused's defense attorney at this time, though the attorney may attempt to contact the victim. Victims may ask the prosecutor if this is likely to occur and find out what they should do or say if so contacted.

There are two possible types of hearings that occur next: a preliminary hearing before a judge or a grand jury hearing. The preliminary hearing is held in open court before a judge to determine if there is sufficient probable cause to have a trial. ("Sufficient probable cause to have a trial" means that the evidence presented is such that it would induce a reasonably intelligent/prudent person to believe that the accused committed the crime.) The victim, suspect, defense attorney, and prosecutor are all present. If the judge determines that, based on the evidence presented, there is not probable cause, the case is dismissed. If the determination is made that there is probable cause, the case is referred for trial.

The procedure followed by a grand jury may vary from state to state and from jurisdiction to jurisdiction, but generally the grand jury hears from individual witnesses who are brought in to testify and then removed. A grand jury hearing is held in private; the suspect and defense attorney are not present. The prosecutor, depending on the jurisdiction, may or may not be present. If present, he or she may present a summation of the evidence to the grand jury. The victim may or may not be present, depending on whether the prosecutor feels that it is necessary for the victim to be there. If the victim is present, she is asked questions about the crime. After the prosecution's evidence has been presented, the grand jury then determines if the case is to be dismissed or tried. If the case is dismissed following either a preliminary or grand jury hearing, the victim's only option is to pursue the matter in civil court.

Following an indictment by the grand jury or the bench, the suspect is arraigned. The victim does not have to be present at the arraignment. The suspect appears before a judge and is informed of the charges filed against him. He is informed of his rights and allowed to plead guilty or not guilty. If the suspect pleads guilty, there is no trial, and a date is then set for sentencing.

Frequently following the indictment for rape, efforts are made on the part of the defense attorney or the prosecutor to obtain a plea bargain—a deal the prosecutor makes with the accused. In most plea bargains, the primary charge is dropped in return for a guilty plea to a lesser charge. This allows the prosecution to avoid a potentially lengthy legal process, ensures that the suspect will be convicted of a crime and will receive at least some punishment, and spares the victim the additional stress of a trial. In many cases, a plea bargain results in a significantly shorter sentence than the accused would have received if convicted of rape. While the victim has no power to authorize or reject a plea bargain, she can generally voice her opinion to the prosecutor beforehand.

If the suspect does not plead guilty and no plea bargain is reached, the case goes to trial. The accused is allowed to select a trial by jury or by bench. At the trial, the prosecutor presents the state's case, followed by the defense attorney's presentation of the suspect's side. Appropriate witnesses are called. The prosecutor asks the victim questions about the crime. The defense attorney then cross-examines. At the conclusion of all testimony, each side makes their final statements. The case then goes to the jury or to the bench for a verdict. For there to be a guilty verdict the prosecution must have proved the case beyond any reasonable doubt. Thus, a returned verdict of not guilty does not necessarily indicate that the accused is innocent. Rather, it indicates only that the evidence presented was not sufficient to remove all doubt.

The pronouncement of sentence in many courts does not happen upon return of a guilty verdict. If the court requires a presentencing report, weeks or even months may elapse between the conviction and the sentencing. While the average number of days between the arrest and the sentencing of a rapist varies from jurisdiction to jurisdiction, in 1988 the national average elapsed time in state court cases in which the suspect pled guilty was 231 days. In cases that went to trial the average was 329 days. (Bureau of Justice Statistics 1990) The victim does not have to be present at the sentencing, but she can generally have an opportunity to express her opinions to the judge prior to sentence being passed.

A case that results in a conviction may only be appealed on the basis of legal errors in the first trial. Accordingly, the victim is not involved in the appeal process. Appeals can last literally years, and the judge may allow the convicted rapist to remain free while appealing the conviction. There can be no appeal of a case in which the accused was found not guilty; however, because civil suits are independent of criminal cases, rape victims can hire an attorney and sue their attacker for damages. Civil verdicts are reached based on the "preponderance of evidence," whereas criminal verdicts require the evidence to establish guilt "beyond a reasonable doubt." As a result, evidence that was not sufficient to obtain a conviction in criminal court may be sufficient to obtain a victory for the plaintiff in civil court. (Hasbrook 1993) Civil suits can extend over a period of years, and they can be very expensive.

Use of DNA as Evidence

The use of deoxyribonucleic acid (DNA) analysis for evidentiary purposes is sometimes referred to as "genetic fingerprinting," and has not been without controversy. Considered to be on the cutting edge of assailant identification, it was first performed in New York in 1986. (Fairstein 1993)

DNA is a substance found in cells that defines an individual's genetic code. Like fingerprints, the genetic code is unique to the individual and is the same throughout the individual's body. For that reason, the DNA sequencing in an individual's semen is the same as that found in his blood. This allows laboratories to compare the DNA evidence found at the crime scene (such as a rapist's semen, skin particles, etc.) with a blood sample drawn from a suspect—following a court order—for similarities. If the evidence and sample match, the lab computes the frequency of the DNA pattern within an appropriate population. For example, in a New York case described by Linda Fairstein (1993), a suspect's DNA pattern had an approximate frequency of 1 in 426,000,000 among black males in North America. Such information greatly assists the prosecution's case by helping to remove any reasonable doubt the jury may have regarding the suspect's guilt.

Legal challenges to the use of DNA evidence in court have been based primarily on the methodology used in determining the population control group and on the laboratory procedures used in making the analysis itself. Much effort, however, has gone into perfecting and standardizing both procedures since the early stages of using DNA evidence, resulting in far greater courtroom acceptance. (Fairstein 1993) Despite its growing legal acceptance, use of DNA analysis for evidentiary purposes continues to be somewhat limited, due to the expense of the process and the limited number of laboratories nationwide that can perform the analysis. (Curtis 1993; Fairstein 1993)

Victim Shield Laws

State victim shield laws, sometimes referred to as "rape shield laws," have usually been modeled after Federal Rule of Evidence 412. This federal rule was promulgated by the Supreme Court in 1978. Rape shield laws are designed to "... protect a sexual assault victim against defense counsel's tactic of presenting degrading and embarrassing disclosure of intimate details about the victim's private life ..." for the purpose of biasing the court against her. (Fisher 1991) They generally prohibit the defense from introducing evidence of the victim's prior sexual conduct with anyone other than the defendant, and they further limit testimony regarding any sexual relations with the defendant that occurred during, or close to the time of, the alleged assault. The defendant does have the right to introduce such evidence in order to rebut evidence of this nature already presented by the prosecution. Determination of what is admissible evidence and what is not is often decided by the judge in an in-camera hearing (a hearing that is conducted with the judge, the prosecutor, and the defense attorney in a private session). The shield laws vary from jurisdiction to jurisdiction in the amount of leeway given a judge in deciding the admissibility of evidence. For example, under Texas Penal Code 22.065, any form of sexual conduct evidence may be admitted as long as the judge approves it, while under New Hampshire Revised Statute Annotation 632-A:6

(1986), no prior sexual history of the victim may be admitted except for that with the defendant. (Fisher 1991) While the rape shield laws have by no means eliminated the introduction of such information, they have served to considerably lessen the courtroom trauma that rape victims previously could have expected as a matter of course. (Fairstein interview 1993)

Correctional System

Housing

According to the *Sourcebook of Criminal Justice Statistics* (Bureau of Justice Statistics 1992b), in 1990 there were approximately 88,647 sex offenders incarcerated in 48 states (Maryland and Montana were excluded), the District of Columbia, and the Federal Bureau of Prisons. Housing conditions and treatment varied from state to state and from prison system to prison system. The majority of the respondents (64 percent) cited in the survey housed sex offenders with the general prison population. The remaining 18 states responded "yes" or a "qualified yes" when asked if sex offenders had separate housing.

Parole Eligibility

The different penal systems also varied considerably in allowing parole eligibility for sex offenders. Fifty-eight percent of the respondents stated that sex offenders would be eligible for parole, while an additional 36 percent stated that sex offenders would be eligible "with exceptions." In some systems, for example, sexual offenders who were "lifers," or who had received mandatory sentences, would not be eligible. Only 6 percent of the respondents (the states of Delaware, Maine, and Florida) did not allow parole eligibility to sex offenders. Of the 94 percent of respondents who did allow parole eligibility, 11 stated that they did not have any special parole provisions specifically for sex offenders. An additional 14 respondents stated that they may or may not have such provisions, depending on resources and facilities available in the individual jurisdictions. (Bureau of Justice Statistics 1992b)

Actual Time Served

According to the *Sourcebook of Criminal Justice Statistics*, the actual time a rapist typically had served in prison before his first release was significantly less than half of the actual sentence length. In state prison in 1988, a rapist served 38 percent of the maximum sentence before being paroled. (This was true of both the mean and median sentence lengths.) The mean time served for other sexual assaults prior to first release was 27 months, 36 percent of the mean maximum sentence, while the median time served was 22 months, or 37 percent of the median. In federal prison the mean time actually served before first release was 53 months, 42 percent of the mean maximum sentence. The median time served was 37 months, or 56 percent of the median maximum sentence. (Bureau of Justice Statistics 1992b)

Rapist's Status in the Prison Population

Within the confines of prison walls there is a strict hierarchy of social standing among inmates. Those at the top of the hierarchy are respected by the other inmates based on the crime they have committed and are usually safe from violence. At the bottom of the hierarchy are child molesters convicts who are frequently singled out for attacks on the basis of their crime. Some self-reports of convicted rapists have indicated rapists have a similar status, just above child molesters in the inmate hierarchy, and are accordingly subject to a large amount of abuse within the prison population. As one convicted rapist put it, "We're the bottom of the barrel, we're (considered to be) the sickos." (Sussman and Bordwell 1981) While any inmate who is not physically intimidating (or who has not established a reputation of extreme violence) is at risk of being raped, convicted rapists may be singled out more often for attack. In the words of the same inmate mentioned above, "You can be subject to a gang rape if you're a rapist. The thing is, it's usually the guys who at one time or another have raped somebody themselves but are here on another charge— they're usually the ones that come up and confront you with it." (Sussman and Bordwell 1981) Despite such reports, observations of both convicts and correctional system employees indicate that a rapist's status in the inmate hierarchy is more a result of the manner in which the individual carries himself among the inmate population (if he is "heavy on the yard," i.e., a power to be reckoned with) and the manner in which he conducts himself within the prison environment (if he is a "stand-up guy," i.e., not an informer; doesn't cooperate with prison authorities). Prisoners who are physically, mentally, or emotionally intimidating, or those who are afforded "protection" by virtue of political connections within the prisoner population, are much less likely to be physically abused by other convicts. ("Bill" 1993; Kishur 1994)

While it is accepted that in the general prisoner population there is a significant amount of male rape, documentation of rape prevalence is impossible. Corrections authorities tend to deny that the problem exists or, at best, to minimize its prevalence. Prisoners frequently tell a different story. Inmates who report offenses by other prisoners to prison authorities are considered to be collaborators or "snitches," and are subject to severe retribution from the inmate population. Fear of a reprisal worse than the rape itself keeps most victims quiet. In all but a few cases it is an unreported crime. In the late 1960s a chief assistant district attorney named Alan J. Davis (1970) did an investigation of sexual assault in Philadelphia prisons. He documented 156 cases of prison rape over a two-year period, but he estimated that the true number of assaults was probably closer to 2,000 during that time.

Ironically, it is in the rape of males in prison that the true dynamics and motivations of rape become most clear—what Susan Brownmiller (1975) calls "a microcosm of the female experience with heterosexual rape." Rape in prison is about dominance, not sexual release. It establishes position within the hierarchy of inmate society. The man who rapes another man in prison is not viewed as a homosexual by other inmates; on the contrary, his "manhood" is asserted by the act of "punking" or "making a girl" out of a weaker male. By such an assertion he identifies himself as one of the strong, not the weak, and as a potential predator, rather than a potential victim. ("Bill" 1993; Kishur 1994)

Medical Treatment of Sex Offenders

Scope and Validity of Studies

According to *Newsweek,* the U.S. Bureau of Justice figures indicate that convicted rapists have a 52 percent recidivism rate within three years of release. (Gelman et al. 1990) (These figures do not distinguish between sexual and nonsexual offenses.) The numerous studies of various methods and programs for the treatment of sex offenders have not yielded a clear, accurate picture of offender rehabilitation. As L. Furby notes, "By selectively contemplating the various studies, one can conclude anything one wants." (Furby et al. 1989) Many studies have been inconclusive, inconsistent, or contradictory when compared to other studies. Many, if not most, have dealt with such a specific type or subset of the offender population that generalization of the programs' efficiency to the larger sexual offender population is impossible. As was noted in chapter 1, the only thing that is clear about the treatment of offenders is that there is no one effective "cure."

Several studies exemplify the difficulties outlined above. Fred Berlin et al. (1991) cites studies done at the Peters Institute in Philadelphia. The Peters Institute did a study with a comparison (but not a control) group and found that, in a follow-up period of two years, the treated offenders had a recidivism rate of 3 percent, while the nontreated offenders had a recidivism rate of 27 percent. When a later study was done with a control group of offenders, the treated offenders had a recidivism rate of 13 percent over a ten-year period, while the nontreated control group of offenders had a rate of 7.2 percent over the same time period. (Berlin et al. 1991; Romero and Williams 1983) In the late 1960s, 24 sex offenders were pronounced "cured" after therapy and were released from prison. They had a 20.8 percent recidivism rate in a follow-up period of over six years. A similar group of offenders who were classified "unamenable to treatment" and were released had an 11.8 percent recidivism rate over a similar period. A third group of offenders who were classified as "nonamenable to treatment and danger-ous" had a recidivism rate of 17 percent. (Dix 1976)

Berlin et al. (1991) identifies three major problems in deter-mining the effectiveness of various treatments: (1) classification in-consistency or generalization of the condition being treated; (2) wide variation in the type of outcome measurement used; and (3) the practical difficulty and, in some instances, the ethical consider-ation of obtaining an appropriate untreated control group for le-gitimate comparison with the treated group. Hypothetical examples may illustrate the first two problems. Identifying a sex offender as a child molester or rapist does not address the specific disorder being treated, nor does it address the primary motivation or common dynamics of the offender's assault. (See chapter 5 for further discussion of primary motivations for rape.) Conclusions based on statistical measurements may not accurately reflect treat-ment effectiveness. In the area of recidivism, some studies (such as Berlin's) consider any arrest for any offense (sexual or not) to be re-cidivism, other studies may consider only arrests for sexual of-fenses, while still others may only count convictions for similar offenses (such as rape). A study that based its definition of recidi-vism on *rape* convictions after treatment would likely produce lower recidivism rates than a study that based its definition on ar-rests for *sexual offenses,* and much lower rates than a study that based its definition on arrests for *any* type of offense. The first study would fail to consider rape cases that were plea-bargained to a lesser offense, while the latter might be more reflective of the offender's anti-social behavior in general rather than of his response to treatment.

Types of Treatment

Most therapies are based on the belief that sexual deviance is a learned or acquired behavioral disorder. Treatment seeks to identify and, at the least, control deviant behavior, while addressing and seeking to change the thought processes that give rise to such behavior. (Association for the Treatment of Sexual Abuses 1993) The effectiveness of any type of treatment is likely to hinge on the level of the offender's desire to change. Treatment programs that seem to have a significant amount of success (such as Berlin's work at Johns Hopkins or the castration programs in Denmark) tend to be those that deal with highly motivated offenders.

Psychotherapy

There are several different types of psychotherapies currently being practiced. Each entails (to one extent or another) helping the offender identify and acknowledge offensive behavior, supporting the offender in his effort to change through individual and/or group therapy, and utilizing support networks to assist the offender in suppressing inappropriate behavior. Some of the major types of psychotherapies associated with the treatment of sexual offenders are cognitive therapy, relapse prevention/support system therapy, and victim empathy. (Association for the Treatment of Sexual Abuses 1993)

Cognitive therapy is based on the belief that offenders have perception distortions that allow them to rationalize and justify their offensive behavior, thereby avoiding responsibility and guilt. Cognitive therapy seeks to enable the offender to recognize such distortions and to modify them appropriately.

Relapse prevention/support system therapy is based on the belief that there are a series of perceptions, emotions, and behaviors that an individual offender experiences prior to committing a sexual offense. Relapse prevention therapy seeks to identify those preceding events for both the offender and support persons (such as a significant other, family members, etc.), so that they may stop the cycle through appropriate coping behaviors.

Victim empathy seeks to enable the offender to empathize with his victims, thereby gaining a recognition of the lasting impact of his actions and a fuller understanding of the severe harm caused by such actions. One form of this approach utilized by some therapists among convicted sex offenders has the rapist reenact the rape from the perspective of the victim. In seeking to reenact the victim's experience, the rapist may choke or strike himself, beg not to be killed, and plead for mercy. The reenactment may be done in the presence of other offenders (in hopes of affording them insight into their own crimes) and videotaped for the purpose of showing it later to the reenacting rapist. While victim empathy may be integrated with other therapies as a matter of course, there are no strong indications of its effectiveness in and of itself. (Association for the Treatment of Sexual Abuses 1993; Kishur 1994)

The primary disadvantage of psychotherapy is its lengthy time requirement, for it is a relatively long process. Furthermore, its success requires a rapist who is suited for it—a motivated offender who is sufficiently intelligent and capable of abstract thought and who is willing to face and experience unpleasant realizations in the process of change. (Groth and Birnbaum 1979)

Arousal Control/Behavior Modification

Arousal control/behavior modification involves the use of external stimuli to effect internal change in the offender, to condition him to adapt socially acceptable behavior, and to control unacceptable behavior. Arousal control frequently makes use of aversive therapy, which can be of a physical or verbal nature. In arousal control therapy utilizing physical aversive therapy, a rapist might be shown a series of scenes depicting a violent sexual encounter. If he is aroused by the scene, he might receive a series of electrical shocks or might be subjected to an offensive odor. Verbal aversive therapy would seek to have the offender associate an image unpleasant to him (such as the offender's mother having to testify in court or having to visit the offender in prison) with thoughts of inappropriate sexual behavior. The goal of the treatment would be to cause the offender to respond adversely to thoughts of, or impulses toward, sexual violence.

One of the more recently developed techniques of arousal control therapy is masturbatory satiation. In this approach the offender's inappropriate behavior is analytically broken down into a series of actions, or steps. Once the segmentation of the action is complete, the offender masturbates to orgasm. Following orgasm, the offender masturbates for an additional 45 minutes to an hour while continually repeating one section only of the analyzed offense. (For example, a sexual abuser of children might repeat "I'm stroking her hair" over and over for the entire time.) The technique attempts to pair a lack of arousal with a part of the offender's inappropriate fantasy, ultimately destroying the appeal of that particular action. The process continues until all segments of the offender's fantasy are addressed.

Arousal control therapy commonly makes use of the penile plethysmograph to measure circumferential penile swelling in response to appropriate and inappropriate stimuli. Plethysmography provides some of the assessment information needed (such as sexual preferences and shifts in preference in response to treatment) to determine effective treatment strategies.

Biomedical Therapies and Castration

Biomedical therapies involve the use of drugs, generally used in conjunction with other forms of therapy, to suppress inappropriate fantasies and compulsive behaviors. Many researchers who believe that biological anomalies are frequently contributors to, if not the cause of, sexual offenses view physical or chemical castration as an effective means of curtailing sexual violence. Surgical castration, a process rarely done today in America, consists of the removal of the testicles, which thereby stops most production of testosterone (the sex hormone secreted by the testes that is responsible for the sexual drive in males) and suppresses the libido, or sex drive. This reduction in testosterone levels is believed to be a major reason for observed behavior changes of offenders who have undergone castration. (Berlin et al. 1991; Frank 1985) As G. R. Kishur (1994) points out, however, testosterone cannot be considered a factor when a prepubescent seven-year-old male successfully rapes a four-year-old female. While a castrated offender can no longer produce semen, he retains the physical ability to achieve an erection. (Groth and Birnbaum 1979; Mayer 1988) In the case of an offender who uses rape as an expression of anger (see chapter 5), removal of the testicles will not automatically prevent him from continuing to use his penis as a weapon.

Chemical castration consists of administering a synthetic hormone (an antiandrogenic medication) that results in suppression of the manufacture of testosterone. Currently the drug most commonly used is called Depo-Provera (medroxyprogesterone acetate), manufactured by the UpJohn Company. Depo-Provera received approval from the Food and Drug Administration (FDA) in 1960 for the treatment of renal and kidney cancer, but it was not approved for use as a contraceptive when the manufacturer applied in 1963, on the grounds that it caused cancer in laboratory animals, was a suspected carcinogen in humans, and possibly caused birth defects in humans. Despite the lack of FDA approval, Depo-Provera was frequently prescribed for nonapproved uses as a means of birth control as well as for treatment of menopause symptoms, menstrual disorders, and endometriosis. (National Women's Health Network 1985) The FDA continued to oppose the use of the drug for use as a contraceptive for the next 19 years, finally granting approval in October of 1992. Depo-Provera has long been used in Third World countries as a means of birth control, and it is endorsed by the International Planned Parenthood Federation and the World Health Organization. The National Women's Health Network continues to oppose the use of Depo-Provera as a contraceptive, primarily because of the possible risk of breast cancer and bone loss. (National Women's Health Network 1992) Depo-Provera has been used in the treatment of sex offenders at Johns Hopkins since 1966. The drug is injected (most commonly into the arm muscles) twice a week. (Rider 1994) Among its numerous side effects are weight gain, lethargy, high blood pressure, and depression. (Frank 1985; Mayer 1988; National Women's Health Network 1985; Rider 1994) Lupron (leuprolide acetate) is being used on a limited basis by Fred Berlin at the National Institute for the Study, Prevention, and Treatment of Sexual Trauma as an alternative drug to Depo-Provera. This drug is believed by Berlin to be at least as effective as Depo-Provera, without the wide range of side effects. It is administered once a month. Its extreme expense is a major drawback; in mid-1994 a single dosage cost between $300 and $500.

There have been several studies of note that have sought to determine the efficacy of castration. G. K. Sturup (1960, 1968) noted a 4.3 percent recidivism rate among 117 physically castrated sex offenders in Denmark over a period of time as long as 18 years, opposed to a 43 percent recidivism rate among 58 noncastrated offenders over a similar time period (Figure 2-4). (Berlin et al. 1991) Cornu in Switzerland found a 7.4 percent recidivism rate among 121 castrated males in 5 years, opposed to a 52 percent recidivism rate among 50 noncastrated men in 10 years (Figure 2-5). Sand et al. reviewed results of castration in Denmark and found a 2.2 percent sexual recidivism rate for 900 castrated men, in a time period as long as 30 years (Figure 2-6). (Heim and Hursch 1979)

It should be noted that the men in the studies included sex offenders of different types, including exhibitionists, pedophiles, and rapists, and that they were voluntarily castrated. (Frank

1985) Given the differences in the nature and motivation of an exhibitionist and a rapist, and given the apparent desire of the offenders to change, it is prudent to view the results of these studies as they apply to a specific study population, rather than applying them to the general sex offender population as a whole.

The most effective treatments are likely those that utilize a variety of treatment methods. One of the most recent and highly regarded surveys to be done in the United States was done by Berlin at the National Institute for the Study, Prevention, and Treatment of Sexual Trauma at Johns Hopkins University (see chapters 4 and 6). His survey tracked recidivism for 626 male sex offenders who had been treated at the sexual disorders clinic. (Berlin et al. 1991) Treatment of the offenders consisted of individual psychotherapy, family therapy, and, in about 40 percent of cases, testosterone-lowering medication. The primary mode of outpatient therapy was one and one-half hours of group therapy a week. The group consisted of 406 pedophiles, 111 exhibitionists, and 109 sexual aggressives (a term coined and defined by G. G. Abel as "men who carry out forced sexual acts against women, which may [or may] not qualify technically as rape." (Abel et al. 1977) The survey tracked recidivism over a period averaging over five years per subject. *Recidivism* was defined as any charge, sexual or nonsexual, resulting in conviction or not (Figure 2-7). Recidivism rates for each category (sexual or nonsexual), however, were noted. In order to be admitted to the program, the offender had to admit to having committed inappropriate sexual acts or of having had urges to commit them and had to express a desire to receive help. The offender may have been referred by officers of the court, by healthcare practitioners, or by himself. It is important to note that the survey was of offenders who had actively expressed a desire to change their ways prior to receiving treatment. It may be surmised that a high degree of motivation can play a significant part in an offender's lack of recidivism.

Of the 109 sexual aggressives Berlin surveyed, 88 percent were first-time sexual offenders, 30 percent had an anti-social personality disorder, and 50 percent had a paraphilic disorder (i.e., thoughts or behaviors of coerced, but not sadistic, sex were more sexually stimulating to them than were thoughts or behaviors of consensual sex). The offenders were classified as either compliant or noncompliant with clinic treatment. Twenty-one percent had one or more prior nonsexual charges. A total of 4.6 percent of the group had sexual recidivism over a mean period at risk (PAR) of just under four and one-half years, representing 2.6

percent of the compliant aggressives and 8.1 percent of the non-compliant aggressives. Only 2 of 85 (2.4 percent) sexual aggressives were charged with a new sexual offense following their discharge from treatment.

Among sexual aggressives, nonsexual recidivism was much higher than sexual recidivism: 14 percent of the compliant sexual aggressives had nonsexual recividism over a mean PAR of just over five and one-half years, while 29.7 percent of the noncompliant sexual aggressives had nonsexual recidivism over a mean PAR of just over four and one-half years.

The sexual recidivism rate for the 406 pedophiles was 7.4 percent, with a PAR of just over five years. A group of 149 heterosexual pedophiles had a sexual recidivism rate of 5.4 percent, while a group of 147 homosexual pedophiles had a sexual recidivism rate of 10.2 percent, and a group of 25 bisexual pedophiles had a sexual recidivism rate of 16 percent (Figure 2-8).

Berlin observed less success in treatment of exhibitionists; of the 111, 23.4 percent engaged in sexual recidivism with a PAR of just over five and one-half years. (Berlin et al. 1991) One possible explanation of why exhibitionists have a much higher recidivism rate than pedophiles or rapists following treatment is that their impulses are much more out of control—their compulsivity is much greater. (Rider 1994) Another possible explanation points to societal and legal reactions to exhibitionism. Society generally does not respond to the exhibitionist with the same intensity as it does to the pedophile or rapist. Exhibitionists are frequently characterized in nonthreatening and comic personna, such as an old man in a raincoat or a streaker on a college campus. In the judicial system an exhibitionist is much less likely to receive a sentence of incarceration (with the exception of aggravated cases) than is a pedophile or rapist. (Fines 1994) The characterization as a "harmless crank" may provide the exhibitionist with less external motivation to change, making it easier for him to give vent to his impulses and thereby contributing to the higher sexual recidivism rate. The counterargument to this theory is that most criminals, including sex offenders, give little consideration in the first place to the potential legal ramifications of their actions and that criminals are primarily focused on the immediate gratification their crime brings, and they are only slightly (if at all) affected by societal mores. (Kishur 1994) In speaking of specific motivation, as with treatment effectiveness, individual differences between offenders make it impossible to make conclusive statements regarding the general offender population.

Figures

Figure 2–1
Projections of Possible Rape Totals in 1991

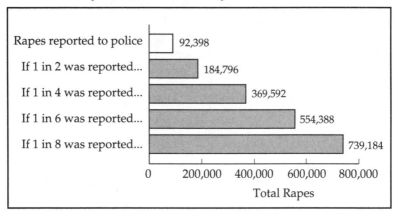

Source: Federal Bureau of Investigation 1992.

Figure 2–2
Rape Arrests by Age, 1991

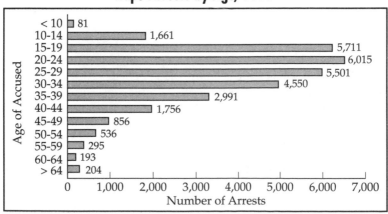

Source: Federal Bureau of Investigation 1992.

Figure 2–3
Ramifications of Rape Reports, State Level

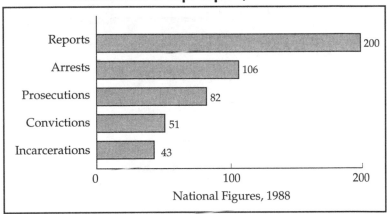

Source: Bureau of Justice Statistics 1992.

Figure 2–4
Recidivism of Castrated vs. Noncastrated Offenders
over an 18–Year Period (Sturup's Study)

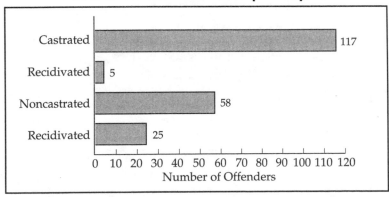

Source: Berlin et al. 1991; Sturup 1960, 1968.

Figure 2–5
Recidivism of Castrated vs. Noncastrated Offenders
over 5-Year and 10-Year Periods (Cornu's Study)

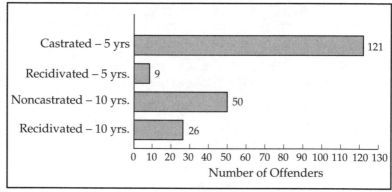

Source: Heim and Hursch 1979.

Figure 2–6
Recidivism of Castrated Offenders in Denmark
over a 30–Year Period (Sand's Study)

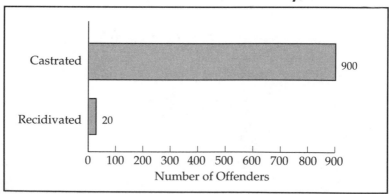

Source: Heim and Hursch 1979.

Figure 2–7
Recidivism Rate of 406 Pedophiles, 111 Exhibitionists, and 109 Sexual Aggressives (Berlin et al. Survey)

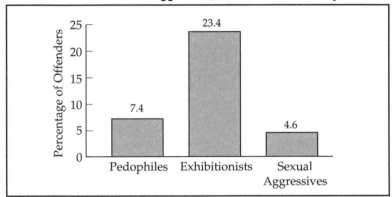

Source: Berlin et al. 1991.

Figure 2–8
Berlin et al. Survey Results: Pedophilia

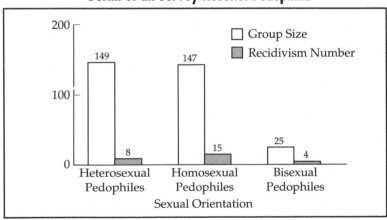

Source: Berlin et al. 1991.

References

Abel, G. G., D. H. Barlow, E. B. Blanchard, and D. Guild. 1977. "The Components of Rapists' Sexual Arousal." *Archives of General Psychiatry* 34: 895–903.

Association for the Treatment of Sexual Abuses (ATSA). 1993. *The ATSA Practitioner's Handbook.* Lake Oswego, OR: ATSA.

Berlin, F. S., W. P. Hunt, M. Malin, A. Dyer, G. K. Lehne, and S. Dean. 1991. "A Five-Year Plus Follow-Up Survey of Criminal Recidivism within a Treated Cohort of 406 Pedophiles, 111 Exhibitionists, and 109 Sexual Aggressives: Issues and Outcome." *American Journal of Forensic Psychiatry* 12: 3.

"Bill" (career criminal). 1993. Interview with the author. Edmond, OK, 6 October.

Boylan, J. (police sketch artist). 1993. Interview on the *Home Program*, ABC-TV, 28 September.

Brownmiller, S. 1975. *Against Our Will: Men, Women, and Rape.* New York: Simon & Schuster.

Bureau of Justice Statistics. 1990. *Felony Sentences in State Court, 1988.* Washington, DC: U.S. Department of Justice, p. 7, table 11.

———. 1991. *Tracking Offenders.* Washington, DC: U.S. Department of Justice. NCJ-129861.

———. 1992a. *National Corrections Reporting Program, 1988.* Washington, DC: U.S. Department of Justice. NCJ-134929.

———. 1992b. *Sourcebook of Criminal Justice Statistics, 1991,* edited by T. J. Flanagan and K. Maguire. Washington, DC: U.S. Department of Justice.

Carlton, T. (captain of the Oklahoma City Police Department Sex Crimes Unit). 1994. Telephone conversation with the author, 17 March.

Curtis, C. (Oklahoma State Bureau of Investigation criminalist/agent). 1993. Lecture on DNA at University of Central Oklahoma in Edmond, OK, 24 November.

Davis, A. J. 1970. "Sexual Assaults in the Philadelphia Prison System." In *The Sexual Scene,* edited by J. Gagnon and W. Simon. Chicago: Transaction/Aldine.

Dix, G. E. 1976. "Determining the Continued Dangerousness of Psychologically Abnormal Sex Offenders." *Journal of Psychiatry and the Law* 3: 372–374.

Fairstein, L. 1993. *Sexual Violence: Our War against Rape.* New York: William Morrow.

———. 1993. Interview on the *Home Program*, ABC-TV, 28 September.

Federal Bureau of Investigation. 1992. *Uniform Crime Report* (1990 and 1991). Washington, DC: U.S. Department of Justice.

Feldman-Summers, S., and G. C. Palmer. 1980. "Rape as Viewed by Judges, Prosecutors, and Police Officers." *Criminal Justice and Behavior* 7: 34–36.

Fines, Phillip U. (assistant commonwealth's attorney). 1994. Telephone conversation with the author, 8 July.

Fisher, P. J. 1991. "*State v. Alvey* [458 N.W.2d 850 (Iowa)]: Iowa's Victimization of Defendants through the Overextension of Iowa's Rape Shield Law." *Iowa Law Review* 76: 835–870.

Frank, J. G. 1985. "Treating Sex Offenders." Unpublished paper on file with the Illinois Coalition Against Sexual Assault.

Furby, L., M. R. Weinrott, and L. Blackshaw. 1989. "Sex Offender Recidivism: A Review." *Psychological Bulletin* 105 (1): 3–30.

Gelman, D., K. Springen, R. Elam, N. Joseph, K. Robert, and M. Hager. 1990. "The Mind of the Rapist." *Newsweek,* 23 July.

Groth, A. N., and H. J. Birnbaum. 1979. *Men Who Rape: The Psychology of the Offender.* New York: Plenum Publishing.

Groth, A. N., and A. W. Burgess. 1977. "Sexual Dysfunction during Rape." *New England Journal of Medicine* 297 (4): 764–766.

Hall, R. 1994. A survey of rape crisis centers in the United States. Unpublished data.

Hasbrook, E. (attorney, Criminal Justice Division, City of Oklahoma City). 1993. Interview with the author. Oklahoma City, OK, 20 October.

Hazelwood, R. R. 1983. "The Behavior-Oriented Interview of Rape Victims: The Key to Profiling." *FBI Law Enforcement Bulletin,* September.

Heim, N., and C. J. Hursch. 1979. "Castration for Sex Offenders: Treatment or Punishment: A Review and Critique of Recent European Literature." *Archives of Sexual Behavior* 8: 281–304.

Kishur, Dr. G. R. 1994. Interview with the author. Oklahoma City, OK, 12 July.

Koss, M. P. 1992. "Defending Date Rape." *Journal of Interpersonal Violence* 7 (1): 122–125.

McCahill, T. W., L. C. Meyer, and A. M. Fischman. 1979. *The Aftermath of Rape.* Lexington, MA: D. C. Health.

Mayer, A. 1988. *Sex Offenders.* Holmes Beach, FL: Learning Publications.

National Institute of Law Enforcement and Criminal Justice. 1978. *Forcible Rape Police Volume IV.* Washington, DC: Law Enforcement Assistance Administration.

National Women's Health Network (NWHN). 1985. *Depo-Provera: A Shot in the Dark* (information sheet). Washington, DC: NWHN.

————. 1992. "Use of Depo-Provera for Contraception." Paper presented to the Fertility and Maternal Health Drugs Advisory Committee, Food and Drug Administration, 19 June. Washington, DC: NWHN.

Novacek, J., R. Raskin, D. Bahlinger, L. Firth, and S. Rybicki. 1993. *Rape: Tulsa Women Speak Out.* Tulsa, OK: Tulsa Institute of Behavioral Sciences.

Rider, M. (executive administrator, National Institute for the Study, Prevention and Treatment of Sexual Trauma). 1994. Telephone conversation with the author, 24 June.

Romero, J., and L. Williams. 1983. "Group Psychotherapy and Intensive Probation Supervision with Sex Offenders: A Comparative Study." *Federal Probation* 47: 36–42.

Sturup, G. K. 1960. "Sex Offenses: The Scandinavian Experience." *Law and Contemporary Problems 1960* 25: 361–375.

————. 1968. "Treatment of Sexual Offenders in Herstedvester, Denmark: The Rapists." *Acta Psychiatrica Scandinavica, Supplement 204.*

Sussman, L., and S. Bordwell. 1981. "Quentin." In *The Rapist File: Interviews with Convicted Rapists.* New York: Chelsea House.

Chronology 3

The following chronology is a listing of significant judicial events and other occurrences, offering a broad overview of the societal history of rape. The legislative events listed are not necessarily the first instances of such legislation in the nation (unless specifically noted), but they are cited to put the creation of such legislation in historical context. Likewise, listings of actual rapes are solely for the purpose of establishing historical context and to demonstrate any patterns of social development. The majority of the significant legislation of the last two centuries in the United States has taken place on the state level, rather than on the federal level.

ca. 1720 B.C.   According to Genesis 39: 7–20, Potiphar was a captain of the guard who bought Joseph as a slave. Joseph impressed Potiphar to the point that Potiphar brought Joseph into the household as the overseer of his house. Potiphar's wife desired Joseph and on several occasions asked him to lie with her. Joseph steadfastly refused. Potiphar's wife ultimately

ca. 1720 B.C. *(cont.)*	aggressed against Joseph in a physical manner and Joseph fled, leaving his garment in her hand. Potiphar's wife then proclaimed that Joseph had sexually assaulted her and cited his discarded garment as evidence. As a result of her false charge, Joseph was thrown into prison. The term *Potiphar's wife* has been used throughout the ages to characterize spurned, vindictive women, and to cast suspicion on rape victims.
17th century B.C.	The Code of Hammurabi, the oldest written laws extant, states that if a man rapes the bride of an inchoate marriage (a status somewhere between an engagement and a contemporary marriage) while she is a virgin and living in her father's house, the penalty is death.
14th century B.C.	Troy falls and is sacked, and the women of Troy are raped. Included among the victims is Cassandra, daughter of King Priam of Troy. She is raped by Ajax, a Locrian ally of the conquering Greeks.
13th century B.C.	The law of Moses, as recorded in Deuteronomy 22: 23–29, states that if a man rapes a betrothed damsel "in a field" (thus out of the hearing-distance of possible rescue), the penalty for him will be death, regardless of whether the woman is a virgin or not. The victim in this case will not be punished. If, however, a man rapes a betrothed virgin damsel in the city (thus in hearing-distance of possible rescue) and she does not cry out, the penalty will be death for them both. If a man rapes a virgin who is not betrothed, he must marry her with no possibility of divorce, and he must pay her father 50 shekels of silver.
A.D. 892	Under the rule of Alfred the Great, if a man rapes a virgin commoner, he must pay 60 shillings. If he rapes a nonvirgin commoner, the fine is 30 shillings. If the victim is not a commoner, the fine is increased according to the wergeld (a monetary value dependent upon social classification, ranging

from a churl to the King, that is paid to the kin or lord of the victim). If a man sleeps with a commoner's wife, the fine is 40 shillings, payable to the husband. If a man sleeps with a noncommoner's wife, the amount of the fine increases dramatically. If a slave rapes a slave, the punishment is castration. (To put the fine system into context: the fine for cutting off a man's nose is 60 shillings; for blinding a person, a little over 66 shillings; for cutting off a man's ear, 30 shillings—60 if the victim is deafened.)

mid-17th century

Lord Matthew Hale (1609–1676) argues in his *History of the Pleas of the Crown* (published posthumously in 1736): "It is true that rape is a most detestable crime, and therefore ought to be severely and impartially punished with death; but it must be remembered that it is an accusation easily to be made and hard to be proved, and harder to be defended by the party accused, tho never so innocent." (This very argument will be heard in courtrooms for the next 300 years.) Hale also comments in the same work on the impossibility of spousal rape when he states: "The husband cannot be guilty of a rape committed by himself upon his lawful wife, for by their mutual matrimonial consent and contract the wife hath given herself in this kind unto her husband, which she cannot retract." (This argument will provide the basis for successful argument against spousal rape laws for centuries to come.)

1838

In New York State a woman accuses a married minister of rape (*People v. Abbott*). The minister declares that the woman has a bad reputation and was willing. There are no other witnesses to the alleged rape. The court acquits the minister, stating that in order for a woman to be believed three conditions must be met. These conditions are: (1) the woman must be of good reputation, (2) the woman must show evidence of physical resistance, and (3) the woman must have tried to call

1838 *(cont.)*   for help. The court makes these conditions on the underlying presumption that once an unmarried woman is sexually active, she is already on her way to being a prostitute and will say "yes" to anyone.

1854   In New York State in the case of *People v. Morrison,* the court declares that the woman not only must resist, but she must resist using "all of her natural abilities" ("natural abilities" referring to her physical abilities). In the absence of such resistance, there is no rape.

1858   In Toronto, Canada, two alleged prostitutes are attacked—robbed and raped—in their home by a gang of 8 to 14 males. (The event becomes known as the Sayer Street Outrage.) The two women identify and charge several of the men with robbery and rape. All the accused are found not guilty, almost exclusively on the basis of the character of the two women, and there is a backlash of antifemale sentiment for years to come.

1874   In New York State in the case of *People v. Dohring,* the court (building on the foundation of *People v. Abbott* and *People v. Morrison*) establishes the degree of physical resistance demanded of the woman. The court declares that the woman must resist to the point of being overpowered "[because of] loss of strength, the number of attackers, duress, or fear of death." *If the woman ceases to resist at any point during the attack, it could be considered consent, and therefore the attack is not rape.*

1931   The Scottsboro Trials begin in Tennessee (to be concluded in their entirety 20 years later). Nine black males, ages 13 to 20, are arrested and charged with the rape of two white women, ages 17 and mid-twenties, on a freight train. During the trial the prosecution presents medical evidence of semen to corroborate the testimony of alleged rape. The judge accepts the prosecution's evidence but excludes evidence presented by the defense that the women had sex the night before the alleged rapes. As a result of this judicial decision, the case gains notoriety throughout the world as a racially based miscarriage of justice, and it gives rise to a significant judicial argument known as the Scottsboro rebuttal, allowing defense attorneys to introduce evidence of sexual activity with others to attempt to demonstrate that the defendant is not the source of semen or the cause of injury.

1971   The first public rape victims' "speakout" is held at St. Clement's Episcopal Church in New York City. It is sponsored by the New York Radical Feminists.

1972   Bay Area Women Against Rape (BAWAR), one of the first rape crisis centers in the United States, is opened in Berkeley, California. (By 1980 there will be over 400 centers nationwide.)

1973   Senator Charles Mathias of Maryland introduces a bill to establish the National Center for the Prevention of Rape. The bill seeks to create a center within the National Institute of Mental Health (NIMH) that will develop programs to help stem the tide of sexual assault. It is passed overwhelmingly by Congress, but vetoed by President Gerald Ford. Later, it is successfully reintroduced, resulting in the establishment of the National Center for the Prevention and Control of Rape in 1975.

1975   The Michigan legislature enacts comprehensive rape law reforms, specifically eliminating the physical resistance requirement and limiting the circumstances and extent to which a victim's sexual history can be introduced. Michigan's laws concerning rape are considered models for other states in the years to come.

1978   Representative Elizabeth Holtzman of New York sponsors the Privacy Protection for Rape Victims Act in Congress. This act seeks to introduce on a national level limits to the circumstances and

1978 *(cont.)*   extent to which a victim's sexual history can be used in court.

The Supreme Court promulgates Federal Rule of Evidence 412, restricting the circumstances under which a victim's sexual history can be introduced in federal court.

National attention is captured when *State v. Rideout*—the first case under Oregon's revised rape statute (which eliminates the exclusion of a husband from the charge of rape)—is presented. John Rideout is accused of beating and raping his wife, but he is ultimately acquitted and the couple reunites, with much fanfare in the press. Several months later the couple is divorced.

The National Coalition Against Sexual Assault (NCASA) holds its first conference in Lake Geneva, Wisconsin. NCASA is begun to create a new national structure for rape crisis centers.

1981   In *State v. Morrison* the New Jersey Supreme Court reinstates the rape conviction of a legally separated husband.

1982   The New York legislature eliminates the physical resistance requirement.

The Kansas Supreme Court rules that the existence of Rape Trauma Syndrome is relevant and admissible as evidence of rape.

1984   *Weishaupt v. Commonwealth* becomes the first Virginia case to consider spousal rape exclusion. The couple had been separated for approximately a year at the time of the rape, but they had not enacted a legal separation or filed for divorce. The defense asks for dismissal of the case based on spousal exclusion. The motion is denied on the grounds that the couple had separated with intent to divorce. Weishaupt is ultimately convicted and sentenced to two years.

1987   State Representative Tom Hayden introduces Resolution 46 to the California legislature, making California the first state to address sexual assault on college campuses. The failure of many schools to establish sexual assault policies and procedures results in passage of further legislation in 1990 requiring compliance.

                The state legislature of North Dakota passes what comes to be known as the date rape bill. Prior to this legislation an assailant could escape being charged with a class A felony of gross sexual imposition if the victim was a "voluntary companion," or if the couple had previously had a sexual relationship.

1988   The Minnesota Vikings professional football team announces that they will be hiring a football player who has recently been released from a Wisconsin prison after serving time for rape. The Minnesota Coalition of Sexual Assault Services takes great exception to the proposed hiring and sends notice over the Associated Press news wire of a scheduled press conference to protest the hiring. Between the time that the coalition's notice goes over the wire and the time of the press conference the next day, the Vikings reverse their decision and announce that they will not be hiring the player.

1989   The Wisconsin state legislature passes Wisconsin Act 177, an act that requires the University of Wisconsin system to include information on sexual assault and sexual harassment in student orientation programs. The act also requires the dean of students of each campus to compile statistics on such incidents on campus and to provide those figures to the Wisconsin State Office of Justice Assistance annually.

1990   The Student Right To Know and Campus Security Act is signed into law as part of Public Law 101-542. The act requires colleges and universities to

1990 *(cont.)*   begin to collect data on campus crime as of 1 September 1991 and to publish those crime statistics by 1 September 1992. Such statistics are to be published on a yearly basis, so that prospective students can make informed judgments in their selection of a college campus. The act also requires institutions to provide students and employees with information about campus security policies and procedures, and it specifically states that institutions are not prohibited from disclosing the results of disciplinary proceedings against alleged perpetrators of violent crimes to the alleged victims.

1991–1992   The Campus Sexual Assault Victim's Bill of Rights Act of 1991, later known as the Ramstad Amendment to the Higher Education Act, is drafted by Frank Carrington and Howard Clery and sponsored by Congressman James Ramstad in the House of Representatives. Senator Joseph Biden sponsors a companion bill in the Senate. The act is later modified, and a revised version is attached by Representatives James Ramstad and Susan Molinari to the Higher Education Amendments of 1992 and signed into law by President Bush in 1992. The amendment requires colleges to develop and publicize a campus sexual assault policy. This policy must: (1) describe the institution's sexual assault prevention programs; and (2) outline post-assault procedures and options, including post-assault procedures students should follow, reporting options and the importance of preserving evidence, procedures for on-campus disciplinary hearings for sexual assault and guarantees of equal rights for both the accusor and the accused within and as a result of the hearings, possible sanctions to be imposed in the event of a guilty finding in a campus disciplinary hearing, existing counseling, mental health or student services for assault victims, and options and available assistance in changing academic and living situations following an alleged sexual assault.

1993   North Carolina and Oklahoma become the last two states to abolish the automatic legal immunity from spousal rape charges for spouses still living with their wives. In many states, however, the removal of automatic exemption does not place spousal rape in the same category of offense as "regular" rape. In Tennessee, for example, a limited spousal exclusion is still in place. Under Tennessee law, in a situation where the spouses are still living together and neither has filed for separate maintenance or divorce, a person cannot be convicted for raping their legal spouse unless the assailant was armed with a weapon (or something the victim believed to be a weapon) or caused serious bodily injury to the victim (in addition to nonconsensual penetration). Furthermore, the penalties are not necessarily the same for spousal rape and "regular" rape. In Tennessee, rape of a nonspouse that results in serious bodily injury or that is committed by an armed assailant is termed aggravated rape, a class A felony punishable by 15 to 60 years in prison. Rape of a spouse under the same conditions is termed spousal rape, a class C felony punishable by 3 to 15 years in prison.

1994   It is discovered that an error in the categorization of sex crimes had resulted in Grand Rapids, Michigan, showing more rapes per capita than any other city in the FBI's *Uniform Crime Report.* In response to the FBI's request for rape (attempted and completed, adult females only) statistics, the Grand Rapids Police Department had submitted the figures it had for criminal sexual assault. The definition by Michigan's criminal code of sexual assault includes a wide range of sexual offenses, including fondling and child molestation. Accordingly, the figures for rape that the *Uniform Crime Report* had listed for Grand Rapids were greatly exaggerated and inaccurate. On the basis of these submitted figures, Grand Rapids had been considered the "rape capital of America" since 1990.

1994 *(cont.)*   The Tennessee General Assembly passes the Sexual Offender Registration and Monitoring Act. This act requires convicted sex offenders to register with the Tennessee Bureau of Investigation (TBI), which maintains a computerized registry of nonincarcerated sex offenders in the state and monitors offenders' whereabouts. The General Assembly also passes legislation mandating that any individual arrested for rape immediately undergo HIV testing at the expense of the arrestee. Offenders convicted of spousal rape or spousal sexual battery are exempt from both pieces of legislation.

An Oklahoma County jury finds Charles Scott Robinson guilty of raping a three-year-old girl. In an effort to ensure that Robinson remain in jail for the rest of his life, the jury recommends a total sentence of 30,000 years. District Judge Dan Owens complies, sentencing Robinson to serve consecutive 5,000-year sentences on each of six counts of lewd molestation. Owens attributes the jury's recommendation to fear that Robinson would be released on parole, and he cites the case as an example of why truth-in-sentencing laws are needed. If the sentence is upheld, Robinson will not be able to leave prison until the year 2084.

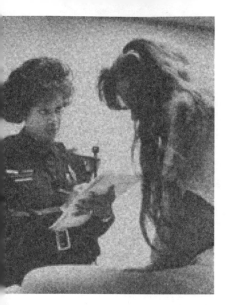

Biographical Sketches 4

I t is impossible to create a comprehensive list of all the "movers and shakers" in the field of sexual assault—a field of largely unsung heroes. The "burnout" rate is tremendous, and the monetary rewards are few. The individuals included in the following list have persevered and excelled in their work to the point of gaining regional, national, and in some cases international recognition for their accomplishments. It is heartening to recognize that these individuals only represent the vanguard in the war against sexual violence; there are literally thousands of women and men who make valuable contributions to the cause on a daily basis.

Cordelia Anderson (1955–)

Through a wide variety of avenues, Cordelia Anderson has actively promoted healthy sexuality as a significant part of sexual violence prevention and recovery. Currently the director of Sensibilities, Inc., a training and consulting business specializing in the areas of sexuality and violence prevention, Anderson was the director of the Illusion Theatre Prevention Program from 1980 until 1993. Before moving to Illusion Theatre in 1980, she was employed for three years at the

Hennepin County Attorney's Office, where she specialized in working with child victims. She coordinated the original Child Sexual Abuse Prevention Project and developed the model and concept of the "Touch Continuum," an educational concept used to help differentiate between nurturing, confusing, and exploitive touch as well as to detect deprivation of touch. This concept has been incorporated into abuse prevention programs throughout the country. Anderson coauthored the play *Touch* with Illusion Theatre while at the attorney's office and, after joining Illusion, she coauthored six other plays dealing with such topics as sexual abuse prevention for adolescents, adult sexuality and violence, and HIV/AIDS awareness and prevention. (Illusion Theatre is discussed in chapter 6.) Anderson has counseled sex offenders, adult survivors of abuse, and prostitutes; has taught classes on sexuality and childhood sexual abuse prevention; and has conducted over 1,200 training sessions on such topics as sexual abuse, sexual harassment, and violence prevention. The cochair of the Violence Prevention Committee of the Minneapolis Public School System, she has been featured on local and national media programs, including CBS *Morning News,* PBS programs, National Public Radio (NPR) programs, and WCCO-TV Minneapolis' *PROJECT ABUSE,* which won a national Emmy Award in 1985. Anderson was the recipient of the 1993 Minnesota Commissioner's Award of the National Conference on Child Abuse and Neglect, the National Camp Fire "On Behalf of Youth" Award in 1989, and the National Council on Family Relations "Distinguished Service to Families 1989" Award, among others. She received her M.A. in human development, with emphasis in sexuality and violence, from St. Mary's College and a criminal justice certificate from the University of Minnesota.

Claudette Baril (1952–)

Since 1984 Claudette Baril has been the executive director of the Susan B. Anthony Project, Inc., a nonprofit agency in Torrington, Connecticut, serving victims of domestic violence and sexual assault. In addition to her usual duties of overseeing three facilities, writing grants, managing budgets and personnel, and speaking publicly, Baril has played a key role in the development and institution of a child abuse investigative team, a transitional housing program, a thrift store, and a permanent office site for the agency. A guest lecturer on violence against women at local colleges and the Yale University School of Nursing, she has served on the board of directors of Connecticut Sexual Assault Crisis Services, Inc. (ConnSACS), since 1985. (ConnSACS is discussed in chapter 6.) In addition, Baril has served on the Aids and Sexual Assault Task Force of the Connecticut Department of Health Services, the Regional Advisory Board of the Connecticut Department of Human Resources, and she is currently on the Advisory Committee on Police Response to Sexual Violence. Baril's approach to combatting sexual violence is rooted in her belief that "[society] can only truly respond to violence against women by understanding it in the context of a culture which is patriarchal. The devaluing of the female lays the foundation for . . . domestic violence and sexual assault."

Fred S. Berlin (1941–)

Fred S. Berlin is currently the director of the National Institute for the Study, Prevention, and Treatment of Sexual Trauma in Baltimore, Maryland, formerly the Johns Hopkins Sexual Disorders Clinic. Berlin has gained national renown for his work with sex offenders, particularly paraphilias, using antiandrogens (see chapter 2). An associate professor in the Department of Psychiatry and Behavioral Science at the Johns Hopkins University School of Medicine and an attending physician at the Johns Hopkins Hospital, Berlin received both his M.D. and Ph.D. from Dalhousie University in Halifax, Nova Scotia. Berlin has published extensively on topics related to sexual disorders in such journals as the *American Journal of Psychiatry*, the *American Journal of Forensic Psychiatry*, and the *British Journal of Psychiatry*. Frequently serving as an expert witness for the defense in sex offense cases, Berlin testified in support of the defendant's plea of insanity in the Jeffrey Dahmer serial murder trial of February 1992.

Nancy Biele (1953–)

Nancy Biele has been active in the field of sexual assault on the local, state, and national levels since 1974, when she cofounded the Program on Aid to Victims of Sexual Assault, the first rape crisis center in northern Minnesota, and the third in the state. For the next 18 years Biele worked with a number of rape crisis centers in Minnesota in a variety of capacities—victim advocate, education coordinator, and executive director (of the Sexual Violence Center of Hennepin, Carver, and Scott Counties). Biele has been extremely active on the state level with the Minnesota Coalition Against Sexual Assault (MCASA), serving for several years as chair and cochair of the Public Affairs (Legislative) Committee and as the urban chair of MCASA's board of directors. She has been a member since 1989 of the Violence Against Women Coalition, a Junior League–sponsored coalition striving to build a community agenda to halt sexual violence in the state. Due to one of her areas of expertise—sexual exploitation by counselors and therapists—Biele served as the chair of the Public Education Work Group of the Minnesota State Task Force on Sexual Exploitation by Counselors and Therapists, and she serves as a member of the Minnesota Council of Churches Committee on Sexual Exploitation within the Religious Community. She is the author of a chapter in *Breach of Trust: Sexual Exploitation by Health Care Professionals and Clergy* (John Gonsiorek, ed., 1994) and several related chapters in the *MCASA Training Manual*. She coauthored *It's Never OK: A Handbook on Sexual Exploitation by Counselors and Therapists for Victims and Advocates* (Minnesota Department of Corrections, [1988], 1993). Biele developed and cotaught one of the first courses on rape ("Sociology of Rape") in the nation at the University of Minnesota at Duluth, from 1975 to 1978. On the national level, Biele served as the regional representative to the National Coalition Against Sexual Assault (NCASA) board of directors from 1985 to 1987, and as the president of the board from 1987 to 1989. Biele operates a Minneapolis consulting firm, specializing in training and consulting on violence and clergy sexual abuse issues.

Carol E. R. Bohmer (1945–)

Carol Bohmer is the coauthor of *Sexual Assault on Campus: The Problem and the Solution* with Andrea Parrot and is a specialist in the fields of sexology, family law, sociology of law, sex discrimination, and mental health law and policy. She has published a number of articles on sexual assault on college campuses, acquaintance rape, and the legal process and rape victims. Since beginning her career at the age of 19 as a law clerk in New Zealand, Bohmer has gone on to serve on the faculty of numerous major universities, including Rutgers University School of Law, Johns Hopkins University School of Medicine, Cornell University, and McGill University of Montreal, Canada. Bohmer is currently an associate professor in the Graduate School of Public and International Affairs at the University of Pittsburgh. She presented a paper entitled "Legal Responses to Complaints of Sexual Assault on the College Campus" with Andrea Parrot at the sixth National Conference on Campus Violence in 1992 in

Baltimore, Maryland, and is currently working on *Must Boys Be Boys?: Sexual Assault and Sexual Harassment in High School* with Parrot. Bohmer served as cochair of the third Annual Conference on Sexual Assault on the College Campus in 1993 in Nashville, Tennessee, and as plenary speaker at the Annual Conference on Sexual Assault on Campus in 1991 and 1992 in Orlando, Florida.

Bohmer was certified as a sexologist by the American College of Sexology in 1980. She received a Ph.D. in sociology from the University of Pennsylvania (1975), a diploma in criminology from the Institute of Criminology, Cambridge University (1969), and an Li.M. (with honors, 1968), an Li.B. (1967), and a B.A. (1965) fromVictoria University in Wellington, New Zealand.

Gail P. Burns-Smith (1946–)

Gail Burns-Smith began her career as a staff nurse at Hartford Hospital in Connecticut, after graduating from Grace New Haven School of Nursing in 1967. She worked as a registered nurse for 12 years, then she began working as the community education project coordinator for the Northeastern Connecticut Sexual Assault Crisis Center (a rape crisis program serving 29 towns). After a year in that position, Burns-Smith became the executive director of the center, serving in that capacity for 3 years. In 1986, she became the executive director of Connecticut Sexual Assault Crisis Services, Inc., the position she currently holds. Burns-Smith is a member of the Governor's Task Force on Sexual Violence, the National Coalition Against Sexual Assault (NCASA), the Adolescent Health Council, and the State of Connecticut Service Provider Task Force. She is also the board director of the National Network for Victims of Sexual Assault, the cochair of the Sexual Assault and HIV Task Force of the Connecticut Department of Health Services, and a member of the Steering Committee of the Connecticut Teen Pregnancy Prevention Coalition. In 1992 Burns-Smith was recognized by the Connecticut Permanent Commission on the Status of Women as a "Connecticut History Maker" and received the Alice Paul Award for Advocacy from the Connecticut chapter of the National Organization for Women (NOW) in 1993.

Linda A. Fairstein (1947–)

Linda Fairstein, author of *Sexual Violence: Our War against Rape*, is chief of the Sex Crimes Prosecution Unit and deputy chief of the Trial Division of the New York County District Attorney's Office.

The publication of *Sexual Violence* in 1993 garnered Fairstein *Glamour* magazine's Woman of the Year Award and catapulted her onto the national television talk show and lecturer circuit, speaking on the judicial perspective of sexual assault. She received her law degree from the University of Virginia School of Law in 1972, and from the same institution she received the Women's Center First Distinguished Alumna Award in 1991. Recognized by the American Bar Association (ABA) in 1991 as one of twenty "outstanding young lawyers" who make a difference, Fairstein has been profiled by *20/20, Ms.*, the *New York Times Sunday Magazine, Esquire, American Lawyer*, and *Time*. She is a member of former Governor Mario Cuomo's Task Force on Rape (formed in July 1989), and in 1992 she was honored for outstanding achievement in the legal profession by the American Association of University Women with their Woman of Achievement Award.

Patricia A. Groot (1952–)

Patricia Groot has been actively working in Virginia to combat sexual assault and its effects since 1980, when she participated in a volunteer training program and became a rape crisis hotline volunteer. She began "self-education" and spent much time attending workshops and training sessions in many areas of sexual assault, including such topics as criminal, civil, and constitutional law, sociology with an emphasis on women's studies, behavioral and cognitive psychology, and health sciences. Groot quickly progressed from being a participant in such sessions to being a presentor. In 1983 she became the public education coordinator of the Charlottesville Rape Crisis Group and spent the next two years acting as the center's law enforcement liaison, conducting training sessions for local law enforcement officials, medical students, obstetricians, and gynecologists. In that position she also conducted media campaigns, trained rape crisis volunteers, and taught classes for high school students on date and acquaintance rape. In 1984 Groot became the executive director of Virginians Aligned Against Sexual Assault (VAASA) and has served in that capacity ever since. In addition to planning and managing the $200,000 budget of the nonprofit organization, Groot is active on the state and national political levels. She monitors, analyzes, summarizes, and disseminates information on public policy development, writes grant applications, provides testimony as requested, and advocates for favorable state and national regulations and policies for funding of sexual assault crisis centers. Groot has served on the staff of the Legal Issues Committee of the Lieutenant Governor's Commission on the Reduction of Sexual Assault since 1992. The committee's efforts resulted in 34 criminal statutory reforms during the 1993 and 1994 Virginia General Assembly sessions.

A. Nicholas Groth (1937–)

A. Nicholas Groth is widely recognized as one of the foremost pioneers in the research of sexual assault and sex offenders. A clinical psychologist, Groth is currently the executive director of Forensic Mental Health Associates, a private enterprise in Orlando, Florida, that provides national education, consultation, and training in regard to sexual assault. He is the founder and former director of the Sex Offender Program at the Connecticut Correctional Institution in Somers (1978–1986) and the former director of psychological services at the Massachusetts Center for the Diagnosis and Treatment of Sexually Dangerous Persons in Bridgewater (1966–1976). The author (with H. J. Birnbaum) of the landmark work *Men Who Rape: The Psychology of the Offender,* Groth developed the standard major classifications of rapists adopted by the FBI and law enforcement agencies throughout the world. He has been a training instructor at the FBI Academy in Quantico, Virginia, the Connecticut Justice Academy in Haddam, and the Massachusetts Criminal Justice Training Council in Boston. Groth has testified before committees of the U.S. House of Representatives, the U.S. Senate, and the California legislature, and he has served as an expert witness in numerous court cases, including *United States v. Patricia Hearst,* in which he testified as a rebuttal witness for the defense. He has been featured on *20/20, The Today Show, Good Morning America, Nighttalk, Donahue,* and the *Montel Williams Show,* among other television programs. He continues to conduct training workshops throughout the nation on working with child victims of sexual abuse, adult survivors of sexual abuse, and juvenile and adult offenders.

Groth received a B.A. in clinical psychology in 1959, an M.A. in psychology in 1960, and a Ph.D. in psychology in 1972, all from Boston University.

Robert R. Hazelwood (1938–)

Robert R. Hazelwood has likely had a greater impact in the area of sexual violence than any other figure in law enforcement. A supervisory special agent with the Behavioral Science Unit at the

FBI's National Center for the Analysis of Violent Crime, Hazelwood has addressed over 150,000 professionals in the disciplines of law enforcement, mental health, corrections, medicine, and the law. He has lectured to law enforcement officials in England, Canada, France, Guam, Switzerland, and Australia, as well as in the United States, and he has received over 50 certificates or awards from civilian and law enforcement organizations. Hazelwood's research and writings have been instrumental in determining investigative procedures followed by law enforcement officers in rape cases throughout the United States. His works, such as "The Behavior-Oriented Interview of Rape Victims: The Key to Profiling" (September 1983), "Rape: The Dangers of Providing Confrontational Advice" (with A. W. Burgess and J. A. Harpold, June 1986), "An Introduction to the Serial Rapist: Research by the FBI" (with Ann W. Burgess, September 1987), and "The Serial Rapist: His Characteristics and Victims, Part I and II" (January 1989, February 1989), all of which appeared in the *FBI Law Enforcement Bulletin,* have had particular impact. Hazelwood has testified as an expert witness in state and federal courts, as well as before a presidential committee and committees of both houses of Congress. In addition to his work with the FBI's Behavioral Science Unit, Hazelwood is currently conducting research with Dr. Park E. Deitz and Dr. Janet Warren on sexual sadism.

Hazelwood received a B.S. in 1960 from Sam Houston State College. He completed a one-year fellowship in forensic medicine in 1969 at the Armed Forces Institute of Pathology in Washington, D.C., and received an M.S. in 1980 from NOVA University. A commissioned officer in the Military Police from 1960 to 1971, he left the Army at the rank of major and joined the FBI. He received additional training at the FBI Academy in Quantico, Virginia, in homicide case management, interpersonal violence, advanced sexual crimes investigation, and criminal personality profiling, among other subject areas.

Lynda Lytle Holmstrom (1939–)

Lynda Lytle Holmstrom has been a prominent author on rape and sexual assault since the mid-1970s, when she wrote *Rape: Victims of Crisis,* with Ann Wolbert Burgess. Holmstrom and Burgess identified traumatic reactions specifically associated with rape and coined the term *rape trauma syndrome,* which would have a tremendous effect on the future treatment of rape victims by the health and legal systems alike. *Rape: Victims of Crisis* was followed by two more major publications: *Sexual*

Assault of Children and Adolescents (with Burgess, A. Nicholas Groth, and Suzanne M. Sgroi), and *The Victim of Rape: Institutional Reactions* (with Burgess). A revised and expanded edition of *Rape: Victims of Crisis* was published in 1979 as *Rape: Crisis and Recovery*, and promptly won the *American Journal of Nursing (AJN)* Book of the Year Award (by category, or type of book). Holmstrom has made numerous presentations at national and international conferences, including congresses in Bulgaria, Israel, Canada, Italy, Sweden, Germany, and Mexico.

Holmstrom received a B.A. in anthropology in 1961 from Stanford University, an M.A. in sociology in 1965 from Boston University, and a Ph.D. in sociology in 1970 from Brandeis University. She has been on the faculty of the Sociology Department at Boston College since 1969, serving as chairperson from 1974 to 1975 and from 1977 to 1982 and as full professor from 1979 to the present.

Carol E. Jordan (1958–)

Carol Jordan is a key figure in the Kentucky state government's efforts to combat sexual and domestic violence. As the director and legislative liaison of the Sexual and Domestic Violence Program of the Department for Mental Health and Mental Retardation Services, she provides consultation and training to the state's rape crisis centers and community mental health centers on the delivery of sexual assault, child sexual abuse, and domestic violence services. Jordan is responsible for evaluating and approving grant proposals from those centers, as well as for developing departmental policies, administrative regulations, and clinical standards of care related to sexual and domestic violence services. She also is responsible for coordinating legislative initiatives of the Division of Mental Health, such as proposed criminal statutes related to sexual and domestic violence. Jordon serves on the Attorney General's Task Force on Child Sexual Abuse, the Governor's Juvenile Sex Offender Treatment Board, and the Steering Committee of the Kentucky Coalition Against Sexual Assault. Among the numerous honors and awards Jordon has received are the Governor's Award for Efforts in the Field of Sexual Assault in 1986, the Outstanding Young Women of America Award in 1988, the Outstanding Advocacy on Behalf of Kentucky Children Award in both 1991 and 1992, and the Kentucky Victim's Coalition Annual Award in 1993. She holds an M.S. in clinical psychology from Eastern Kentucky University (1983) and a B.S. in psychology from Texas A&M University (1980).

Mary P. Koss (1948–)

Mary Koss is renowned as one of the foremost researchers of acquaintance rape and sexual assault, particularly among college students. She served as the director of one of the most widely cited studies of sexual violence to date and published its results in "The Scope of Rape: Incidence and Prevalence of Sexual Aggression and Victimization in a National Sample of Higher Education Students" (with C. Gidycz and N. Wisniewski, 1987). This study, funded by the National Institute of Mental Health and conducted in collaboration with *Ms.* magazine, collected data from 6,159 college students on 32 campuses across the nation. It is from this study that the often-quoted statistic that "one in four women will have experienced sexual assault in her life by the time she gets out of college" is derived. Koss has testified before the U.S. Senate Committee on the Judiciary on the quality of federal rape statistics and before the U.S. Senate Committee on Veteran's Affairs on rape of women in the military. In addition to authoring numerous publications on the prevalence, causes, and ramifications of sexual assault, Koss coauthored *The Rape Victim: Clinical and Community Interventions* with Dr. Mary Harvey. She also is the associate editor of the journals *Psychology of Women Quarterly* and *Violence and Victims* and a consulting editor for the *Journal of Interpersonal Violence, Violence Update, Journal of Child Sexual Abuse,* and *Criminal Behavior and Law.* Koss is the recipient of the Stephen Schaefer Award for Outstanding Research Contributions to the Victim's Assistance Field (1989) from the National Organization for Victim's Assistance and the Research Career Development Award (1991–1996), given by the National Institute of Mental Health. Koss received her Ph.D. from the University of Minnesota.

Virginia A. Lynch (1941–)

Virginia A. Lynch, M.S.N., R.N., spearheaded the concept of forensic nursing and is in the forefront of the movement to educate and prepare forensic nurses for use as sexual assault nurse examiners. A forensic clinical nurse specialist with extensive experience and education in the forensic arena, she has worked in surgery, psychiatric/mental health nursing, emergency nursing, oncology, and clinical forensic nursing. She was a medical investigator for 6 years in Texas and is a certified coroner in the state of Georgia. Having served as a rape crisis counselor for 12 years, she played a major role in the development of rape crisis programs in

Texas and Georgia. Lynch was instrumental in the designing of the graduate program in forensic nursing at the University of Texas at Arlington, where she was the first student enrolled in the program. Her master's thesis, *Clinical Forensic Nursing: A Descriptive Study in Role Development*, was the first publication to present and identify the concept of the forensic clinical nurse specialist as a separate professional discipline. She is currently at the University of Louisville, School of Nursing, in Kentucky helping to develop the curriculum for the first master's degree program in clinical forensic nursing in the nation.

Having received a B.S. in nursing from Texas Christian University in 1982, Lynch went on to receive the first M.S. in nursing and the Certificate in Forensic Nursing as a Clinical Nurse Specialist Award from the University of Texas at Arlington in 1990.

Elected the first president of the International Association of Forensic Nurses in 1993, Lynch is a member of the American Nurses Association and the International Homicide Investigators Association. She is also a fellow of the American Academy of Forensic Sciences. Her numerous presentations of scientific papers on forensic topics have been at such organizations as the American Academy of Forensic Sciences, the Academy of Criminal Justice Sciences, the National Organization for Victim Assistance, and (in Great Britain, Scotland Yard) the Association of Police Surgeons, the World Police Medical Officers, and the Royal College of Nursing.

Carol Middleton (1948–)

Carol Middleton is one of the most respected women martial artists in the United States. A practitioner of karate for over a quarter of a century, Middleton is the founder and chief instructor of (Washington) D.C. IMPACT Self Defense and D.C. Self Defense Karate Association (DCSDKA). (The IMPACT program is discussed in chapter 6.) She began D.C. IMPACT in 1989 with the intention of helping women overcome psychological obstacles to defending themselves and of providing a full-contact women's self-defense course that utilized simple, effective physical and verbal self-defense techniques. Middleton is very firm and verbal in her belief that anyone can learn to protect and empower herself. As a result, DCSDKA welcomes students of all ages, backgrounds, and abilities, including persons with disabilities.

Middleton holds an M.S. in microbiology from the University of Oklahoma (1971), an M.S. in bacteriology from the University of Wisconsin (1975), and an M.S. in exercise physiology from the University of Maryland (1981).

Susan Molinari (1958–)

Congresswoman Susan Molinari has sponsored some of the most controversial anti-rape bills introduced to the House of Representatives in recent years. A Republican representing the Thirteenth District of New York (Staten Island), Molinari introduced Bill HR688, the Sexual Assault Prevention Act of 1993. The Senate equivalent was sponsored by minority leader Bob Dole of Kansas. The bill, among other things, mandated the death penalty in sex-murder cases, required HIV testing for accused sex offenders, and broadened admissibility of evidence to include evidence that the accused had committed other sex crimes. The bill was opposed by the American Civil Liberties Union and gay groups, on the grounds that mandatory HIV testing is an invasion of privacy and violates the constitutional right of the accused to be presumed innocent. Molinari justified mandatory testing by pointing out that "probable cause is sufficient basis for arresting and detaining a person, and for taking blood samples for evidentiary purposes." She suggested that conducting an HIV test on the blood of an accused rapist is a logical extension of "probable cause" doctrine. She further maintained (echoing Justice Oliver Wendell Holmes) that "constitutional rights are not absolute when the safety of the general public is threatened." Molinari expressed a belief that a positive test result from the accused would allow the victim to immediately begin medical and psychological treatment in anticipation of her possibly developing the AIDS virus and dying. A negative test result, Molinari stated, would alleviate "much of (the victim's) legitimate fear" and allow her to progress with psychologically recovering from the rape. The National Organization for Women (NOW) did not endorse the proposed legislation, primarily due to the mandatory death penalty clause. Molinari is currently focusing on the Republicans' "Contract with America," placing priority on maintaining funding for the Violence Against Women Act.

Bonnie Bliss Palecek (1944–)

Bonnie Bliss Palecek, executive director of the North Dakota Council on Abused Women's Services/Coalition Against Sexual Assault in North Dakota, has been a major figure in the movement against sexual assault and abuse in North Dakota for nearly two decades. A self-described "hopeless workaholic" who sees her "life and work as one," Palecek was the founder and director of the Abused Women's Resource Closet, and a founding member of the North Dakota Children's Caucus, the Coalition Against Sexual Assault in North Dakota, the North Dakota Women's Network, and the North Dakota Council on Abused Women's Resources. She is a member of the Governor's Committee on Children and Youth and the Supreme Court's Team on Domestic Violence. She established the Children's Nurturing Network, the Children's Advocacy Network, and the Campus Violence Project. Palecek has been the recipient of numerous awards, among them the Child Advocate of the Year Award from the North Dakota Children's Caucus, the Outstanding Victim Advocate Award of the North Dakota Attorney General's Office, the Fargo Rape and Abuse Crisis Center's Healing the Hurt Award, and a Crime Victims Service Award/Certificate of Appreciation from the Department of Justice. A rape crisis center worker commented, "Bonnie makes the Governor nervous just by walking down the halls of the Capitol."

Andrea Parrot (1953–)

Andrea Parrot, coauthor of *Sexual Assault on Campus: The Problem and the Solution* with Carol Bohmer, is a specialist in acquaintance rape prevention, a sexologist, and a sex educator certified by the American Board of Sexology and the American Association of Sex Educators, Counselors, and Therapists (A.A.S.E.C.T.). Parrot received her M.S. (*summa cum laude*) from the State University of New York (SUNY) at Albany in 1977 and her Ph.D. from Cornell University in 1981. Parrot is currently an assistant professor in the Department of Human Service Studies at Cornell University, and she teaches human sexuality, health issues and sexual concerns of the adolescent, and sexual abuse and assault prevention, among other classes. She has received numerous awards for scholarship and teaching excellence. Parrot taught a women's self-defense class at Cornell for three years and is the cofounder and current chair of the Cornell Coalition Advocating Rape Education. Parrot has been a consultant to the Zuni Indians of Zuni, New Mexico, on acquaintance rape prevention since 1992, and she is currently preparing another book with Bohmer titled *Must Boys Be Boys? Sexual Assault and Harassment in High School.*

Polly Poskin (1947–)

Polly Poskin has actively combatted the causes and ramifications of violence since the 1970s. The director of the Illinois Coalition Against Sexual Assault (ICASA)—one of the largest and most respected coalitions in the country—since 1982, she works with over 30 sexual assault centers across Illinois to serve sexual assault victims. Under Poskin's leadership ICASA's budget has grown from $148,000 in 1982 to $3.1 million in 1993. During her tenure ICASA has worked, with considerable success, to acquire revision of Illinois' sexual assault laws and has conducted a statewide training program regarding those changes. In April of 1994, Poskin received a national award from President Bill Clinton and Attorney General Janet Reno in recognition of her service to victims and their families. Prior to becoming the director of ICASA, Poskin worked in a domestic violence shelter, first as the volunteer coordinator, then as the executive director. She has been active for 18 years as a community educator on lesbianism and homophobia, working with high school, college, and adult audiences to examine and alter personal and cultural biases against homosexuals. In concert with this work, Poskin joined the Springfield Area AIDS Task Force in 1985 and helped create its "buddy network" in 1988. Participants in this network provide personal support and care to people with AIDS. Poskin has had a buddy since 1988.

Rosemary Richmond (1945–1994)

Rosemary Richmond was a driving force in anti–sexual assault work on both the state and national levels, waging war against sexual violence with her pen. A prolific writer, she wrote numerous essays and stories about women's social roles and violence, such as "100 Ways To Blame a Mother" and many articles on Take Back the Night. For several years she edited and contributed to the newsletters of both the Illinois Coalition Against Sexual Assault (ICASA) and the National Coalition Against Sexual Assault (NCASA). Although Richmond came from a life of poverty, she worked her way through school, ultimately receiving her M.A. in English from Sangamon State University in Springfield, Illinois. A single parent, she raised two children. Richmond died in 1994 at the age of 49. The Rosemary Richmond Scholarship for female fiction writers was established at Sangamon State University in her honor.

Patricia Scott Schroeder (1940–)

Democratic Congresswoman Patricia Scott Schroeder of the First Congressional District of Colorado is arguably one of the most powerful women in the country and a staunch advocate of women's rights. Born in Portland, Oregon, she attended grade school in Texas, junior high in Ohio, high school in Iowa, college in Minnesota (University of Minnesota, 1961, *magna cum laude*), and law school in Massachusetts (Harvard Law School, 1964, J.D.). Prior to her political career, Schroeder practiced law in Colorado and taught at Denver colleges.

A member of the House of Representatives since her election in 1972, Schroeder is the senior woman in Congress and the cochair of the Congressional Caucus for Women's Issues, a bipartisan group of representatives devoted to advancing women's legislation in Congress. She is a member of the House Armed Services Committee, the House Judiciary Committee, the House Committee on Post Office and Civil Service, and the House Select Committee on Children, Youth, and Families. A primary sponsor of the Family and Medical Leave Act and the current Equal Rights Amendment, Schroeder is the leading House sponsor of House of Representatives Bill 1133, The Violence Against Women Act of 1993. Highlights of this act include the authorization of $200 million in grants to reduce violent crimes against women, in addition to $136 million over three years for rape prevention programs, $500,000 to establish a national board on violent crimes against women, $200,000 to study the problem of campus sexual assaults, and $1.3 million to educate judges and court personnel to ensure equal justice for women in the courts, and to create new and extend old evidentiary rules to protect victims from character assassination in court.

Laura Slaughter (1946–)

Laura Slaughter is revolutionizing the examination process of rape victims and the collection of forensic evidence for use in prosecution. In addition to holding a private practice in rheumatology and internal medicine, Slaughter is the medical director of the Suspected Abuse Response Team (SART) of the county of San Luis Obispo, California, and on the clinical staff at the Barbara Sinatra Children's Center in Rancho Mirage, California. She is a pioneer in the use of the colposcope in the examination of adult victims of sexual assault, documenting and characterizing genital findings in cases of forced sex in order to clinically compare them with those of consensual sex. This research allows prosecutors to more effectively present evidence of rape, and it significantly undermines a rapist's claim of consensual sex.

Slaughter enrolled at the University of Michigan at age 16, entered the university's Medical School without a degree, and received her M.D. in 1970. She served her residency at the University of Oregon Medical School in Portland, and at the University of California, Davis. She later was both a clinical and a research fellow in rheumatology at Scripps Clinic and Research Foundation in La Jolla, California. Since 1980 Slaughter has presented lectures, seminars, and papers in the United States, Guam, and Canada on such topics as the recognition, examination, and evaluation of child physical and sexual abuse, adult and child sexual assault/rape, consensual versus forced sex, preparation of courtroom testimony, and the establishment and function of sexual assault response teams. Among Slaughter's many awards are commendations from numerous district attorneys' offices (1982, 1990), the California District Attorney's Association (1986, 1989, 1990–1991), the California Sexual Assault Investigators' Association (1992), and the International Association of Forensic Nurses (1993) for her work in the field.

Susan J. Xenarios (1946–)

Susan J. Xenarios' sphere of influence not only encompasses the state of New York, but it also extends internationally. One of the original founders in 1977, Xenarios has served as the director of the Rape Intervention Program/Crime Victim Assessment Project at St. Luke's-Roosevelt Hospital Center—the largest sexual assault program in New York City, and one of the largest hospital-based programs in the United States—since 1987. A member of the Executive Committee of the New York City Task Force Against Sexual Assault since 1987, Xenarios also serves as cochair of the New York State Downstate Coalition for Crime Victims and is a member of the New York State Crime Victims Board Advisory Council and the New York State Department of Health Rape Crisis Advisory Board. Xenarios helped design and implement uniform collection of evidence protocol (a specified manner or order of evidence collection) for sexual assault in New York State, and has organized major lobby days in both the state and federal legislatures for Women Against Violence. Having received her M.S. in 1982 from the Columbia University School of Social Work, Xenarios became an adjunct professor of the university in 1986 and continues to teach for the School of Social Work, the University's College of

Physicians and Surgeons. Xenarios has provided professional training and consultation locally to such groups as the New York City Board of Education, the New York Police Department, and the New York State Department of Health, as well as internationally to the Government of Australia and the Congress of South African Trade Unions.

In the fall of 1993 Xenarios organized training teams and traveled to Croatia and Bosnia, where she conducted training seminars on rape trauma for medical doctors, psychiatrists, and women activists. She is a member of the Steering Committee of the New York City Balkan Rape Crisis Response Team. At the bequest of the Bahamian government, Xenarios provided training and consultation for staff and volunteers at the hospital-based Women's Crisis Center in Nassau, the Bahamas. She is currently providing consultation and technical assistance to the Women's Crisis Center at the University of the Philippines, as they seek to establish a hospital-based rape crisis and domestic violence program. The recipient of the Susan B. Anthony Award from the New York City chapter of the National Organization for Women (NOW) in 1993, Xenarios has also received awards from both the governor of New York (1988) and the mayor of New York City (1987). She has been featured on CNN, PBS, NPR, and all other major television networks, as well as in *Ms., New Woman, Ladies Home Journal, The Village Voice,* and the *New York Observer.* In addition to carrying out her duties at St. Luke's-Roosevelt Hospital, Xenarios operates a clinical practice in general psychotherapy with specialization in sexual trauma/abuse and domestic violence in New York City.

5

Types of Rape/Rapists

A lthough statistics are available on over
30,000 adults charged with forcible rape
in 1991 and comparisons can be made as
to the age, race, and sex of those charged,
there is nothing to outwardly distinguish a
rapist from any other individual. He can and
often does appear as an average citizen and
can be found in any community, at any time.
Rapists can be "typed" on the basis of the
apparent primary motivation of the assailant, though even this categorization acknowledges that each classification contains
elements of other classifications. For example, an "anger rapist" will likely share some
of the same motivations as those of a "power
rapist," or a "sadistic rapist." The assault itself can be classified, with categories within
categories. Under the general heading of
"acquaintance rape" can be found rapes
committed by friends, family members (incest), spouses (marital rape), dates (date
rape), and passing acquaintances. The following chapter identifies and describes
some of the more commonly used classifications of rape and rapists.

Demographic Profile of Arrested Rapists

There are figures regarding the sex, age, and race of suspects charged with forcible rape, supplied by law and judicial authorities, and found in the *Uniform Crime Report*, which states that in 1991 a total of 29,964 men and 386 women were charged with forcible rape of females. For both sexes, 33 percent of those charged were between 25 and 34 years of age, 18 percent were between 25 and 29 years old, and 15 percent were between 30 and 34 years old. A greater percentage of males than females were 18 or older: 84 percent of the men were 18 or older, while 77 percent of the women were 18 or older.

On a national level, 55 percent of those charged with forcible rape were white, while 44 percent were black. (Federal Bureau of Investigation 1992) Percentages were much closer in city arrests: 51 percent of those under 18 arrested were white, 48 percent were black, while slightly more suspects over 18 were black (50 percent) than white (49 percent). (Federal Bureau of Investigation 1992) It should be remembered that these figures only reflect the percentage of reported rapes that resulted in both arrest and formal charging with forcible rape (versus a lesser charge) and that the number of reported rapes by all estimates is considerably less than the number of those that go unreported.

External and Internal Characteristics of Rapists

There is no demographic picture of a "typical" rapist that serves to outwardly differentiate him from a "typical" man in the street. Studies of convicted rapists, serial rapists, and sex killers have found the majority to be of average or above average intelligence, to have obtained the equivalent of a high school diploma or better, to have been married at least once, and to have had an income well above the poverty level. (Langevin et al. 1988; Warren et al. 1991) There are, however, internal and historical differences that have been noted in several studies. In the landmark book *Men Who Rape*, A. N. Groth and H. J. Birnbaum (1979) stipulate that "rape is not a symptom of mental illness but of personality dysfunction." In a study of over 500 convicted sexual offenders, Groth and Birnbaum observed that the most apparent personality dysfunction of rapists was the inability to form or maintain emotionally intimate relationships with other human beings. Rapists observed displayed little ability to trust, to sympathize or empathize, or to display warmth with others. Their relationships lacked reciprocity and mutuality. Groth and Birnbaum's studies in the penal system reflect Patricia Groot's observations from dealing with survivors that "no one can assault someone they consider of equal value to them." (Groot 1994)

Childhood Sexual Trauma

In J. I. Warren, R. R. Hazelwood, and R. Reboussin's study of serial rapists (1991), it was observed that 76 percent of the 41 rapists studied had experienced some sort of sexual abuse as children, ranging from forced watching of sexual acts to physical penetration. Groth and Birnbaum (1979) found that in a study of 250 convicted rapists, approximately one-third had experienced sexual trauma, and that 45 percent of that third had been sexually assaulted. Nearly half of those assaulted had been assaulted by a family member, while another third had been assaulted by a known assailant such as a teacher, neighbor, or friend. Of those who had been sexually assaulted, 68 percent were victimized before age 13. According to D. Finkelhor, approximately 10 percent of nonoffending adult males have experienced sexual trauma. (Finkelhor 1979)

Alcohol

Alcohol abuse is another common denominator among convicted rapists. R. Langevin's study (1991) of sexual assailants, rapists, and sex killers found over 50 percent of the number to be alcoholics. J. I. Warren, R. R. Hazelwood, and R. Reboussin (1991) found 63 percent of the studied serial rapists to be alcoholics, while Groth and Birnbaum (1979) found 40 percent of the 250 studied rapists to have a history of chronic drinking and another 33 percent of the group to have a history of steady but moderate drinking. Groth and Birnbaum further determined that in 50 percent of the cases, the rapist had been drinking and/or using drugs at the time of the assault. It was observed, however, that the rapists generally were not drinking or using drugs any more at that time than was typical for them. Groth and Birnbaum suggest that alcohol may only play a contributive role in rape, not a causal one; that it may ". . . serve as a releasor only when an individual had already reached a frame of mind in which he is prone to rape."

Sexual Dysfunction

The most frequently cited source of information regarding sexual dysfunction among rapists is a study published in 1977 by A. W. Burgess and A. N. Groth entitled "Sexual Dysfunction during

Rape." The study combined data received by Burgess from sexual assault victims with that received by Groth from convicted rapists. The widely cited statistic from that study is that 34 percent of the assailants experienced sexual dysfunction in the form of impotence, premature ejaculation, or retarded ejaculation. It should be noted that the number from which that percentage is drawn includes a significant number of cases in which no data were available—21 percent of the total. If that percentage is removed to allow consideration of only those cases in which data were available, the percentage of assailants experiencing sexual dysfunction rises to 43 percent. The new total, however, still includes a significant percentage of cases in which the dysfunction was not applicable due to interruption, resistance, or a lack of attempt on the part of the assailant. If these figures are removed from consideration, leaving only those cases in which it is known whether dysfunction was or was not present, just under 58 percent of the assailants experienced some type of sexual dysfunction.

The indicated high prevalence of sexual dysfunction among rapists does much to combat the common rape myth of "no sperm, no assault." Historically, law enforcement officials and states' attorneys have interpreted the presence of sperm in a sexual assault victim as being supportive of the allegation that the assault did take place. Conversely, defense attorneys have sometimes been able to use the absence of sperm to cast doubt on the victim's claim of assault. (Young et al. 1992) As indicated above, and as will be discussed further in this chapter under Physical Ramifications of Rape, the presence or absence of sperm may be more indicative of sexual functioning on the part of the rapist or the post-assault behavior of the assailant and/or victim than of the legitimacy of the allegation of rape.

Rapist Typology

"Rape is not a symptom of mental illness but of personality dysfunction. It is the result of defects in human development." (Groth and Birnbaum 1979)

With the publication of *Men Who Rape: The Psychology of the Offender* by A. N. Groth and H. J. Birnbaum in 1979, guidelines for the categorization of rapists were established. While others have occasionally developed subcategories of, or variations on, this blueprint, the major categories of "anger," "power," and "sadistic" rapists remain intact. They provide the terminology used by the majority of researchers, from psychiatrists to the FBI, which has developed a system of profiling rapists on the basis of their core behavior—verbalizations, sexual actions, and physical force used—which in turn gives insight into the assailant's underlying motivation. (Hazelwood and Burgess 1987) While the use of categories indicates the predominant nature of the rape and rapist, it is important to note that the elements of power, anger, and sexuality are present in all cases of forcible rape to one degree or another. (Groth and Birnbaum 1979) Differences are noted in the form in which sexuality is expressed. That is not to say that rape should be considered a sexual act. Contrary to the social myth, rape is not a result of uncontrollable sexual desire. Groth and Birnbaum identifiy rape as a ". . . pseudosexual act, a pattern of sexual behavior that is concerned much more with status, hostility, control, and dominance than with sensual pleasure or sexual satisfaction. It is sexual behavior in the primary service of non-sexual needs." The anger rapist uses sexuality to express hostility, while the power rapist uses sexuality to express conquest. The sadistic rapist combines and eroticizes the two. Groth and Birnbaum found 40 percent of their subjects to be primarily anger rapists, 55 percent to be primarily power rapists, and 5 percent to be sadistic rapists. It is likely, however, that the percentage reported in the study of anger rapists may be inflated in terms of the prevalence of anger rape in society as a whole, and the reported percentage of power rapists is likely to be deflated in the same context. Groth and Birnbaum's subjects were over 500 incarcerated rapists, studied over a 15-year period. Because of the nature of the assault by the anger rapist, there is more likely to be obvious evidence of physical assault than in the case of an attack by a power rapist. A prevalence of physical evidence of attack is more likely to result in conviction of a rapist than in cases where such evidence is lacking.

The Anger Rapist

"His intent . . . is to hurt and degrade his victim. His weapon is sex, and his motive is revenge." (Groth and Birnbaum 1979)

Anger rapes are impulsive, sudden, physically brutal attacks and are of relatively short duration. The anger rapist uses more physical force than is necessary to overpower the victim, resulting in physical trauma to the victim extending beyond that typically sustained as a result of the act of rape itself. The assailant is often not sexually aroused by attack and accordingly may experience impotence. As a result of this impotence, the anger rapist frequently forces the victim to perform oral sex in an attempt to achieve an erection.

The anger rapist typically considers sexuality to be "dirty," and therefore a suitable weapon to be used to defile and humiliate the victim in addition to the physical assault. His mood is one of anger, and possibly depression. The rapist's language commonly contains obscenities and is abusive toward the victim.

The anger rapist seeks retribution for perceived wrongs and injustices done to him, particularly by women. Anger rapes are more likely to be committed by strangers than by acquaintances, with the exception of spousal rapes in which there is a history of battering. Because of the spontaneous nature of the attack, anger rape victims tend to be selected by virtue of circumstance (i.e., their physical surroundings and vulnerability) rather than by specific physical appearance or type.

The Power Rapist

"The intent of the power rapist . . . is to assert his competency and validate his masculinity. Sexuality is the test and his motive is conquest." (Groth and Birnbaum 1979)

The power rapist generally uses only as much force as is necessary to gain and maintain control over the victim; any bodily injury other than that typically sustained in nonconsensual sex would be inadvertant, rather than intentional, on the part of the rapist. As opposed to anger rapes, power rapes may be for an extended period of time.

Power rapes are premeditated. Power rapists are typically operating on a variation of a fantasy regarding sexual conquest and rape. In this fantasy the victim initially resists the assailant, but is overpowered and soon becomes sexually aroused and desirous of the assailant. Over a period of time the power rapist may become increasingly frustrated by the failure of the fantasy to materialize, resulting in an increase in the frequency and severity of assaults.

The power rapist frequently projects his own desires on the victim, thereby interpreting her resistance as a facade of noncompliance and the resulting rape as consensual sex. It is not uncommon for power rapists to seek to continue to socialize with the victim following the rape—offering to go out for a drink, seeking to make a date for a later time, etc.

The power rapist's mood is one of anxiety, and his language is instructional (seeking to maintain and exercise control of the victim) and inquisitive as to the victim's responses (seeking to validate his fantasy of a willing victim). He seeks to compensate underlying feelings of inadequacy by sexual conquest.

Power rapes most frequently are committed by acquaintances, especially in the context of social situations ("date rape"). Victims may be specifically selected, based on the rapist's assessment of the victim's personal vulnerability and availability.

The Sadistic Rapist

"The intent of the sadistic rapist . . . is to abuse and torture his victim. His instrument is sex, and his motive is punishment and destruction." (Groth and Birnbaum 1979)

Sadistic rapes are planned and calculated. A type of serial rapist, the sadistic rapist may show a pattern of increasing aggression and violence in his attacks over time. His victims may be kidnapped, held prisoner for extended periods of time, sexually assaulted, tortured in a ritualistic manner (bites, burns, flagellation, etc., particularly to the sexual areas of the body), and in extreme cases, mutilated and/or killed. Sex killers form a major subset of sadistic rapists. It can be argued, in fact, that sadistic rapists are simply sex killers who have not quite completed their full, eventual evolution. Studies have noted a greater interest in anal intercourse among sexually sadistic criminals than "regular" rapists. (Dietz et al. 1990; Warren et al. 1991) The sadistic rapist has eroticized the blending of anger and power; he is sexually excited by the pain and suffering of the victim, and he seeks to prolong both. The sadistic rapist's mood is one of intense excitement, and his language is commanding and degrading, reflecting a feeling of omnipotence.

The sadistic rapist is often extremely personable and "normal" in outward appearance and conduct, contrary to the societal stereotype of a sadist as an obvious psychotic madman. In fact, his "charm" is frequently what gains him access to his victims, who are usually strangers with common traits, such as age and appearance. (Groth and Birnbaum 1979)

The Sex Killer

Research conducted in the late 1980s did much to compare and contrast sex killers, "regular" killers, serial rapists, and "regular" rapists/sexual assailants. A comparison of the demographics of sex killers and regular killers revealed no significant differences in level of education, alcohol abuse, intelligence, occupation, marital history or criminal record. (Langevin 1991; Warren et al. 1991) Major differences were noted in their relationship with their victim(s) and the manner used to kill. R. Langevin (1991) found that 69 percent of the sex killers studied had murdered a stranger, while only 8 percent of the regular killers had not known their victim. A firearm was used by almost half of the regular killers, while none of the sex killers used a gun; in all likelihood, such a method would have been too fast. The method of murder preferred by 71 percent of the sex killers was strangulation, since it allowed them to maintain control over the victim. He could start and stop at will, thus prolonging his pleasure as well as the suffering of the victim.

Langevin et al. (1988) found that over half of the sex killers studied had engaged in transvestism. In a study of serial rapists, one-fifth of whom had displayed sexually sadistic behavior, Warren et al. (1991) found 23 percent had cross-dressed at some time in their life.

The "big three" in childhood—enuresis (bed wetting), cruelty to animals, and fire-setting—have often been asserted to be predictors of extreme, violent behavior in later life. While research has shown that these may be indicators, such behaviors are by no means universal among sex offenders and other violent criminals. In one study, Langevin et al. (1988) found that 62 percent of the sex killers had experienced enuresis after age five, compared with 33 percent of both the regular rapists/sexual assailants and regular killers. Little difference was noted in the history of cruelty to animals between sex killers (39 percent) and regular rapists/sexual assailants (40 percent), but only 10 percent of the regular killers had displayed such behavior. Less difference between the three groups was found in the final category, with 39 percent of the sex killers, 33 percent of the regular rapists/sexual assailants, and 20 percent of the regular killers having a history of fire-setting (Figure 5-1).

The Serial Rapist

". . . all rapists are potential serial rapists; some just get caught before they become serial offenders." (Hazelwood and Burgess 1987)

One of the most extensive studies of the serial, or multiple, rapist was conducted by the FBI's National Center for the Analysis of Violent Crime (NCAVC) and a team from the University of Pennsylvania's School of Nursing in the mid-1980s. Interviews ranging from 4-1/2 to 12-1/2 hours in length were conducted by FBI special agents with 41 incarcerated serial rapists in 12 states. Each of the rapists had committed 10 to 59 rapes and had exhausted all judicial appeals. (Hazelwood and Burgess 1987) The 41 rapists had committed 837 rapes, over 400 attempted rapes, and over 1,237 sexual assaults. The group consisted of 35 Caucasians, 5 blacks, and 1 Hispanic.

Basic demographic information did little to distinguish the serial rapist from the nonraping male population. Contrary to the "loner" stereotype, 71 percent had been married at least once, 34 percent had been married more than once, and 79 percent had been living with someone (spouse and/or kids, parents, or other) at the time of the last rape. (Warren et al. 1991) This supports Groth and Birnbaum's (1979) earlier study, in which one-third of the incarcerated rapists had been married and sexually active with their wives, and the remaining two-thirds had active, consensual sexual relationships at the time of their rapes. Slightly over half of the serial rapists in the NCAVC study had served in the military, with 50 percent of those receiving honorable discharges, 25 percent receiving a general or medical discharge, and 25 percent receiving an undesirable or dishonorable discharge. Over 60 percent of the rapists had a high school diploma or G.E.D., while an additional 22 percent had either an associate's or bachelor's degree. Intelligence scores showed 36 percent of the group to be of average intelligence, while 51 percent tested at above average intelligence. Over half of the criminals had grown up in homes that were rated either average or advantaged.

An examination of the rapists' childhood, however, revealed that most of the offenders had displayed recognized social maladjustment, either in the form of juvenile delinquency, emotional disturbance, or both. Sixty-seven percent of the offenders had been institutionalized prior to adulthood in either a detention center or a mental health facility. An additional 27 percent had lived in either an orphanage, foster home, boarding school, or military academy. Almost three-quarters of the felons had stolen as children, often through breaking and entering. Obscene phone calls had been made by 38 percent of the group, while 68 percent had been voyeurs. Paraphilic behavior had been committed by 84 percent of the serial rapists in addition to their rapes.

Sadistic masturbatory fantasies were a significant part of the serial rapists' development. Of the 70 percent of the serial rapists who responded to questions regarding such fantasies, 52 percent began to fantasize about rape between the ages of 9 and 15, and

28 percent began between 16 and 22. This was particularly relevant as it related to the time elapsed between the onset of the fantasy and an attempt to carry it out. Fifty-nine percent of the responding offenders acted on their fantasy in less than a year. For the remaining 41 percent, it took 1 to 14 years to act on the fantasies, with an average delay of 5.2 years. These facts indicate a rough division between rapists with sadistic masturbatory fantasies: those who act on their fantasies in relatively short order and those who significantly delay acting on their fantasies.

In over 80 percent of the cases the victim was a stranger to the serial rapist, and in 79 percent of the cases the victim was alone. Half of the rapes took place in the victim's home. (As noted above, many of the serial rapists were experienced voyeurs and burglars as children; this early "training" may well have facilitated their career as rapists.) In slightly less than half of the rapes the offender displayed a weapon.

In better than three-quarters of the assaults, the rapist used "minimal" force (i.e., force designed to intimidate and control, rather than punish); however, 25 percent of the rapists were "increasers" in the amount of force used as their history of rape grew. It was also noted that the increasers were three times more likely to have anally raped their victims than were the other rapists in the study. These increasers starting raping at a slightly earlier average age than the other rapists (20 versus 22 years old), and finished at a slightly older average age (30 versus 28). Additionally, this group assaulted more victims (an average of 40 victims each versus 22.4 victims) in a shorter period of time (19.7 days between assaults versus 55.2 days) and increasingly got more pleasure from his assaults. (Warren et al. 1991)

The FBI identified three primary methods of operation used by all rapists to gain access to overcome their victims: (1) the con, (2) the blitz, and (3) the surprise. The con method involves subterfuge; the rapist poses as a policeman, a good samaritan, a lost motorist, etc. In a blitz approach the rapist simply assaults the victim without warning, overpowering and raping her. The surprise method involves the selection and observation of a specific victim to determine when she is vulnerable (such as sleeping or home alone). Once assured of the victim's vulnerability, the rapist gains control over the surprised victim by threats and/or the use of a weapon. The FBI researchers wanted to determine if serial rapists change their standard method of operation over time. To assist in this determination, they gathered information about the offender's first, a middle, and last assault. In the initial rape, slightly over half of the rapists used the surprise approach, while the remaining half were equally divided between the con and blitz approaches. Rapes occurring in the middle, as well as the last rape of the offender's series, saw a decrease in the amount of blitz and surprise approaches and an increase in the con approach. This may have been reflective of increasing confidence on the part of the rapist. Despite the shift toward the con approach, however, surprise remained the most frequently used approach (Figure 5-2).

The Acquaintance or Date Rapist

"On some level, the acquaintance rapist is always a man who has tricked you into thinking you're safe with him." (Bart 1994)

It has long been believed that acquaintance rapes account for the majority of unreported rapes, as well as the majority of total rapes. (Hall 1994; Koss et al. 1988; McDermott 1979; National Institute of Law Enforcement and Criminal Justice 1977; Williams 1985) Acquaintance rape is committed by an assailant known to the victim, and it may or may not be in the context of a romantic or social situation. Date rape is a subcategory of acquaintance rape and takes place in a romantic or social situation.

Women are particularly vulnerable to acquaintance rape for several reasons. Because the assailant is someone who is known to the victim, he is likely to be trusted more than a stranger. Victims frequently do not recognize, or choose to ignore, warning signs because of the identity of the attacker. Depending on the circumstances of the initial assault, victims may often be too embarrassed to resist in a manner that might increase their chances of avoiding rape. For example, the initial assault from a best friend's boyfriend might be viewed as "joking around" and not recognized as a genuine sexual assault until it is too late. In a dating situation in which the victim has been kissing the assailant, the rapist may be able to capitalize on the victim's confusion over where sexual play ends and sexual assault begins. The lack of recognition of danger, coupled with embarrassment and confusion, frequently cause resistance to be delayed until it is too late to avoid the attack. A study funded by the National Institute of Mental Health in the early to mid-1980s found that, while 31 percent of the victims of an assault by a stranger screamed for help, only 11 percent of the acquaintance rape victims did so. The study also found that stranger rape victims were twice as likely to have attempted to flee their assailant than were acquaintance rape victims. Environment also plays a significant part in acquaintance rape; attacks by known assailants frequently occur in the victim's own home, or in a similar environment where the victim is less likely to receive outside assistance. Studies indicate that alcohol usage has been present in approximately half of the reported acquaintance rapes. (Jacoby 1994)

In a major study of rape among college women, 89 percent of the rape victims who provided information on their attacker were assaulted by someone they knew. Of those acquaintance rape victims, 60 percent were assaulted in a dating situation—25 percent by casual dates, 35 percent by steady dates. Nonromantic acquaintances were responsible for 29 percent of the acquaintance rapes, while spouses or family members accounted for 11 percent (Figure 5-3). (Koss et al. 1988) College-age women are particularly vulnerable to acquaintance rape in a romantic/social setting, since they are most often single and dating. Accordingly, the percentage of those victims assaulted in a dating situation would likely decrease in a study of older victims. Likewise, the percentage of those victims assaulted by spouses or nonromantic acquaintances might increase with an older group.

The Marital Rapist

". . . [Rape is] when a person has sex with another by force and without his or her consent. A rape is 'marital' simply when the attacker is the husband of the woman being attacked." (Finkelhor and Yllo 1985b)

Definitions of marital rape, as with other types of rape, vary in specificity from researcher to researcher. Susan Brownmiller (1975), in *Against Our Will*, defines rape in general terms as ". . . any sexual intimacies forced on one person by another," while Diane Russell (1982) in *Rape in Marriage* insists on using the term *wife rape* and specifies that it includes ". . . forced oral, anal, and digital penetration. . . ." (Finkelhor and Yllo 1985b) Physical force may be considered a key element, as in A. Nicholas Groth's definition of marital rape as a ". . . forcible sexual assault on an unwilling spouse," (Groth and Birnbaum 1979), or it may be totally absent and considered unnecessary for an act of rape to occur. Suzanne Brogger (1976) states in *Deliver Us from Love*, "All the women who copulate to keep peace in the house are the victims of rape. All our grandmothers who just 'let it happen' were essentially force-fucked all their lives." (Finkelhor and Yllo 1985a) Kersti Yllo and David Finkelhor identify two specific types of possible coercion in marital rape that contain no threat of physical force at all ("social coercion" and "interpersonal coercion"), but concede that objective identification of such coercion is impossible for the researcher.

While victims of acquaintance rape have had to combat myths of not being victims of "real rape," victims of marital rape have been faced with the cold reality that until recently it was legally impossible for a wife to be raped by her husband. In 1985 over half of the states exempted husbands from prosecution for raping their wives if they were living with them at the time of the rape. While most states had changed their laws by the end of the decade, as late as 1993 North Carolina and Oklahoma did not legally recognize marital rape if the married couple were living together. North Carolina eliminated the automatic exemption as of 1 July 1993, Oklahoma as of 1 September 1993 (see chapter 3).

Finkelhor and Yllo describe the commonly held societal view of marital rape as a "sanitary stereotype"; a "petty conflict" that arises as a result of differing opinions about sexual frequency. "He wanted to, she didn't, they did anyway." (Finkelhor and Yllo 1985a) The entertainment industry has successfully capitalized on this view on several occasions. *Gone with the Wind* contained probably the most famous marital rape scene in motion picture history and presented marital rape as an appropriate and successful way to reconcile marital disputes. *General Hospital* made television soap opera history in the early 1980s when a relationship began with a rape and culminated with a marriage.

Contrary to the myth that marital rape is not quite "real" rape (due to the previous sexual history and intimate relationship between the parties) and is not as severe an experience as rape by a stranger, many psychologists believe that the long-term effects of the trauma may be greater than those of either stranger or acquaintance rape. Marital rape victims experience the same violation, loss of control, and violence as stranger rape victims, and they suffer additionally from the complete betrayal of trust in their spouse. "The person to whom (the victim) looks for protection and caring is her victimizer." (Groth and Birnbaum 1979) Recovery from such an assault is further complicated by the fact that, in many cases, the victim is still living with the rapist.

Societal attitudes and legal codes notwithstanding, there is a growing conviction among researchers that marital rape may be the most common type of sexual assault. (Finkelhor and Yllo 1985a and b; Groth and Birnbaum 1979) The National Women's Study indicated that 61,000 women are raped each year by their husbands or ex-husbands. (Kilpatrick et al. 1992) As D. Finkelhor and K. Yllo (1985b) discovered in their research, "The slowly accumulating evidence is that marital rape is widespread. With prevalence estimates ranging between 3 percent and 14 percent of married women, with much higher rates among battered women, it is clear that millions of women in the U.S. have been raped by their husbands. It appears that marital rape is, in fact, the most common form of rape."

In one of the most often cited studies to date, D. Russell (1982) surveyed 930 women, ages 18 and older, selected randomly in San Francisco. Of the women who were currently or formerly married, 14 percent said they had been raped by their husband or (now) ex-husband (see Russell's definition of rape, above). Twice as many women had been raped by their spouse than had been raped by a stranger.

The reported incidence of marital rape in studies of battered women is significantly higher than among women who are not battered. (Finkelhor and Yllo 1985a) In the Russell study, 35 percent of the women who reported being raped by their spouse also reported being victims of domestic violence. A study of 304 battered women in ten shelters in Minnesota found 36 percent of them reported they had been raped by their husband or cohabitating partner. (Spektor 1980) In I. Frieze's study (1983) of 137 battered women in Pittsburgh, 73 percent of the group reported having been pressured by their husbands to have sex, and 34 percent of the group reported having been raped. In a group of 403 self-identified battered women studied by the Battered Women's Research Project in Denver, 59 percent of them reported marital rape. (Thyfault 1985)

Studies have shown that marital rape victims tend to be found in a lower socioeconomic class, especially victims who remain with the assaulting spouse. Within this class, high school dropouts are four times more likely to be raped than are graduates, and victims who were sexually victimized as children are three times more likely to be subjected to marital rape. The frequency of marital rape is also significant. In the Russell study (1982), 71 percent of the victims reported being raped more than once, and 34 percent said it had occurred 20 or more times. Frieze (1983) found 59 percent of the marital rape victims had been raped more than once, while R. Thyfault (1985) reported 83 percent of the marital rape victims studied said it occurred more than once.

Marital rape often occurs near the end of the relationship, as a result of a spouse's anger or desperation regarding the termination of the relationship, or possibly as an outgrowth of already present marital problems, particularly regarding sex. (Finkelhor and Yllo 1985a; Groth and Birnbaum 1979) As Groth and Birnbaum observed, ". . . the refusal of sex is not, in and of itself, the reason for (marital rape): rather it is how such denial is experienced by the offender in the context of the marital relationship. . . ." He goes on to identify possible motivations of marital rape as an attempt on the part of the offender to regain control of the relationship, an attempt to forcefully reaffirm their spouse's love for them (sex of any type being equated with love), an attempt to assuage self-doubts about their virility, an attempt to "solve" the marital problems (in a manner similar to that in the *Gone with the Wind* scenario), or an attempt to punish their spouse. Victims in relationships where violence is chronic are more likely to be subjected to forced anal or oral sex. (Finkelhor and Yllo 1985a)

Factual and Statistical Data on Victims

Aside from general demographics, it is impossible to draw a conclusive profile of a rape victim. Rape victims range in age—infants and elderly individuals alike are rape victims—and represent all races and socioeconomic categories of the population. Uncertainty of reporting accuracy frequently results in statistics of limited value; however, studies have shown that the physical and psychological ramifications of sexual assault—both immediate and long-term effects—are common to most victims. The recognition that rape trauma syndrome (RTS) is a post-traumatic stress disorder (PTSD) has led to major advancements in the treatment of victims. Guidelines for dealing with sexual assault victims have been developed and are being used successfully by rape crisis advocates and others throughout the country.

Profile of Rape Victims

The nature of rape precludes any possibility of ascertaining with any degree of certainty the number of assaults each year. Estimates of the percentage of rapes that go unreported each year range from 40 percent to 90 percent. (Bastian 1992; Kilpatrick et al. 1992) Government figures of reported rapes are affected by incomplete data, estimates, and varying reporting factors. (Federal Bureau of Investigation 1992) Government surveys are affected by survey environment factors, while other studies are affected by sample size and nature, survey methods and wording, and research bias. The *Uniform Crime Report* (*UCR*) figures supply a reasonably accurate number of the rapes and attempted rapes (statutory rapes and other sex offenses are not included in the number) that are reported to the police each year. The National Crime Victimization Survey (NCVS) suggests that not all assaults are reported to the police and indicates the reasons why. The NCVS indicates that from 1985 to 1988 between 35 percent and 53 percent of forcible rapes were not reported to the police. The 1991 NCVS found that 50.6 percent of the surveyed victims of rape reported the crime, while 45 percent did not. Data were unavailable for 4.3 percent of the rape victims. Victims of attempted rape were more likely to report the assault; 64.2 percent told the police, while 35.8 percent did not. (Bureau of Justice Statistics 1992) Data from rape crisis centers around the country document that many of the victims that contact the crisis centers do not contact the police (and therefore are not included in any governmental figures). For example, figures from a rape crisis center in a college town in Virginia indicate that of the 118 rapes reported to them in 1991, 30 percent of them were not reported to the police. In the fiscal year ending on 30 June 1993, 52 percent of the 214 sexual assaults reported to the Nebraska Domestic Violence Sexual Assault Coalition were also reported to the police. The Boston Area Rape Crisis Center received reports of 659 sexual assaults in 1992; less than 19 percent were reported to the police (Figure 5-4). One survey of over 120 rape crisis centers around the country indicated a wide range of reporting, with 5 percent to 100 percent of known assaults reported to the police. An average of 49 percent of the rapes the centers had learned of in the past year had been reported to the police. (Hall 1994) It is important to note that a significant percentage of rape victims tell no one of the assault when it happens, and accordingly are not represented by figures from law enforcement officials or from rape crisis centers. For example, a major study of 3,187 female college students found that 27 percent of the stranger rape victims and 46 percent of the acquaintance rape victims did not tell anyone of their assault, and only 21.2 percent and 1.7 percent, respectively, told the police (Figure 5-5). (Koss et al. 1988) It is impossible to determine the number of victims who are raped each year and choose not to tell anyone; it becomes a matter of pure speculation.

The commonly touted estimates that the ratio of actual forcible rapes to reported rapes is 1:3, 1:4, or 1:5 have their origins in area-specific data collected in 1967, 1964, and 1950, respectively. (Minnesota Department of Corrections 1964; President's

Commission 1967; Subcommittee on Sex Crimes 1950) There is no way to determine how the changing social climate has affected the actual ratio or what that ratio actually is today. Seven large-scale studies conducted between 1979 and 1991, however, have resulted in estimates that 15 percent to 25 percent of the women in the United States have been raped. (Burt 1979; Kilpatrick et al. 1987; Kilpatrick and Best 1990; Koss et al. 1991; Russell 1982; Sorenson et al. 1987; Wyatt 1990) Additionally, a national study of 3,187 college women in 1987 indicated that 15 percent of the group had been raped at least once since their fourteenth birthday, and an additional 12 percent had been victims of attempted rape. (Koss et al. 1987)

According to the *Uniform Crime Report,* there were an approximate total of 106,593 forcible rapes in the United States in 1991, an increase of 3.9 percent over 1990, and 17 percent over 1987. By the *Uniform Crime Report*'s "crime clock," that averages out to a rape committed every five minutes. The figures indicate that an average of 80 of every 100,000 women were raped in 1990, an average of 83 of every 100,000 in 1991. It should be noted that the figures were national averages, however; in 1991 in the Metropolitan Statistical Areas the number was 91 of every 100,000 women. (Federal Bureau of Investigation 1992)

The 1990 National Crime Victimization Survey was a survey of 47,000 housing units, inhabited by 95,000 individuals. The rape and attempted rape figures reflected the experiences within the past year of females aged 12 and older. Assaults in which the victims were 12 to 15 years old were most likely to be reported (65 percent), followed by forcible rapes of victims over 20 (53 percent), and cases in which the victim was between the ages of 16 and 19 (47 percent). (Bureau of Justice Statistics 1992) While the majority of reported rapes are stranger rapes, it is commonly believed that nonstranger rapes are greatly underreported.

It is believed that between 61 percent and 77 percent of reported rapes are reported by someone other than the victim or, if reported by the victim, are reported as a direct result of the decision or advice of a third party. (Holmstrom 1985; Holmstrom and Burgess 1983; McCahill et al. 1979) Figures from Tulsa, Oklahoma (named "America's most typical city" in a 1990 study for *American Demographics* magazine), support this data. A study published in 1993 by the Tulsa Institute of Behavioral Studies of 294 rape victims found that only 16 percent reported the rape to the police. Of the 84 percent who did not report the rape, four out of five did not speak to anyone before making the decision not to report. (Novacek et al. 1993) L. S. Williams (1985) determined that victims were more likely to report if: (1) the attacker was a stranger or an acquaintance versus a friend or relative, and (2) the victim was attacked in her own environment (home, car, workplace, etc.) versus on a date or other social situation (bar, party, etc.). M. J. McDermott's (1979) analysis of a national crime survey conducted between 1974 and 1975 supports findings that victims of strangers are more likely to report the crime than are victims of nonstrangers. A 1992 study of 294 rape victims found that victims of stranger rapes were two and one-half times more likely to report the rape to the police than were victims of acquaintances. (Novacek et al. 1993)

According to the 1991 NCVS, there were three primary reasons for rape victims reporting the crime to the police. Of those victims who reported, 19.6 percent did so to prevent further crime by the offender against the victim. A desire to punish the offender motivated 15.7 percent, while 10.5 percent wanted to prevent further crimes by the offender against anyone else. (Bureau of Justice Statistics 1992) Due to a small sample size, the survey's data on the primary reasons for not reporting the assault cannot be considered statistically reliable, though it may suggest reasons. A study of 980 Tulsa women found that 88 percent of the rape victims who reported the assault did so because they wanted the rapist to be punished. Fear that the offender would rape others motivated 72 percent of the victims, while 63 percent were afraid the rapist would try to rape them again. (Novacek et al. 1993) Of those who did respond to the 1991 NCVS, a little over one-fourth cited the "private or personal" nature of the crime as the reason for not reporting. A little over one-fifth of the respondents indicated feeling that the police would be indifferent, biased, or ineffective. (Bureau of Justice Statistics 1992) The Tulsa study found that the primary reason 84 percent of the victims did not report the rape was their embarrassment at having been raped. Twenty-four percent of the victims did not want to have to deal with a male police officer, and 43 percent were afraid the police would not believe them. (Novacek et al. 1993)

Victims of rape range in age from a few months to women in their nineties. The 1991 NCVS indicated that women aged 16 to 19 were at greatest risk (3.5 per 1,000 women), followed by females aged 20 to 24 (1.7 per 1,000 women), and then 12 to 15 (1.1 per 1,000 women) (Figure 5-6). Women aged 25 to 49 were assaulted at about the frequency of the NCVS national average (1 per 1,000 women), but were more likely to be threatened with a weapon and to be the victim of a completed rape than were victims aged 12 to 24. Not surprisingly, there was a clear relationship between socioeconomic classification (as determined by household income) and the likelihood of a woman being raped: the less the household income, the greater the risk of rape. Women on the lower end of the socioeconomic scale were more likely to live in unsafe areas, depend on public transportation, and have less secure dwellings. White and black women were raped with about the same frequency in their respective socioeconomic groups. It is important to note, however, that much of the listed statistical estimates in the NCVS on black women were the result of much lower sample sizes than that of white women. Rape occurred most frequently during the summer months, with two-thirds of the rapes taking place between the hours of 6 P.M. and 6 A.M. (30.7 percent took place between 6 P.M. and midnight, 31.5 percent between midnight and 6 A.M. and 4.4 percent took place sometime at night). (Bureau of Justice Statistics 1992; Federal Bureau of Investigation 1992)

Physical and Psychological Ramifications of Rape

The physical and psychological ramifications of rape extend far beyond the immediate trauma sustained in the attack itself. The long-term effects on the mental and emotional health of rape victims may extend into years or even decades following the assault. (Benedict 1985) One study found that rape victims were three times more likely to report their physical health as "poor," and five times more likely to report their mental health as "poor" than were women who had never been raped. The same study found that while the negative impact of rape does diminish over time, women who were raped over ten years earlier were still four times more likely to report poor mental health than were women who had never been raped and three times more likely to report poor physical health. (Novacek et al. 1993)

Physical Ramifications of Rape

Sexually Transmitted Diseases It is extremely difficult to estimate the likelihood of a sexually transmitted disease (STD) being contracted as a result of a sexual assault. Studies have yielded wildly divergent results, indicating the presence of at least one STD at the initial emergency room examination in 11 to 43 percent of rape victims, and the presence of a new STD in 1 to 37.5 percent of the victims who returned for a follow-up examination.

C. Jenny et al. (1990) conducted a study of 204 victims who came to the emergency room. The victims were tested for eight separate STDs, and the results were staggering. Forty-three percent of the victims tested positive for at least one STD on the initial examination. Of the 109 victims who returned for a follow-up examination, 37.5 percent had a new STD. This study was later criticized because it did not provide an STD rate for the general population of Seattle. It is unknown if the victims in the study represented a segment of the population that would normally be considered at "high risk" for contracting an STD.

J. T. Sturm et al. (1990) conducted another study of a slightly larger group of victims, and found that 11 percent tested positive for an STD on the initial examination. Of the 73 victims who returned for a follow-up examination, only 1 percent tested positive for a new STD. It is important to note that, while this study was of more victims (235), it only tested for two separate STDs.

L. E. Ledray (1991) conducted a study of 110 adolescent victims, ages 12 through 16. The adolescents were tested at the initial examination for five separate STDs. The testing revealed that 13 percent of the victims tested positive for at least one STD at that time. Of the 51 percent who came back for a follow-up examination, 13 percent had a new STD.

It is difficult to draw any conclusions from such studies for several reasons. First, there is considerable variation in the STDs tested for in each group of victims. Early studies tended to focus only on gonorrhea and syphilis, while more recent studies usually included a greater number of STDs. (Ledray 1991) Secondly, there is uncertainty as to whether a positive gonorrhea culture taken at the initial examination is a result of the rape or indicative of a pre-existing condition. Earlier medical thinking (and rape victim studies) assumed the latter to be true, which in turn served to support the myth that rape victims were generally promiscuous and sexually irresponsible. There have been recent indications, however, that a positive culture may have as its source the assailant's seminal fluid still present in the victim. The third difficulty is a result of limited follow-up testing. Because generally less than half of the rape victims return for such testing, the percentage of those returning victims that have developed a new STD may not be representative of the entire victim population. Victims who suffer symptoms are more likely to return for follow-up treatment, whereas victims who do not perceive any symptoms may be less likely to return.

While there have been no conclusive studies regarding pregnancy as a result of rape, there are physiological reasons why the possibility of pregnancy from a single act of unprotected nonconsensual intercourse is less than that of a single act of unprotected consensual intercourse. In consensual intercourse, the uterus elevates and tilts backward to form a reservoir to retain the semen. In an act of violent, nonconsensual intercourse the uterus does not form that reservoir, thereby allowing the semen to drain out much more quickly. Furthermore, if the victim walks or runs following the attack, drainage of the semen can occur. If the rapist continues to thrust following orgasm, his penis can literally drag the semen out of the vagina. While the risk of pregnancy from a single act of unprotected sex is between 4 percent and 6 percent for the general population, the risk of pregnancy from rape is believed to range between 1.5 percent and 3 percent for victims. (Slaughter 1994b)

Psychological Ramifications of Rape

Symonds (1975) describes four phases of response that victims of violent crime commonly go through. While Symonds' studies did not focus on rape victims exclusively, an examination of the four phases makes it clear that the rape victim's experience follows the same sequence as that of a victim of any other violent crime. Phase I occurs at the onset of the victimization and is characterized by an inability on the part of the victim to accept the reality of the attack. Because of the victim's initial shock and disbelief, she may be temporarily unable to respond. Rape victims frequently report that they could not believe at the onset of the sexual assault that it was happening to them. (Ribera 1993) Phase II also occurs during the attack, when the victim can no longer deny the assault and is overwhelmed by the reality. As a result of terror, she may exhibit or feel a removal from the reality of the assault, a temporary detachment from her emotions. (Symonds 1975) Rape victims have described this phase as watching the rape as if it were happening to someone else. (Ribera 1993) Phase III takes place following the end of the assault, when the victim experiences a wide range of fluctuating emotions and nervous reactions as well as disruption of sleep patterns through insomnia and/or dreams. As discussed in the following section on rape trauma syndrome, such reactions are very common among women who have been raped. Phase IV involves the victim's regaining her personal power and control as she comes to terms with the assault and is able to successfully integrate the experience into her ongoing behavior and life. (Symonds 1975)

The psychological damage done by a sexual assault lasts far longer than the immediate concerns of the attack. In addition to experiencing fluctuating emotions and disturbed sleep, rape victims are extremely prone to depression following the assault. Two separate national studies found at least three out of ten sexual assault victims considered suicide (Kilpatrick et al. 1992; Koss et al. 1988), as did a recent study in a major midwestern city. (Novacek et al. 1993) This depression may be most severe during the first month and can, along with a loss of self-esteem and feelings of nervousness, fear, or outright terror, lead to additional physical problems. Loss of appetite, nausea, vaginal or oral pain and irritation, and stress-induced illness commonly follow a sexual assault. Victims frequently develop phobias related to the attack, such as a fear of men or a certain color of car. In addition to the suffering that the fear itself causes the victim, such phobias can lead victims to question their sanity, further injuring their mental health. Novacek's study of rape victims in Tulsa found that 23 percent of the victims increased their use of alcohol or drugs as a result of the assault. (Novacek et al. 1993) Victims of sexual assault commonly have problems resuming sexual activity, often in the form of a lower sexual drive or arousal level, an inability to have an orgasm, or an aversion to sex entirely. Specific sexual activities or positions may cause the victim to have a flashback of the assault. (Benedict 1985)

Studies have indicated that the majority of rape victims do not seek follow-up counseling. (Hall 1994; Koss et al. 1988; Novacek et al. 1993) A 1992 study conducted in Tulsa suggests victim denial and lack of education about the benefits of rape counseling are the principal reasons victims did not seek help. Of the 79 percent of the rape victims who did not seek counseling, the primary reason given by 84 percent was that they wanted to forget the rape experience. The second most common reason was embarrassment; 67 percent did not want anyone to know of the assault. Almost half of the noncounseled victims believed they could not afford counseling (46 percent), and 42 percent did not know how to get counseling or did not know that counseling could help rape victims. (Novacek et al. 1993) These later figures are of particular concern because they underline the need for greater education and awareness regarding rape and its aftermath. In a recent survey of services of over 200 rape crisis centers in the United States, nearly 100 percent of the centers offered victim counseling at no charge or on a sliding scale. (Hall 1994) The demographics of the Tulsa study serve to emphasize the need for rape awareness and education; 94 percent of the survey participants had a high school education, 81 percent had attended college, and 36 percent were college graduates. (Novacek et al. 1993)

Rape Trauma Syndrome In 1974 Burgess and Holmstrom coined the term *rape trauma syndrome* (RTS)—sometimes called sexual assault trauma syndrome (SATS) (Ruch et al. 1991)—to describe a predictable stress response pattern a victim of sexual assault typically displays following an assault. While later research has utilized more rigorous psychological measurement methods (Becker et al. 1983; Ruch et al. 1991) than the basic observation of the presence or absence of symptoms (Holmstrom and Burgess 1975), the work of Burgess and Holmstrom did much to revolutionize the perception of rape and its ramifications. Their establishment of the validity of RTS as a post-traumatic stress disorder (PTSD) has had a major effect on the treatment of victims by law enforcement and judicial officials, since it has done much to explain behavior of victims that seemed incongruous with the societal stereotype of how a sexual assault victim should act following an assault. (Borgida and Brekke 1985)

Four cardinal criteria must be met for a diagnosis of post-traumatic stress disorder. First, the source of the stress must be of sufficient magnitude (such as the death of a loved one, a major car accident, or a tragic fire) to cause distinguishable symptoms in almost anyone experiencing it. Second, the source of stress must generate intrusive imagery—recurring, intrusive memories of the event such as daydreams and dreams. Third, the victim must experience a "numbing," or a lack of interest or involvement with her environment or former activities. In this stage the victim may behave in extremes, displaying emotional reactions such as great anger or fear or displaying an extreme control of her emotions, indicating shock or denial. Fourth, the victim should display at least two of the following six symptoms: (1) an extreme startle response of hyperalertness, such as crying spells or paranoia; (2) a disturbed sleep pattern, such as nightmares or insomnia; (3) guilt over some aspect of her involvement with the event, such as a perceived responsibility for not preventing it, for her behavior during it, or even for her survival of it; (4) difficulty remembering or concentrating; (5) complete avoidance of activities that serve to remind her of the incident, such as sexual relations (often a victim experiences a lower sexual drive or arousal level, an inability to have an orgasm, or an aversion to sex entirely); or (6) an increase in symptoms that resemble or symbolize the incident during sexual relations. (Burgess and Holmstrom 1985)

Burgess and Holmstrom made it clear that the behavior of rape victims meets these criteria. Victims of sexual assault have every aspect of their lives disrupted to one degree or another as a result of the attack. Burgess and Holmstrom (1974) divided RTS into two phases: the acute, or disruptive, phase and the reorganization phase. During the acute phase the victim displays general stress response symptoms such as wildly fluctuating mood swings, laughing, crying, panic, or feeling removed from reality. This phase can last several days to several weeks or longer. Following the acute phase the victim enters the reorganization phase. During this phase the victim attempts to regain the sense of control that was stripped from her by the rapist. In this phase the symptoms displayed by the victim, such as sleep disorder, sexual dysfunction, and phobias, are more specifically rape-related, and they can last for several years. In Burgess and Holmstrom's (1974) study of 146 rape victims, 74 percent took four to six years to recover. (Benedict 1985; Burgess and Holmstrom 1985; Ferris 1983; Ruch and Leon 1986)

Rape victims frequently experience three types of dreams in the weeks, months, or years following the assault: nonmastery dreams, symbolic dreams, and mastery dreams. Nonmastery dreams—dreams in which the victim relives an assault and is powerless and ineffective in her resistance—are the most common until the victim recovers. Symbolic dreams frequently involve a surrealistic theme drawn from the assault itself. Mastery dreams replay the attack in a variation in which the victim is able to gain control, often taking extreme vengeance on her attacker. (Burgess and Holmstrom 1985)

Rape victims frequently have severe emotional reactions following their victimization and may deal with those emotions in an atypical manner. They may display anger, hostility, defensiveness, or fear in an extreme manner with little or no apparent provocation, or they may exercise rigid control over their emotions by acting indifferent to the experience, joking, or being objective for fear of losing control altogether. Victims may become very withdrawn or constrained in their normal activities and aggressively avoid any activity or location that reminds them of the assault. This defensive reaction may leave them afraid to leave their home or to travel on public transportation. Victims may go to the other extreme and take unusual risks, such as walking alone in a park at night, in an attempt to prove to themselves that they have not been intimidated by the assault. Efficiency at, and interest in, school or work may diminish. (Benedict 1985; Burgess and Holmstrom 1985) As a result of societal conditioning, embarrassment and self-blame are two extremely common reactions to rape. This assumption on the part of the victim of partial or full responsibility for the rape greatly influences the number of sexual assaults that are reported to the police or to anyone else. (Koss et al. 1988; Novacek et al. 1993)

No description of the psychological symptoms of rape trauma syndrome can capture the emotional destruction caused by sexual assault. The common saying "the rapist got ten years; the victim got life" holds true. Sexual assault is a life-altering experience—the victim's perception of the world is forever changed.

Guidelines for Dealing with the Sexual Assault Victim

A victim of rape experiences a great deal of depression and, in many cases, embarrassment and shame. The circumstances of the assault, coupled with the victim's societal conditioning, may also generate self-blame and feelings of guilt. Such feelings can greatly delay the victim's recovery at best, or lead to suicidal tendencies at worst. A sympathetic and supportive listener can do much to counteract the generation and negative impact of these feelings and can facilitate the victim's healing. Conversely, an insensitive response or reaction on the part of a confidant can cause tremendous harm to an already traumatized victim and greatly impede her ultimate recovery. The following guidelines have been compiled from fliers, brochures, and training manuals from numerous rape crisis centers throughout the United States.

> **Do believe the victim.** Many rape victims do not tell anyone of the assault for fear that they will not be believed. Let the victim know you believe her.

> **Do be supportive.** Many rape victims feel great embarrassment as well as a feeling of isolation. Let the victim know that you are willing to listen to whatever she wants to say, whenever she wants to say it.

> **Listen to the victim.** Allow her to express her feelings in her own manner, without trying to talk her out of any of

those feelings. Offering suggestions as to how she should feel ("you don't have anything to be afraid of now") or as to what she should do with her feelings ("think about something else") may cause her to feel that her reactions to the trauma are being negated or judged.

Do allow the victim to be silent. Do not press for details; allow the victim to decide how much she feels comfortable discussing and allow her to talk at her own pace.

Do respect the victim's privacy. Let her decide who is to be told of the assault.

Do let the victim know that the assault was not her fault. Stress the fact that the responsibility is solely that of the assailant.

Do not physically hug or touch the victim. You must first check to see if she is comfortable with such contact.

Do not ask questions ("why didn't you scream?") or make suggestions ("you should have hit him") that second-guess the victim's actions. Such critical remarks shift the responsibility for the rape to the victim and can compound any feelings of shame or self-blame she may have, greatly impeding her future recovery.

Do help the victim regain control of her life. Do not make decisions for the victim. Involve her as much as possible in decision making. The assault forcibly robbed her of personal power and control. By making decisions for her ("you'll come and stay at my house tonight") in an attempt to help, you may inadvertently reinforce her feelings of helplessness. Offer options, let the victim make her own choices, and support those choices.

Do offer to be available to the victim to accompany her to the hospital, counseling, the police station, or the district attorney's office. Offer to be available by phone or in person whenever she wants to talk.

Do ask the victim what her needs are. Make it clear that she is encouraged to voice those needs at any time. Do respect her wishes, even if they are in conflict with yours.

Do not vent your frustration and anger at the rapist in the presence of the victim. Doing so will only increase her anxiety and increase the turbulence in a life that has already been traumatized. If the assailant is known, do not seek personal revenge. Doing so will only severely damage your life and cause further damage to the rape victim.

Do help the victim recognize and acknowledge that any extreme reactions she may be having following the assault are likely symptoms of rape trauma syndrome (RTS). Stress that RTS is a natural reaction to the trauma of the assault.

Do encourage the victim to contact a rape crisis center to seek professional counseling as well as information on her possible options. Such services are free and provide invaluable assistance in the healing process.

Do contact a rape crisis center. It is important to talk about your feelings and to get advice on how best to help the victim.

Medical Procedures

In 1988 the United States Department of Justice, Office for Victims of Crime, sponsored the creation of a model protocol (a specified manner or order of procedure) for medical and evidence gathering examination of victims of sexual assault. (Goddard 1988) In 1989 New Hampshire became the first state to develop a statewide uniform protocol using the model. (Matheson 1989) Within three years, a total of 13 states and Puerto Rico had adopted statewide protocols using the national guidelines. (Young et al. 1992)

While protocol may vary slightly from state to state, the protocol may also vary from facility to facility, depending on the equipment used by each facility to collect evidence, such as a colposcope and camera. Within the medical facility itself general evidence gathering protocol may occasionally be reordered to respond to variables presented by the specific case. For example, if there is debris or other foreign evidence present on the victim that could be lost if collection is delayed, that evidence may be collected earlier in the protocol than would ordinarily be the case. (Valento 1994)

Another frequent variation in protocol concerns the treatment of victims for possible contraction of a sexually transmitted disease (STD). There is currently a controversy in the medical community regarding STD protocol, namely the administering of STD testing and follow-up care versus the administering of prophylactic antibiotics, or antibiotics that are prescribed prior to medical detection of an infection as a precaution. The argument for STD testing and follow-up care is twofold. First, such protocol avoids the unnecessary use of antibiotics. This is a concern because extensive use of antibiotics has resulted in the development of antibiotic resistant bacteria. Second, collection of STD information may later have use in court as evidence of sexual assault.

The first argument for the administering of prophylactic antibiotics focuses on the behavior of the rape victims. As was noted previously, the majority of all the rape victims in the studies did not return for any follow-up treatment (308 victims out of 549, or 61 percent, did not return). A significant number of the victims that did return had new STDs. This raises the possibility that a number of the victims who did not return for a follow-up exam eventually developed STDs. By administering the prophylactic antibiotics at the time of the initial examination the need for return visits (and the attendant expenses) can be greatly reduced along with the victim's fear of contracting an STD. (Ledray 1990) The psychological benefit of such treatment should not be taken lightly. The Sexual Assault Resource Service in Minneapolis, Minnesota, found that 98 percent of their clients wanted antibiotics rather than cultures with follow-up visits; prophylactic treatment ". . . (made them) feel cleansed from the inside out." (Ledray 1990)

There are two immediate disadvantages to such treatment, however. By eliminating the follow-up visit, further study on the likelihood of contracting an STD as a result of a sexual assault is prevented. Also, prophylactic antibiotics are not 100 percent effective on all STDs, and such treatment may give the victim a false sense of security.

The second argument in favor of administering prophylactic antibiotics is a rebuttal of the value of STD information as evidence. Evidence obtained by STD tests can actually work against the victim in court. If the victim does not test positive for an STD at the initial examination but later develops one, the defense attorney can argue that it cannot be proven that the accused was the source of the disease, particularly if the accused tests negative. Given the amount of time that generally passes between the rape and actual trial (see chapter 2), the assailant may have had sufficient time to seek anonymous testing and treatment. If the victim does test positive at the initial examination, the defense attorney may seek to use that information to discredit her in the eyes of the jury by asserting that it was a pre-existing condition. (Ledray 1990)

The following is a general summation of procedures hospitals and other healthcare facilities follow in the course of a sexual assault examination.

Upon the victim's arrival at the medical facility, a hospital representative (usually a nurse) inquires if there is anyone the victim needs notified. At this time the victim should be notified of the nature and availability of an advocate from a local sexual assault center, and that advocate should be contacted if the victim desires. In some areas the advocate is automatically called by the facility and allowed to meet and explain to the victim the nature of their service. It is then up to the victim to decide whether or not she wants the advocate to remain with her.

There is the requisite paperwork—consent for treatment, insurance, and medical report release authorization forms. In some states, for the cost of the examination to be covered by state funds it is necessary for the victim to agree to pursue legal action, while in other states there are less stringent requirements for compensation. It is not uncommon for a state fund covering the expenses of rape victims to have been depleted before the end of the fiscal year. In such a case, the victim, who is ultimately responsible for all expenses, may have to cover the medical expenses. The state's delay in payment or failure to make payment can adversely affect the victim's credit rating, thereby traumatizing the victim again.

A preliminary medical assessment of the victim is performed, and any pressing medical needs (such as bleeding) are addressed. Pictures are taken of any apparent injuries.

If the victim's clothes were worn at the time of the assault, they are taken and preserved as possible evidence. Aside from the condition of the victim's clothing possibly serving as evidence of force, microscopic pieces of evidence such as hairs, fibers, or bodily fluids that could help identify the assailant may be present. If necessary, replacement clothing is provided by the hospital or the advocate.

Any obvious debris on the victim's body, such as soil, plant matter, semen stains, hair, etc., is collected and saved.

A number of specimens are collected for a variety of purposes. Blood will be drawn for typing and enzyme work. The victim is asked to swirl a small amount of saline in her mouth (an oral wash) and to give a saliva sample. The head hair and pubic hair are combed to acquire any foreign hairs or debris that might later assist in identifying the assailant. A number of hairs are pulled from various locations on the victim's head and pubic area for comparative study. It is necessary that these hairs be pulled, rather than cut, in order to obtain the roots of the hairs. The roots of hairs are best for forensic comparison and supply the needed material for deoxyribonucleic acid (DNA) analysis (see chapter 2). The national model protocol for sexual assault examinations calls for samples of 25 to 100 head hairs and 10 to 50 pubic hairs. (Young et al. 1992)

Several swabs are taken from the external genitalia, the cervix, and the anal canal. These swabs are used to check for P30 and acid phosphatase (seminal plasma components whose presence indicates semen), motile (living) or nonmotile spermatozoa (sperm), various types of venereal disease, such as gonorrhea and chlamydia (the most common bacterially transmitted venereal disease), and for possible future use in DNA analysis. If the assailant licked any other part of the victim, such as her breasts or neck, a swab of that area may be done as well. A vaginal wash is done with sterile saline solution to check for motile spermatozoa. A Woods lamp (a process using ultraviolet light to illuminate semen) may be done to check for semen, and Toluedin Blue (a dye used to highlight injuries) or a colposcope may be used to determine and document the nature and extent of injuries not immediately apparent to the naked eye. (Use of the colposcope is discussed in detail later in this chapter.)

Attention is paid to the victim's hands in order to obtain additional forensic evidence. Fingernails are scraped in case the victim scratched the assailant and got skin or fiber particles under them. If a fingernail was broken in the assault, the nail of that finger is clipped to preserve the tear pattern on the broken nail. Some protocols may call for the clipping of all the fingernails on the same hand to allow the striations of the other nails to be checked for identification purposes.

Some hospitals test for pregnancy, most commonly through a urine test. If the victim is not already pregnant and if there is a chance that she may become so, an abortifacient—a drug administered to cause the body to discharge, or abort, a fertilized egg—may be offered. As noted above, some hospitals prescribe prophylactic antibiotics to prevent certain venereal diseases as a matter of course, while others prefer to take a culture for STDs and depend on follow-up treatment.

Forensic Nurses/Sexual Assault Nurse Examiners

The treatment required by a sexual assault victim from the healthcare community extends beyond meeting the victim's immediate physical needs. Caregiving must attend to the psychological needs resulting from extreme trauma as well as preserve the victim's legal rights through the proper discovery, collection, and preservation of evidence. Traditionally, the medical community has had difficulty in meeting all the physiological, psychological, and legal needs of rape victims. This shortcoming has largely been due to the environment and logistics of the emergency room (covered below), coupled with a lack of emergency room physicians and nurses with backgrounds in forensic medicine and medicolegal issues. Caregivers who lack knowledge of evidence protocol requirements of the criminal justice system can inadvertently affect the outcome of a trial, which can have major ramifications for the rape victim's psychological recovery.

The traditional process of receiving medical treatment and examination in an emergency room can present numerous complications for the emotional and physical comfort of a rape victim. The first difficulty the victim may be faced with is finding a hospital emergency department that will perform a sexual assault examination. Many hospitals are reluctant to handle sexual assault cases and may, in fact, refuse to do so. A forensic examination that follows proper evidence collection protocol usually lasts a minimum of two and one-half hours, and can average two or three times that length in an emergency room setting. Often hospital administrations feel it is not medically or financially feasible to pull an emergency room physician away from the influx of cases for several hours. Even in major cities there are frequently only a few hospitals that stock sexual assault evidence collection kits and offer services to sexual assault victims. As a result the victim may be forced to travel some distance from her home to receive a sexual assault examination. Unless the victim has suffered obvious physical injury that mandates immediate medical treatment, other medical emergencies take priority in the emergency room. Accordingly, the victim may be required to wait for several hours before receiving medical attention. (Carlton 1993) Conversations with victim advocates in three major metropolitan areas in the Midwest and the Southwest found waits of two to ten hours not uncommon, while the average wait in an emergency room in California was eight hours.

(Slaughter 1994a) In hospitals other than the few that have established separate waiting rooms for sexual assault victims, this lengthy wait takes place in the public waiting area, thereby adding to the victim's discomfort and distress. Regardless of the waiting time, the victim is not supposed to use the bathroom, wash, or change clothes. Once the victim has been processed to an examination room, the examining physician may well be called away for additional periods of time to attend to more pressing medical emergencies, thus increasing the emotional trauma of an already traumatized victim and possibly compromising the chain of evidence. This further delay may also serve to tie up needed facilities, the attending police officer, and the rape crisis counselor.

The emergency department physician may have extremely limited training and experience in performing forensic gynecological examinations and evidence collection protocol. This inexperience can result in problems for the prosecution (and by extension, the victim) should the case go to court. The emergency room doctor may be reluctant to perform a sexual assault examination, knowing that if the case goes to court, he or she may be pulled away from normal hospital duties to testify. (Derryberry 1994; Prichard 1994; Zachritz 1993)

The development of the discipline of forensic clinical nursing, specifically the sexual assault nurse examiner (S.A.N.E. nurse), is serving to bridge the gap between the victim's biomedical, psychological, and legal needs. Sexual assault nurse examiners are registered nurses who have been specifically trained in the collection of forensic evidence from sexual assault victims. The use of a S.A.N.E. nurse, through coordinated actions by legal, medical, and advocate agencies, alleviates many of the difficulties outlined above. (Lynch 1994) In several areas around the country, programs utilizing sexual assault nurse examiners have succeeded in removing the victim from the emergency room environment altogether. In Tulsa, Oklahoma, a suite has been set aside by Hillcrest Medical Center specifically for rape examinations by forensic nurse examiners. (See S.A.N.E. in chapter 6.) The rooms in the suite provide a private setting for the examinations, toilet and shower facilities, and fresh clothing, as well as separate waiting areas with refreshments for the victim's family or friends. Rape victims are either brought directly to the facilities by the police or directed to go there by the local rape crisis center, Call Rape, Inc. The victim is met there by a qualified and specially prepared nurse examiner and a counselor, both of whom have been dispatched by the crisis center. The examination can begin in a timely manner without interruption or distraction, since the examiner has no other professional duties.

The S.A.N.E. nurse has been specifically trained to collect forensic evidence following legal chain of custody procedures as well as to tend to the special needs of sexual assault victims (such as administering an aftercare protocol to treat and prevent sexually transmitted diseases). The quality and consistency of evidence collection is very high, because the S.A.N.E. nurse conducts sexual assault examinations on a regular basis. The combination of proper education and quality examination results has resulted in S.A.N.E. nurses being designated by district attorneys as expert witnesses in most of the jurisdictions in which they operate. (Zachritz 1993)

The Use and Ramifications of the Colposcope in Sexual Assault Examinations

The increasing use of a colposcope with a camera attachment to gather forensic evidence in sexual assault examinations is having tremendous ramifications in the investigation and prosecution of rape cases. Sometimes referred to as a "microscope on wheels," the colposcope magnifies up to 15 times and has been in use since the early 1970s in diagnostic testing for uterine cancer. In the late 1980s the device began to be used in examinations of children who had been sexually abused, and its use was extended to adult victims of sexual assault in the early 1990s with profound effect. (Swindell 1994)

Prosecutors have long recognized the difficulties inherent in cases where the victim exhibits no external physical injury or outward sign of having been sexually assaulted; such is the case in over two-thirds of all reported rapes. (Fairstein 1993) Medical literature has established that examination of rape victims by gross visualization (i.e., the naked eye) alone yields positive physical findings, or existence of evidence, in only 10 percent to 30 percent of the cases. (Cartwright 1987; Tintinalli and Hoelzer 1985) Recent research showed that examinations of rape victims that utilized a colposcope had positive physical findings in 87 percent to 92 percent of the cases when conducted within 48 hours of the assault. Colposcopy can lengthen the time in which forensic evidence can be collected. While the percentage of positive findings dropped to slightly over 50 percent in examinations conducted between 3 and 181 days after an assault, the percentage still surpassed the results of visual exams conducted within the initial 24-hour period. (Slaughter 1994a)

Laura Slaughter, medical director of the Suspected Abuse Response Team (SART) for San Luis Obispo County, California, has pioneered the use of colposcopy to evaluate sexual assault victims. The research of Slaughter and others has served to establish the typical location, number, and type of injuries sustained in a sexual assault. Injury most frequently occurs at the point of initial contact of the penis, digit, or external object to the vagina, somewhere in the 3-6-9 o'clock position of the vaginal area, and most commonly within the 5-6-7 o'clock position. These injuries, known as mounting injuries, usually consist of tears, abrasions, and ecchymosis (bruising). Through the study of 160 rape victims who sustained genital trauma, Slaughter identified the most frequent type and site of injury to be tears to the posterior fourchette. The second most frequent site was the labia minora, where abrasions were most common. Ecchymosis to the hymen was the third most common trauma observed, followed by tears to the fossa navicularis. Trauma was observed at more than one site in 72 percent of the injured victims, with the mean number of sites being 2.3. (Slaughter and Brown 1991)

In addition to categorizing typical injuries from sexual assault, Slaughter's research has served to contrast such injuries with those sustained through consensual sex. In a study of 52 women who were examined within 24 hours of consensual sex, Slaughter found evidence of genital trauma in 15 percent of them, as opposed to 89 percent of the rape victims that were examined within the same time frame. (Slaughter and Crowley 1993) The mean number of injury sites on women who sustained genital trauma through consensual sex was one, while the mean number of injury sites on rape victims was three. (Slaughter and Shackleford 1993) While there are some similarities between the two types of injuries, there are marked differences in the extent and nature of the injuries incurred. Injury sustained through consensual intercourse is of a demonstrably lesser degree than that caused by rape, primarily due to the position of the pelvis. The presence of lubrication in a rape victim does not prevent trauma; Slaughter found the same injury pattern of nonlubricated victims when she examined a woman who had been raped during her period. The pattern was also consistent in cases where the victim was drunk, unconscious, or otherwise nonresistant. (Slaughter 1994a)

Legal Application

In a judicial context, the documentation through pictures (obtained by use of a colposcope) of trauma associated with rape can help belie a defendant's claim of "consent" and/or "rough sex." (Such defenses are particularly common in cases of acquaintance rape.) The presentation of this kind of evidence to a defense attorney has often resulted in a request for a plea bargain. (Swindell 1994)

The use of the colposcope can also assist in obtaining evidence used to help identify the assailant that would otherwise be lost. In one recent case in San Luis Obispo County, California, the colposcope found a piece of lint (invisible to the naked eye) in the vagina of a child who had been assaulted and murdered. The lint matched the fabric of the suspect's sweatpants. The suspect pled guilty to sexual assault and murder. Justice was served and thousands of dollars in trial costs saved. In another case the colposcope was used to locate a pubic hair in a fold of the vagina. A comparison of the hair served to exonerate a suspect. (Slaughter 1994a)

Absence of Evidence

There are several theories regarding the lack of "rape injuries" in some cases. (Slaughter found that 31 percent of the rape victims in her study did not display any genital trauma.) The simplest is the possibility of fraudulent reporting. (As noted in chapter 2, the 1991 *Uniform Crime Report* states that 8 percent of the reports of forcible rapes were unfounded.) Perhaps a more likely possibility involves cases in which the victim was raped by a current or former boyfriend or spouse. In that instance, the victim would be more likely to have the knowledge and ability to move her body to minimize injury. Additionally, the amount of force used in the rape itself might be of a lesser amount; the victim may still be raped, but the actual act may follow the precipitating intimidation or physical violence that set up the act in the first place. Conversely, a victim being overpowered by a stranger, perhaps while simultaneously being threatened by a weapon, would be much less likely to shift her body in any manner that would lessen her injury. In other words, she would be too frightened to move.

The Role of the Victim Advocate

A rape victim advocate is a specially trained individual connected with a local rape crisis center, either as a paid member of the staff or as a volunteer. Advocates are trained to help victims deal with the trauma of sexual assault as well as with post-assault logistics.

The function of the advocate is to serve as a source of information, comfort, and support for the sexual assault victim. The advocate is familiar with the manner in which the medical, law enforcement, and court systems work and is able to serve as a guide for the victim in dealing with the aftermath of an assault. The advocate can tell the victim what is involved in each process and what will happen next. The advocate helps the victim understand her choices and the ramifications of her decisions. If the victim desires, the advocate will stay with her during the rape examination and accompany her to report to the police, to meet with the state's attorney, and to appear in court. The victim is under no obligation to use the services of an advocate if she does not care to do so. Use of an advocate does not require the victim to follow any prescribed course of action, such as reporting the assault to the police or pressing charges, nor does the victim have to pay for the advocate's services. The advocate does not make any decisions for the victim. Rape advocacy's purpose is to empower the victim by allowing her to make her own choices and by assisting her in that process by supplying needed information. Rape advocacy is a free service.

It is frequently at the hospital that the rape victim first comes in contact with the advocate. Advocates can be acquired by the victim by calling the rape crisis center. In many instances the center is notified by the hospital or the police that a sexual assault victim is at the hospital. The crisis center then dispatches an advocate to the hospital, where the advocate waits with the victim and explains the upcoming medical examination and evidence collection procedures. The advocate will contact any family or friends the victim wishes to contact and will supply the victim with clothes to wear home from the hospital if her clothes are kept for evidence. If the police are present at the hospital, the advocate will talk with the police if the victim so desires. Otherwise, anything the victim reveals to the advocate is confidential.

If the victim elects to report the assault to the police, she can request that the advocate accompany her for the initial report and any follow-up interviews. The advocate can explain to the victim what her rights are during the interview as well as what type of questions she is likely to be asked. The advocate takes no part in the actual investigation of the attack. If a police line-up is needed to identify the assailant, the advocate can go with the victim. With proper authorization from the victim, the advocate can follow up with the police to determine if the case has been presented to the state's attorney and, if so, what the outcome was of that presentation.

If the case is not accepted by the state's attorney, the advocate can assist the victim in finding out why and determining any other options. If the case is accepted for prosecution, the advocate can accompany the victim to her meetings with the state's attorney to discuss the case and how it will be handled. The advocate does not function as the victim's lawyer; the advocate's function is to help the victim as she helps the state's attorney prepare the case. The advocate can assist the victim in understanding the trial process, keep her informed as to the progress of the case, and ensure that the victim's rights are respected. In order to maintain the victim's right to confidentiality, the advocate does not testify in court.

If the assailant is found guilty, and if it is allowed in the state, the advocate can assist the victim in filing a Victim Impact Statement—a victim's written statement, detailing the impact the crime has had on her life, which is considered by the court before sentencing of the assailant. The advocate can also assist the victim in getting information on any appeals the assailant files, as well as on his release date and any parole conditions.

Coalitions against Sexual Assault

Function

Coalitions commonly serve as monitors of policies and legislation that have direct impact on victims of sexual assault. Such monitoring can range from the elimination of the spousal exemption for rape made by the state legislature to the revision of the recommended protocol for hospital evidence collection made by the state crime commission. Coalitions commonly serve as resources, providing input (when requested) on policy and legislative development, and they may or may not serve as a lobbyist force. The more financially stable and developed coalitions may have one or more staff members who are specifically assigned the task of tracking pertinent legislation. Some of the larger coalitions are able to retain one or more attorneys or paralegals on staff.

Coalitions serve their member crisis centers by facilitating networking among the centers; providing administrative advice and assistance in the development of centers, funding, and operations;

and by seeking on a state government level additional services for new centers. Coalitions frequently organize information gathered from individual centers and present that data to the appropriate state agency, inviting them to join with a locality and the federal government in providing services.

The other major function of coalitions is providing educational services to a number of groups who interact with victims of sexual assault, specifically the general public, rape crisis centers, and allied professionals such as police departments, district attorney's offices, and healthcare professionals. This educational emphasis may take the form of publications, "Take Back the Night" type rallies, training seminars for professionals, studies and reports for legislators, or all of the above.

Stages of Development

Coalitions generally pass through three stages in their development as viable entities. The first is when a nucleus of a coalition develops from the rape crisis centers already present. Historically, volunteers from different centers begin meeting on a regular basis to discuss their needs and means of addressing them. An organization of volunteers is formed and gradually articulates a mission as the needs of each member center are identified. The second stage sees the acquisition of a paid staff, though in several instances this staff has consisted originally of a part-time coalition director. The appointment of a director usually has a major impact on the level of services provided by the new coalition; the director serves as a centralizing point of communication. The third stage is reached as more staff is added. The addition of more coalition staff often results in more funding for the member centers from state sources. Rape crisis center staff are usually overwhelmed with the demands of local level services and therefore need someone who can write grant proposals and seek other funding. A fully staffed coalition is able to at least assist in those endeavors.

Impact of Coalitions via Rape Crisis Centers

Rape has historically been viewed by society as a "woman's problem." By extension, rape crisis centers are perceived as serving females only, with little or no societal impact beyond the sexual assault victim and possibly her immediate family. While this stereotype is slowly being expanded to include the occasional male victim, far less attention has been given to the economic impact of sexual assault than that of, say, asbestos in public buildings. Pat Groot, executive director of Virginians Aligned Against Sexual Assault (VAASA) coalition, equates the need for rape crisis centers with the need for police or fire departments. She notes that the needed location and size of the latter are determined by population demographics and are designed to serve the needs of all citizens of the state. Groot maintains that the establishment and staffing of crisis centers should follow similar criteria, because all citizens, regardless of sex or age, have potential need of the services offered by such centers. (Groot 1994)

The presence of a rape crisis center, along with its attendant services, has far-reaching impact. A study conducted by a sociology class at Mary Washington College in Fredericksburg, Virginia, suggests that the presence of a rape crisis center increases the number of rapes that are reported to law enforcement officials. The economic impact of rape is lessened if victims have immediate access to sexual assault support services. For example, the facilitation of such services can lessen time lost from work, decrease the development of compounded psychological problems, and reduce the spread of sexually transmitted diseases. The funding, staff size, and effectiveness of the center, as well as the positive impact the center has on the surrounding population, are all interrelated.

Attack Response Options

"Different motives operate in different offenders and, therefore, what might be successful in dissuading one type of assailant might, in fact, only aggravate the situation with a different type of offender." (Groth and Birnbaum 1979)

As awareness of rape has increased in recent years, there has been a proliferation of self-defense programs, devices, and theories made available to the general public. These self-defense options generally fall in one or more of the following categories: compliance and/or nonresistance, verbal resistance, auditory resistance, physical resistance, use of weapons, and use of bodily functions. (Hazelwood et al. 1986; Ribera 1993)

The use of compliance and/or nonresistance as an attack response option ranges from actively cooperating with the demands of the assailant, to going limp. It is interesting to note that while such self-defense tactics have been attacked by defense attorneys in rape trials as being evidence of consent, such has generally not been the case when these same tactics have been used by victims of other types of crimes. As Linda Fairstein noted in speaking of a bank hostage situation, ". . . everyone knew that the deal that had to be cut was simple: Tell us what you want, and we'll give it to you—*just don't hurt anyone*. . . . Why couldn't a rape victim, like any other kind of hostage, say, 'I'll do anything you want, just don't hurt me?'" (italics in original) (Fairstein 1993)

Verbal resistance as an attack response option includes attempting to reason with the assailant, pleading or begging, using a pretext (such as being pregnant or having a venereal disease) in an attempt to appeal to the assailant's humanity or to capitalize on the fears of the attacker to dissuade him from continuing the assault, responding assertively to the aggression (such as shouting "no!"), and screaming for assistance.

Auditory resistance makes use of noisemaking devices such as whistles, air horns, and sirens to distract the attacker and draw attention to the assault.

Physical resistance is generally considered to include physically fighting with the attacker in an attempt to end the assault or to effect an escape. Some studies have included running away in evaluating the prevalence and effectiveness of physical resistance, while others have not included it in the physical resistance category in the compilation of data. (Koss et al. 1988; Smith 1986) Such variance in definition requires that the outcome of studies be considered on an individual, rather than on a universal, basis. Some women's self-defense instructors advocate and include in this category physically attacking the immediate environment (such as an apartment or dormitory room) if applicable, particularly in the case of an acquaintance rape. Attacking the environment by breaking windows, knocking over chairs, tearing down curtains or pictures and the like, can serve to discourage the assailant from continuing his assault, to provide sufficient distraction for the victim to escape, or to attract the notice of others in the area. (Ribera 1993; Smith 1986)

The response option of weapons includes the use of guns; knives; chemical weapons such as tear gas, mace, and pepper spray; and "found" weapons such as stickpins, keys, and umbrellas. The function of such weapons is to disable or distract the attacker, enabling the victim to escape.

The use of bodily functions as a response option includes voluntary defecation, urination, and/or vomiting by the victim in an attempt to disgust and repel the rapist to the point where he discontinues his assault.

Response Option Selection Parameters

Faculty of the Behavioral Science Unit at the FBI Academy have identified three parameters that need to be considered when selecting a response to a sexual assault: the personality of the victim, the environment, and the type and motivation of the assailant. (Hazelwood et al. 1986)

A potential victim must honestly assess her personal strengths and weaknesses as part of determining and selecting appropriate attack response options. A woman who has been socially conditioned to be passive in the presence of aggressive men, who has been conditioned to equate passivity with being "ladylike," might experience a great deal of difficulty in responding to an assault with aggressive verbal resistance. Conversely, a woman who has been raised to actively assert her personal rights and privileges might have an equally difficult time utilizing the response option of nonresistance/compliance.

The environment might automatically rule out specific response options, or it might provide a wealth of opportunities for successful rape avoidance. For example, a chemical spray may be rendered useless or even counterproductive on a windy day, but it could be quite effective on a calm one. Screaming for help might be futile in a remote house, but it could result in assistance in an occupied dormitory.

While each rapist is an individual, their core motivation and resulting behavior will type them in one of the categories described earlier in this chapter—"power," "anger," or "sadistic." The response option that effectively stops one type of rapist might serve to exacerbate another. Interviews with convicted rapists have served to confirm this notion; while one rapist might advise victims to fight their assailant, another will urge total compliance as a means of avoiding further injury. (Groth and Birnbaum 1979; Hazelwood et al. 1986)

Clearly, there is no single response to sexual assault that will be correct in all situations. While there may be similarities in various sexual assaults, there are always numerous variables that will be unique to specific attack—variables that will require a unique response. While a specific response—physical resistance, for example—might be the best possible choice to ensure the survival of the victim in one instance, it might result in severe injury or death in another. Total faith in a weapon as a sufficient means of defense can result in a false sense of security. It can be proven tragically misplaced if the weapon is not readily at hand or is not effective in halting the assault. (Hazelwood et al. 1986) Claiming to have a sexually transmitted disease might dissuade a power rapist on a date, while the same pretext might serve to further enrage an anger rapist, who already sees women as "dirty," and result in anal rape instead. The use of bodily functions might destroy a date rapist's rationalization that the victim is "just playing hard to get," but the same response option might be used by a sadistic rapist to further torture the victim. (Hazelwood et al. 1986; Ribera 1993)

Statistically speaking, the most effective response in avoiding rape has been physical resistance. (Bart 1979; Marchbanks et al. 1990; Novacek et al. 1993) Studies have indicated that physical resistance has had the greatest success when initiated at the onset of, or early in, the assault. (McIntyre 1980; Smith 1986) The least effective self-defense option has been pleading or trying to reason with the attacker. (Levine-MacCombie and Koss 1986; McIntyre 1980; Novacek et al. 1993) These statistical findings may be reflective of A. N. Groth's observation that in many cases the victim is an "object" to the rapist and Groot's belief that "no one can assault someone they consider of equal value. . . ." (Groot 1994; Groth 1979)

Statistics gathered in a study conducted in the late 1980s by the U.S. Centers for Disease Control have indicated that certain types of active resistance (such as fighting) are more likely to result in increased physical injury. This study, however, did not determine whether such active resistance on the victim's part was in response to escalating violence on the part of the assailant. (Marchbanks et al. 1990; Ullman and Knight 1992) Other studies that have noted a greater likelihood of additional injury have failed to describe the nature and severity of the injuries received. (Novacek et al. 1993) In any physical confrontation injuries are unavoidable (knees scraped from falling, arms bruised from being grabbed, knuckles cut from striking the mouth, etc.). In a sexual assault situation, such injuries may well be a trade-off for avoiding rape. (Ribera 1993) Other studies have indicated that sustaining *significant* additional injury as a result of active resistance is rarely the case, if at all. The same studies have found that active physical resistance significantly increases the victim's chances of avoiding rape. (Bart 1981; McIntyre 1980; Ullman and Knight 1992)

The objective of physical resistance to a sexual assault is twofold: to stop the immediate assault and to provide the means by which the victim is able to escape further assault. There are three prerequisites for maximizing the possibility of success in using physical resistance that must be considered before any such confrontation takes place. First, the victim must have a mental attitude that will permit her to cause significant injury to, or possibly the death of, the assailant, depending on the circumstances. The victim who is likely to have the most effective physical resistance is the one whose response does not simply meet the level of the assailant's aggressiveness, but exceeds it. Second, the victim must have the mental and emotional ability to continue a forceful resistance when injured. As noted above, it is extremely likely that the victim will sustain some amount of injury in the course of defending herself, if not in the onset of the attack itself. Third, the victim's response must be done with effective techniques—techniques that will serve to injure and/or immobilize the attacker, allowing the victim to escape rape, severe injuries, or death. Ineffective techniques might dissuade the assailant who is utilizing the rationalization of perceived consent, or they might discourage the rapist who is not willing to go to great lengths to complete the assault; however, against an angry, determined rapist ineffective techniques will do little more than extend the assault and result in more injury to the victim. (Wood 1990)

Figures

Figure 5–1
Presence of the "Big Three" in Childhood

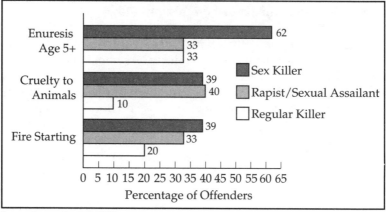

Source: Longevin et al. 1988.

Figure 5–2
Serial Rape – Method of Approach Frequencies

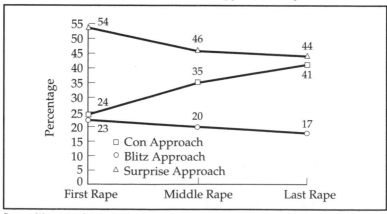

Source: Warren et al. 1991.

Figure 5–3
Relationship of Rapists to 489 Victims

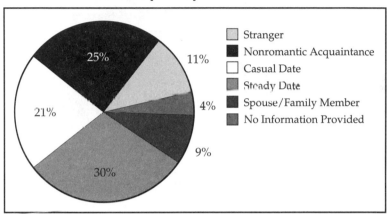

Source: Koss et al. 1988.

Figure 5–4
Boston Area Rape Crisis Center – Number of
Rapes/Assaults Reported to Police

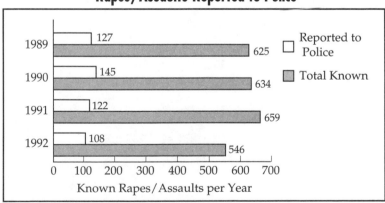

Source: Boston Area Rape Crisis Center, Boston, MA, 1992.

Figure 5–5
Post-Rape Response of 489 Victims

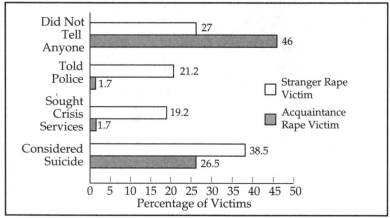

Source: Koss et al. 1988.

Figure 5–6
Occurrence of Rape by Victim Age Group, 1991

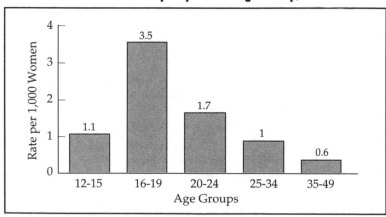

Source: Bastian 1992.

References

Bart, P. 1979. "Avoiding Rape: A Study of Victims and Avoiders." Final report presented on National Institute of Mental Health Grant MH-12931, University of Illinois Medical Center, Chicago, August.

————. 1981. "A Study of Women Who Both Were Raped and Avoided Rape." *Journal of Social Issues* 37: 4.

————. 1994. Quoted in S. Jacoby, "How To Spot and Resist the Rapist You Know." *Glamour*, February.

Bastian, L. D. 1992. *Criminal Victimization 1991.* Bureau of Justice Statistics Bulletin. Washington, DC: U.S. Department of Justice.

Becker, J. V., L. J. Skinner, and G. G. Abel. 1983. "Sequelae of Sexual Assault: The Survivor's Perspective." In *The Sexual Aggressor: Current Perspectives on Treatment,* edited by J. G. Greer and I. R. Stuart. New York: Van Nostrand Reinhold.

Benedict, H. 1985. *Recovery: How To Survive Sexual Assault for Women, Men, Teenagers, and Their Friends and Families.* New York: Doubleday.

Borgida, E., and N. Brekke. 1985. "Psycholegal Research on Rape Trials." In *Rape and Sexual Assault,* edited by A. Burgess. New York: Garland Publishing.

Brogger, S. 1976. *Deliver Us from Love.* New York: Delacorte.

Brownmiller, S. 1975. *Against Our Will: Men, Women, and Rape.* New York: Simon & Schuster.

Bureau of Justice Statistics. 1992. *Sourcebook of Criminal Justice Statistics 1991,* edited by T. J. Flanagan and K. Maguire. Washington, DC: U.S. Department of Justice.

Burgess, A. W., and A. N. Groth. 1977. "Sexual Dysfunction during Rape." *New England Journal of Medicine* 297: 4.

Burgess, A. W., and L. L. Holmstrom. 1974. "Rape Trauma Syndrome." *American Journal of Psychiatry* 131: 981–988.

————. 1985. "Rape Trauma Syndrome and Post Traumatic Stress Response." In *Rape and Sexual Assault,* edited by A. Burgess. New York: Garland Publishing.

Burt, M. R. 1979. "Attitudes Supportive of Rape in American Culture." Final report presented to the National Institute of Mental Health, National Center for the Prevention and Control of Rape, University of Minneapolis. Unpublished manuscript.

Carlton, T. (captain, Oklahoma City Police Department Sex Crimes Unit). 1993. Quoted in "Nurses Fight Injustice of Rape," by J. Kuhlman. *The Sunday Oklahoman*, 7 November.

Cartwright, P. S. 1987. "Factors That Correlate with Injury Sustained by Survivors of Sexual Assault." *American Journal of Obstetrics and Gynecology* 70: 44–46.

Derryberry, S. (Call Rape, Inc. volunteer coordinator). 1994. Telephone conversation with the author, 16 March.

Dietz, P., R. Hazelwood, and J. Warren. 1990. "The Sexually Sadistic Criminal and His Offenses." *Bulletin of the American Academy of Psychiatry and the Law* 18: 163–178.

Fairstein, L. 1993. *Sexual Violence: Our War against Rape*. New York: William Morrow.

Federal Bureau of Investigation. 1992. *Uniform Crime Report 1991*. Washington, DC: U.S. Department of Justice.

Ferris, E. 1983. "Long-Term Consequences of Adult Rape." *Response* 6 (January/February): 1.

Finkelhor, D. 1979. *Sexually Victimized Children*. New York: The Free Press.

Finkelhor, D., and K. Yllo. 1985a. *License To Rape: Sexual Abuse of Wives*. New York: Holt, Rinehart & Winston.

———. 1985b. "Marital Rape." In *Rape and Sexual Assault*, edited by A. Burgess. New York: Garland Publishing.

Frieze, I. 1983. "Investigating the Causes and Consequences of Marital Rape." *Signs* 8: 532–553.

Goddard, M. A. 1988. *Sexual Assault: A Hospital/Community Protocol for Forensic and Medical Examination*. Washington, DC: U.S. Department of Justice.

Groot, P. (Virginians Aligned Against Sexual Assault executive director). 1994. Telephone conversation with the author, 22 January.

Groth, A. N., and H. J. Birnbaum. 1979. *Men Who Rape: The Psychology of the Offender*. New York: Plenum Publishing.

Hall, R. 1994. A survey of rape crisis centers in the United States. Unpublished data.

Hazelwood, R. R., and A. W. Burgess. 1987. "An Introduction to the Serial Rapist: Research by the FBI." *FBI Law Enforcement Bulletin*, September.

Hazelwood, R. R., A. W. Burgess, and J. A. Harpold. 1986. "Rape: The

Dangers of Providing Confrontational Advice." *FBI Law Enforcement Bulletin*, June.

Holmstrom, L. L. 1985. "The Criminal Justice System's Response to the Rape Victim." In *Rape and Sexual Assault*, edited by A. Burgess. New York: Garland Publishing.

Holmstrom, L. L., and A. W. Burgess. 1975. "Assessing Trauma in the Rape Victim." *American Journal of Nursing* 75: 1288–1291.

———. 1983. *The Victim of Rape: Institutional Reactions*. Reprint. New Brunswick, NJ: Transaction. (New York: Wiley, 1978.)

Jacoby, S. 1994. "How To Spot and Resist the Rapist You Know." *Glamour*, February.

Jenny, C., et al. 1990. "Sexually Transmitted Diseases in Victims of Rape" (Seattle study). *New England Journal of Medicine* 322 (11): 713–716.

Kilpatrick, D. G., and C. L. Best. 1990. "Violence as a Precursor of Women's Substance Abuse: The Rest of the Drugs-Violence Story." Paper presented at 98th Annual Convention of the American Psychological Association in Boston, August.

Kilpatrick, D. G., C. N. Edmunds, and A. K Seymour. 1992. *Rape in America: A Report to the Nation*. Arlington, VA: National Victim Center.

Kilpatrick, D. G., B. E. Saunders, L. J. Veronen, C. L. Best, and J. M. Von. 1987. "Criminal Victimization: Lifetime Prevalence, Reporting to the Police, and Psychological Impact." *Crime and Delinquency* 33: 479–489.

Koss, M. P., T. E. Dinero, V. A. Seibel, and S. L. Cox. 1988. "Stranger and Acquaintance Rape: Are There Differences in the Victim's Experience?" *Psychology of Women Quarterly* 12: 1–24.

Koss, M. P., C. A. Gidycz, and N. Wisniewski. 1987. "The Scope of Rape: Incidence and Prevalence of Sexual Aggression and Victimization in a National Sample of Higher Education Students." *Journal of Consulting and Clinical Psychology* 55: 162–170.

Koss, M. P., W. J. Woodruff, and P. Koss. 1991. "Criminal Victimization among Primary Care Medical Patients: Prevalence, Incidence, and Physician Usage." *Behavioral Sciences and the Law* 9: 85–96.

Langevin, R. 1991. "The Sex Killer." In *Rape and Sexual Assault III*, edited by A. Burgess. New York: Garland Publishing.

Langevin, R., M. H. Ben-Aron, P. Wright, M. Marchese, and L. Hardy. 1988. "The Sex Killer." *Annals of Sex Research* 1: 263–301.

Ledray, L. E. 1991. "Sexual Assault and Sexually Transmitted Disease: The Issues and Concerns." In *Rape and Sexual Assault III*, edited by A. Burgess. New York: Garland Publishing.

Levine-MacCombie, J., and M. P. Koss. 1986. "Acquaintance Rape: Effective Avoidance Strategies." *Psychology of Women Quarterly* 10: 311–320.

Lynch, V. (president, International Association of Forensic Nurses). 1994. Telephone conversation with the author, 14 April.

McCahill, T. W., L. C. Meyer, and A. M. Fischman. 1979. *The Aftermath of Rape*. Lexington, MA: D. C. Health.

McDermott, M. J. 1979. *Rape Victimization in 26 American Cities*. Albany, NY: U.S. Department of Justice.

McIntyre, J. 1980. *Victim Response to Rape: Alternative Outcomes*. Washington, DC: Bureau of Social Science Research.

Marchbanks, P. A., K. J. Lui, and J. A. Mercy. 1990. "Risk of Injury from Resisting Rape." *American Journal of Epidemiology* 132: 3.

Matheson, S. 1989. *Sexual Assault: A Hospital/Community Protocol for Forensic and Medical Examination*. Concord, NH: Office of the New Hampshire Attorney General.

Minnesota Department of Corrections. 1964. *The Sex Offender in Minnesota*.

National Institute of Law Enforcement and Criminal Justice. 1977. *Forcible Rape: A National Survey of the Response by Police, Police Volume 1*. Washington, DC: U.S. Department of Justice.

Novacek, J., R. Raskin, D. Bahlinger, L. Firth, and S. Bybicki. 1993. *Rape: Tulsa Women Speak Out*. Tulsa, OK: Tulsa Institute of Behavioral Sciences.

President's Commission of Law Enforcement and Administration of Justice. 1967. *The Challenge of Crime in a Free Society*. Washington, DC.

Prichard, T. (former counselor, Rape Crisis Program, Tarrant Co., TX). 1994. Telephone conversation with the author, 15 March.

Ribera, L. A. (instructor, Rape Prevention/Women's Self-Defense). 1993. "Identifying and Preventing Date and Acquaintance Rape." Lecture presented at University of Central Oklahoma in Edmond, OK, 8 November.

Ruch, L. O., J. W. Gartrell, S. R. Amedeo, and B. J. Coyne. 1991. "The Sexual Assault Syndrome Scale: Measuring Self-Reported Sexual Assault Trauma in the Emergency Room." *Psychological Assessment* 3 (1): 3–8.

Ruch, L. O., and J. J. Leon. 1986. "The Victim of Rape and the Role of Life Change, Coping, and Social Support during the Rape Trauma Syndrome." In *Stress, Social Support, and Women*, edited by S. E. Hobfall. New York: Hemisphere Publishing.

Russell, D. 1982. *Rape in Marriage*. New York: Macmillan, Collier Books.

Slaughter, L., 1994a. Telephone conversation with the author, 24 February.

————. 1994b. "When 'No' Means 'No': The Medical Evaluation of the Adult Sexual Assault Victim." Seminar presented to the Sexual Assault Nurse Examiners Program in Tulsa, OK, 8 March.

Slaughter, L., and C. V. Brown. 1991. "The Forensic Evaluation of Sexual Assault Victims: A Revised Protocol." *Annals of Emergency Medicine* 20 (9): 951.

Slaughter, L., and S. Crowley. 1993. "Correlates of Genital Injury in Rape." Paper presented to the North American Association of Pediatric and Adolescent Gynecology, April.

Slaughter, L., and S. Shackleford. 1993. "Genital Injury in Rape." Paper presented to the American College of Obstetricians and Gynecologists in Washington, DC, May.

Smith, S. E. 1986. *Fear or Freedom: A Woman's Options in Social Survival and Physical Defense.* Racine, WI: Mother Courage Press.

Sorenson, S. B., J. A. Stein, J. M. Siegel, J. M. Golding, and M. A. Burnam. 1987. "Prevalence of Adult Sexual Assault: The Los Angeles Epidemiologic Catchment Area Study." *American Journal of Epidemiology* 126: 1154–1164.

Spektor, P. 1980. Testimony delivered to the Law Enforcement Subcommittee of the Minnesota House of Representatives, 29 February.

Sturm, J. T., M. E. Carr, M. G. Lexenberg, J. K. Swoyer, and J. Cicero. 1990. "The Prevalence of Neisseria Gonorrhoeae and Chlamydia Trachomatis in Victims of Sexual Assault." *Annals of Emergency Medicine* 19 (5): 587–590.

Subcommittee on Sex Crimes of the Assembly Interior Committee on Judicial Process. 1950. Preliminary report. State of California.

Swindell, B. 1994. "New Equipment Expected To Help Convict Rapists." *Tulsa World,* 10 February.

Symonds, M. 1975. "Victims of Violence." *American Journal of Psychoanalysis* 35: 19–25.

Thyfault, R. 1985. "Sexual Abuse in the Battering Relationship." Paper presented to the Rocky Mountain Psychological Association in Tucson, AZ, 1980. Cited in D. Finkelhor and K. Yllo, *License To Rape: Sexual Abuse of Wives* (New York: Holt, Rinehart & Winston, 1985).

Tintinalli, J. E., and M. Hoelzer. 1985. "Clinical Findings and Legal Resolution in Sexual Assault." *Annals of Emergency Medicine* 14: 447–453.

Ullman, S. E., and R. A. Knight. 1992. "Fighting Back: Women's Resistance to Rape." *Journal of Interpersonal Violence* 7 (March): 1.

Valento, T. (S.A.N.E. nurse). 1994. Telephone conversation with the author, 10 June.

Warren, J. I., R. R. Hazelwood, and R. Reboussin. 1991. "Serial Rape: The Offender and His Rape Career." In *Rape and Sexual Assault III*, edited by A. Burgess. New York: Garland Publishing.

Williams, L. S. 1985. *The "Classic" Rape: When Do Victims Report?* Seattle: University of Washington (Department of Sociology).

Wood, R. (director of Combatives at West Point). 1990. Quoted in J. D. Brewer, "Martial Arts at West Point." *TaeKwonDo Times* 11 (November): 1.

Wyatt, G. E. 1990. "The Circumstances and Disclosure of Rape." Testimony before the U.S. Congress, Select Committee on Children, Youth, and Families, June.

Young, W. W., A. C. Bracken, M. A. Goddard, S. Matheson, and the New Hampshire Sexual Assault Medical Examination Protocol Project Committee. 1992. "Sexual Assault: Review of a National Model Protocol for Forensic and Medical Evaluation." *Journal of Obstetrics and Gynecology* 80: (November): 5.

Zachritz, H. (S.A.N.E. coordinator). 1993. Telephone conversation with the author, 16 March.

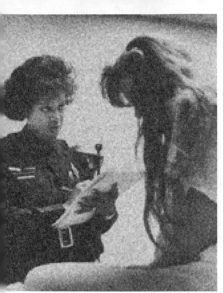

Directory of Organizations 6

The organizations described in this chapter are all actively involved in some aspect of the war against sexual violence. Some work with other organizations to facilitate the development of anti–sexual assault programs, some work to rehabilitate offenders, and some work with local victims of sexual assault. All of the organizations listed, however, have an impact regionally, nationally, or internationally. For example, the National Institute for the Study, Prevention, and Treatment of Sexual Trauma receives patient (both offender and victim) referrals from across the nation. The Rape Treatment Center at Santa Monica Hospital in California and the Sexual Assault Nurse Examiners Program (S.A.N.E.) in Tulsa, Oklahoma, are both model interagency programs that receive international recognition and acclaim. Each of the state coalitions is committed to assisting in the development of and solidarity among rape crisis centers in their respective states. Organizations such as the National Coalition Against Sexual Assault (NCASA) work toward the same goals for their members on a national level. While no such directory can ever be exhaustive (due to the continuous creation, dissolving, or merging of organizations), the organizations

125

included here can refer the reader to other organizations appropriate for their specific needs.

Abused Deaf Women's Advocacy Services (ADWAS)
2366 Eastlake Avenue, East, Suite 201
Seattle, Washington 98102-3366
Business/Education/Outreach Line: (206) 726-0093 TTY
Sexual Assault/Domestic Violence Crisis Line: (206) 236-3134 TTY
Washington State TDD Relay Service: (800) 833-6384

The Abused Deaf Women's Advocacy Services (ADWAS) was incorporated in early 1986. Recognizing the difficulties existing crisis centers experienced in attempting to serve deaf victims, ADWAS was created as a support agency for deaf, deaf-blind, and hard-of-hearing victims of sexual assault and domestic violence. Since the creation of its 24-hour crisis line staffed by volunteers in November 1986, ADWAS has grown to include a paid staff of seven, including an executive director, a therapist, and volunteer, education, and community advocacy coordinators. In addition to the crisis lines, services include support groups for both female and male victims of physical, sexual, or emotional abuse and educational programs and workshops on date rape and teen battering that are taken to high schools with deaf programs. ADWAS is the first non-mainstreamed agency of its kind, but it is actively working to help establish similar agencies in the United States and Canada. Each state operates a TDD/TTY (telecommunication device for the deaf/telecommunication typewriter for the deaf) relay service, whereby the hearing caller can contact a TDD/TTY anywhere in the country, have their audible conversation converted into printed format for the party with the TDD/TTY, and have the response read to them by an operator.

Association for the Treatment of Sexual Abusers (ATSA)
P.O. Box 866
Lake Oswego, OR 97034-0140
(503) 233-2312
FAX (503) 238-0210

The Association for the Treatment of Sexual Abusers (ATSA), a nonprofit, interdisciplinary organization, was incorporated by a small group of Oregon clinicians in 1984. Since its founding ATSA has become an international organization, boasting a membership of over 550 treatment providers and professionals from allied fields, dedicated to the prevention of sexual assault through effective management of sexual offenders. The organization seeks to foster research and information exchange, to further professional education, and to provide for the advancement of professional standards and practices in the field of sexual offender evaluation and treatment. ATSA sponsors an annual research and treatment conference.

Publications: In 1993 ATSA published *Practitioner's Handbook,* containing extensive standards of practice, guidelines for use of the penile plethysmograph, and a code of professional ethics that seeks to protect the integrity of the field and the safety of the community. ATSA also publishes a quarterly newsletter (*The Forum*) and a journal (*Sexual Abuse: A Journal of Research and Treatment*).

Illusion Theatre
528 Hennepin Avenue, Suite 704
Minneapolis, MN 55403
(612) 339-4944

The Illusion Theatre Prevention Program uses theatre as a catalyst for personal and social change. Through the use of original plays and workshops presented in an educational format, the company addresses such issues as sexual abuse, interpersonal violence, sexual harassment, and HIV/AIDS. The Illusion Theatre developed its first such work in 1977, when it collaborated with the Hennepin County Attorney's Child Sexual Abuse Prevention Program to create "Touch," a play about nurturing, confusing, and exploitive touching. The play remains in the company's repertoire, along with works geared toward adolescents, families, high school and college students, and adults. Workshops are available, and are changed quarterly. They are approximately two and one-half hours in length, relate to specific plays and the company's mission, and cost $500. The cost of play presentations ranges from $800 to $2,500, depending on the play.

Publications: The company has available several video versions of its plays, as well as print resources for students and educators.

IMPACT International, Inc. (I.I.I.)
D.C. IMPACT
701 Richmond Avenue
Silver Spring, MD 20910-5225
(301) 589-1349

BAMM IMPACT (San Francisco area)
(415) 592-7300

IMPACT Personal Safety (Los Angeles area)
(818) 546-5477

IMPACT International, Inc. (I.I.I.) was fully incorporated as a non-profit organization in July 1991 to oversee the development of the IMPACT women-only self-defense programs and to make those programs "accessible to as many women as possible." I.I.I. screens and certifies all IMPACT program instructors after an extensive training and certification process, conducts in-service training to maintain certification, and establishes specific course curricula. The instructor certification process is one of the strictest in the nation, requiring a prescreening psychological examination, a criminal background check, and an interview with a therapist (all for $200), a medical release from a physician, participation in (women) or observation of (men) an IMPACT basic self-defense course ($400 to $700 for women), attendance at a two-week certified instructor training program in California (approximately $1,000 tuition), coteaching of at least one course with a certified instructor trainer, supervised teaching, and the purchase of a special protective suit ($1,800). Membership fees for chapters range from $250 to $1,000, plus dues of $10 to $20 per student. Having invested several thousand dollars at a minimum, IMPACT instructors are highly trained, dedicated professionals. The Women's Basics self-defense course consists of 25 hours of training, with an emphasis on full-contact techniques that are designed to incapacitate an attacker in a matter of seconds. Classes are taught in a supportive group atmosphere, and they are not open to spectators (with the exception of the final "graduation," which permits spectators but no children, video cameras, or flash pictures). Classes are taught by female/male teams, with the female instructor as the class leader and the male instructor (in the protective suit) serving as the primary attacker. Tuition ranges from $400 to $700, depending on the course location; though reduced tuition courses may be available through specific women's shelters. IMPACT chapters are located in Washington, D.C., Chicago, Los Angeles, and San Francisco, among other locations.

International Association of Forensic Nurses, Inc. (IAFN)
c/o SLACK Incorporated
6900 Grove Road
Thorofare, NJ 08086
(609) 848-8356
FAX (609) 848-5274

The International Association of Forensic Nurses, Inc. (IAFN) evolved in Minnesota in 1992 and elected Virginia Lynch as its first president in 1993. An association composed primarily of registered nurses who work in the legal nursing field, its stated mission is to ". . . develop, promote and disseminate information about the science of forensic nursing nationally and internationally." IAFN members include sexual assault nurse examiners, forensic nurse investigators and educators, nurse coroners/death investigators, correctional nurses, and emergency/trauma or critical care nurses, among others. Members are actively involved in the establishment of Sexual Assault Nurse Examiners (S.A.N.E.) programs, the unification of standards of forensic nursing practice, and the development and implementation of undergraduate and graduate curricula in clinical forensic nursing. IAFN provides members with free copies of forensic protocol and guidelines for identification of crime victims and evidence collection, access to a research database, an annual directory of membership, and networking resources with other professionals in the field. Annual membership for registered nurses is $100.

Publication: IAFN publishes *The Journal of Forensic Nursing* quarterly.

King County Sexual Assault Resource Center (KCSARC)
304 Main Avenue, South, Suite 200
Renton, WA 98055
(206) 226-5062 business line (TDD available)
(206) 226-7273 crisis line (for King County)
(800) 825-RAPE crisis line (for King County)

The King County Sexual Assault Resource Center (KCSARC), formerly the King County Rape Crisis Center, has evolved in its 20-year history into a center admired and emulated throughout the world. Begun in 1974 and incorporated in 1976, the KCSARC's twofold mission is to provide support services to victims of sexual assault and their families and to provide programs to increase awareness and eliminate sexual assault in the community. In its early years the education program was underwritten by sales of publications, particularly *He Told Me Not To Tell* (reviewed in chapter 7, along with several other resources from KCSARC). This particular work was marketed to various states' Department of Human Services, and it included laws specific to each state. KCSARC's education materials have won national acclaim, are currently being used in 51 countries, and continue to be a source of revenue for the center. The center's education department is active in training educators, mental health providers, and other professionals whose work brings them in contact with victims of sexual assault. The center's continued success is due in large part to the calibre and dedication of the staff (several key staff members have been at KCSARC for over a decade) and to the composition of its board of trustees; the business-oriented board is composed of individuals active in marketing, sales, financial planning, advertising, and banking. KCSARC's budget for 1992 was in excess of $1 million.

Publications: In addition to *He Told Me Not To Tell*, KSARC publishes *Top Secret: Sexual Assault Information for Teenagers Only, So What's It to Me?*, *Sexual Assault Information for Guys, Be Aware. Be Safe.*, and *Helping Your Child To Be Safe.*

**National Clearinghouse on Marital
and Date Rape (NCMDR)**
2325 Oak Street
Berkeley, CA 94708
(510) 524-1582

The National Clearinghouse on Marital and Date Rape (NCMDR) is a business supplying phone consultation, research, and document location and acquisition relevant to the subjects of marital and date rape. NCMDR also operates a speakers bureau featuring Laura X, the nationally known director of the company. NCMDR maintains copies of relevant and current federal and state legislation and sells a chart ($3) depicting the marital rape laws of each state. A year's subscription to their services is $10 for students, senior citizens, and the unemployed; $15 for faculty, researchers, librarians, and social workers; $25 for attorneys; and $30 for organizations. A phone consultation and/or document search and delivery fee is $7.50 per 15 minutes. Photocopying charges are $.25 per page. NCMDR has a volunteer internship program for students in a wide variety of areas.

National Coalition Against Domestic Violence (NCADV)
P.O. Box 18749
Denver, CO 80218-0749
(303) 839-1852

The National Coalition Against Domestic Violence (NCADV), formed in 1978, is the oldest national organization representing grass-roots organizations and individuals working to assist and empower battered women and their children. It is governed by a board of directors who are active in domestic violence programs in their own communites. NCADV provides general information to the public, referrals to and for individuals and other organizations, and technical assistance to domestic violence shelters and related service organizations. On the national level, NCADV sponsors "National Domestic Violence Month" yearly and a national conference on domestic violence every other year. NCADV functions as a legislative watchdog and provides a national voice for battered women and their children through their public policy advocate in Washington, D.C. NCADV also offers training and educational services. It works with numerous agencies and organizations to develop posters, fact sheets, and printed materials. NCADV has five membership categories: (1) active (for organizations such as shelters, safehomes, and state coalitions); (2) supportive organizational; (3) supportive individual; (4) incarcerated women (a free membership open to battered women in prison); and (5) youth (open to individuals under 18 and requiring a pledge statement).

Publications: NCADV develops and distributes general information packets, media and public relations packets, a quarterly newsletter titled *NCADV VOICE*, and informational bulletins on the issue of domestic violence, including marital rape.

National Institute for the Study, Prevention, and Treatment of Sexual Trauma
104 East Biddle Street
Baltimore, MD 21202
(410) 539-1661

The National Institute for the Study, Prevention, and Treatment of Sexual Trauma is an outgrowth of work begun by John Money in 1966 at Johns Hopkins Hospital. Money's research at that time focused on the effect of antiandrogenic medication on sex offenders (see chapter 2). In 1980 the Sexual Disorders Clinic was established at Johns Hopkins to treat sexual disorders and foster related research and teaching. In 1991 Johns Hopkins Hospital discontinued its Sexual Disorders Clinic and the director of the clinic, Fred S. Berlin, established the National Institute for the Study, Prevention, and Treatment of Sexual Trauma as a free-standing private clinic. While the institute provides care to both patients with sexual disorders and victims of sexual trauma, it has gained national recognition for its work with sexual offenders, particularly paraphilias (see chapter 2). The institute performs evaluations of offenders and victims, and offers group therapy for victims, offenders, and the mentally retarded. It also provides support group therapy for offenders' families, significant others, and friends. The institute is one of the major clinics in the United States offering pharmacotherapy for sex offenders (see chapter 2). In addition to offering professional consultations, the institute conducts a yearly teaching seminar for legal and medical professionals and a week-long training seminar twice yearly for professionals whose work concerns paraphilias.

National Organization for Victim Assistance (NOVA)
1757 Park Road, NW
Washington, DC 20010
(202) 232-6682 (232-NOVA)
(800) 879-6682 (TRY-NOVA)
FAX (202) 462-2256

The National Organization for Victim Assistance (NOVA) is a nonprofit organization of victim and witness assistance programs and practitioners, criminal justice agencies and professionals, mental health professionals, researchers, former victims and survivors, and others committed to the recognition and implementation of victim rights. NOVA was founded in 1975 by a group of individuals who had been working in various capacities with victims of crime, and it was initially supported through volunteer efforts and the financial donations of its founders. By 1992 its membership had increased to include approximately 3,500 agencies and individuals. Governed by a board of 22 elected and 7 appointed directors, NOVA has four stated purposes:

1. National advocacy for victims in state and national legislatures
2. Direct services for victims through 24-hour and follow-up assistance for victims in areas where local programs are unavailable

3. Professional development through education and training services for professionals involved in victim assistance
4. Services for members through publications, national conferences, and networking

NOVA has been a primary force in the establishment of victim compensation programs in the United States and the Virgin Islands, and it has played a significant role in the passage of federal legislation, such as the Victim/Witness Protection Act of 1982, the Victims of Crime Act of 1984, and "victims' rights" bills and constitutional amendments on the state level. NOVA operates a Community Crisis Response Institute that maintains a roster of trained volunteers of varied backgrounds. In the event of a natural or man-made disaster (such as earthquakes or mass murders), NOVA checks with the appropriate state agency to see what assistance services are needed. If a need exists and NOVA is invited by the local or state government or agency, a volunteer crisis team is compiled and sent to the disaster area to supplement available services. Volunteers are not paid, receiving only transportation, lodging, and board. NOVA also maintains a catalogue of publications, training manuals, selected topic briefs, information packets, audiocassettes, and accessories for sale, in addition to offering national training institutes. Membership fees are $20 for seniors and students and $30 for individuals.

Publications: NOVA periodically publishes a newsletter entitled *NOVA NEWSLETTER* and *Legislative Alerts*, a publication that alerts readers to relevant current or pending legislation. Both publications are available free of charge to members.

National Organization for Women (NOW)
P.O. Box 96824
Washington, DC 20090-6824
(202) 331-0066
(202) 331-9002 TTY

The National Organization for Women (NOW) was founded in 1966 and has since become the largest women's rights organization in the country, with a membership in excess of 275,000. As part of its organizational purpose to bring about full equality for women, NOW actively campaigns on the national and state levels for legislative change. NOW has pioneered model rape and spousal assault legislation and actively lobbied for passage of such legislation. Though no longer active on a national level with the establishment of local rape crisis centers, local chapters and state organizations are often involved in legislative efforts. NOW has a representative structure, operating on the national, regional, and state level. Local chapters of ten or more members operate on the grass-roots level. Regular national, state, and local dues are $35 per year except in Arizona, California, Illinois, and Michigan, where they are $40. A sliding scale is available for those unable to pay the full amount.

Publication: NOW publishes *National NOW Times,* a quarterly newspaper.

Rape Treatment Center
Santa Monica Hospital Medical Center
1250 16th Street
Santa Monica, CA 90404
(310) 319-4000

The Rape Treatment Center, begun in 1974 at Santa Monica Hospital, is nationally recognized for its pioneering work as a model program serving sexual assault victims and their families. It offers many services, all of which are free, including specialized therapy, individual and group counseling, emergency medical treatment, and legal assistance. The center's Stuart House, a model interagency program for sexually abused children, has been internationally recognized. The center's staff offers rape awareness and crime prevention programs for various age groups and audiences, such as the elderly, college students, adolescents, and the Hispanic community.

Publications: The Rape Treatment Center produces and offers many materials (films, videos, books, and posters), at very reasonable cost, for use in sexual assault prevention programs in schools and colleges. One video of particular note is *Campus Rape,* which features Susan Dey and Corbin Bernsen (reviewed in chapter 7). The Rape Treatment Center has also developed special educational films, seminars, and publications for medical personnel.

Safer Society Program (SSP)
P.O. Box 340
Brandon, VT 05733-0340
(802) 247-3132

The Safer Society Program (SSP), a nonprofit project of the New York State Council of Churches, is a national research, advocacy, and referral center on the prevention and treatment of sexual abuse. It serves as a clearinghouse/network center for newly emerging topics related to these issues, and it maintains the only computerized nationwide database of agencies, institutions, and individuals identified by the program as providing specialized assessment and treatment for youthful and adult sex offenders. Interested parties can call SSP in the afternoon during the work week for free individual referrals of juvenile and adult sex offenders to specialized community-based and residential treatment programs throughout the United States. SSP conducts a number of specialized training institutes for professionals each year in Vermont.

Publications: Every two years SSP publishes the *Nationwide Survey of Juvenile and Adult Sex Offender Treatment Programs and Models,* a survey that provides information about sex offender treatment and professionals throughout the country that provide such treatment. SSP maintains a file of programs treating abuse-reactive children. The program publishes a number of sexual abuse related materials through five ongoing series. These publications include studies of treatment programs for professionals, self-help workbooks for offenders, research papers and monographs on pertinent issues, and audio- and videotapes for clinicians and offenders.

Sexual Assault Nurse Examiners Program (S.A.N.E.)
Tulsa Police Department
600 Civic Center
Tulsa, OK 74103
(918) 596-7608

The Sexual Assault Nurse Examiners Program (S.A.N.E.) was initiated by Mayor Roger Randle of Tulsa, Oklahoma, in July of 1991 in response to a community crisis. Local hospitals and healthcare facilities were expressing extreme reluctance—and in some cases refusing outright—to perform sexual assault examinations, due to the amount of time it demanded of the attending physician both in the emergency room and possibly in court. The Tulsa Police Department became actively involved in the recruiting and training of registered nurses to perform forensic rape examinations. Hillcrest Medical Center in Tulsa provided a suite of rooms and medical supplies, enabling the examinations to be done away from the emergency rooms of local hospitals. As a result of this program, sexual assault victims are no longer subjected to waiting long periods of time (up to 12 hours) in a public setting for medical attention, law enforcement officials are no longer delayed for an equal period of time while awaiting the collection of evidence, evidence is collected in a timely manner, and physicians are freed to attend to medical emergencies. Since the incorporation of the program, the quality of forensic evidence collection has greatly improved, facilitating the prosecution efforts of the district attorneys' offices. The S.A.N.E. program is unique in that it is administered from within the police department; the coordinator's office is located in the Sex Crimes Department. The program received a U.S. Justice Department Award for Public Service in 1991, and, as one of ten winners from a field of 1,300 applicants in the 1994 Innovations in State and Local Government Awards program of the Ford Foundation and Harvard University, received a $100,000 award.

Women's Funding Alliance (WFA)
119 South Main Street, Suite 330
Seattle, WA 98104
(206) 467-6733 V/TDD
FAX (206) 467-7537

According to the National Network of Women's Funds, programs specifically designed for women receive less than 5 percent of all corporate and foundation philanthropic funds. Accordingly, rape crisis centers that are not supported by state government often experience a great deal of financial instability from one fiscal year to the next. One solution to the problem has been the establishment of specialized funding organizations; there are now over 50 women's funding organizations in the United States. A registered nonprofit corporation, the Women's Funding Alliance (WFA) was founded in 1983 to serve as a supplement and alternative to traditional funding sources for services to women and children. Composed of ten nonprofit organizations that provide essential services to women and children, WFA is one of only three federations of women's organizations whose members have a voice in its operations. The primary mission of WFA is fund-raising: it raises and distributes funds to its member organizations, thereby contributing to a consistent financial operating base that ensures their continued existence. In 1993 WFA began awarding special grants to nonmember organizations specifically targeted to aid women and children throughout the state of Washington. WFA pursues its secondary mission of raising public awareness of women's issues through speaking engagements, literature, information booths, and workplace charitable campaigns. It also provides networking opportunities for its member organizations. In 1989 the National Committee for Responsive Philanthropy recognized WFA with several awards for community service.

Publications: WFA publishes various flyers, handouts, and other informational material.

Sexual Assault Coalitions

Sexual assault coalitions nationwide have many similarities—basic philosophy, aim and focus, services provided, and dedication of their members in combatting sexual violence. There are, however, numerous differences—size, history, organizational structure and methods, and visible accomplishments, to name a few. The following descriptions of coalitions seek to put primary emphasis on those differences, since their differences are what make each coalition unique. While most coalitions do not provide direct services to victims of sexual assault, they all provide references to local crisis centers throughout the state.

National Coalition Against Sexual Assault (NCASA)
P.O. Box 21378
Washington, DC 20009
(202) 483-7165

Established in 1978 by representatives from 20 rape crisis centers, the National Coalition Against Sexual Assault (NCASA) currently has a membership of approximately 600 rape crisis centers and individuals concerned about sexual violence. It is governed by a national board of directors. NCASA's stated purpose is:

> To eliminate sexual violence and, until that is achieved,
> To ease the suffering and facilitate the recovery of its victims.

NCASA promotes and advocates a national course of action based on the sexual assault victim's/survivor's perspective within a feminist framework, and it works toward the empowerment of all victims/survivors. The organization holds an annual national conference of therapists, rape crisis counselors, and interested individuals. A series of seminars and workshops are presented, with topics ranging from counseling specifics to organizational structuring. Dues for individuals are $35 per year.

Publication: NCASA publishes *NCASA Journal,* a quarterly journal (included with membership).

**Alaska Network on Domestic Violence
and Sexual Assault**
130 Seward Street, Suite 501
Juneau, AK 99801
(907) 586-3650
FAX (907) 463-4493

The Alaska Network on Domestic Violence and Sexual Assault had its beginning in the winter of 1977, with the executive directors of the five existing centers in Alaska. Those directors met in Anchorage to discuss possible development and funding of resources for battered women and sexual assault victims, and the Alaska Shelter Alliance was born. (The Alliance was incorporated in 1978 as the Alaska Council on Family Violence, and as the Alaska Network on Domestic Violence and Sexual Assault in 1980. The network currently consists of 22 nonprofit programs that provide services to victims of domestic violence and sexual assault.) The directors articulated three specific goals for the new organization: (1) to secure adequate funding for all existing programs; (2) to develop a mechanism to facilitate networking between programs; and (3) to provide a model of social service delivery more humane than that of the traditional male model, a model that emphasizes empowerment of women in its management style. Regarding the first goal, the original founders felt that funds should be acquired and distributed among the centers in a cooperative, noncompetitive manner without regard to political considerations or pressures. Practical application of that philosophy came in July 1978, when the network received an appropriation of $736,000 in a lump sum, with no statuatory authority by any state department to administer or monitor the funds. The network divided the funding among its programs on a consensus basis, with each program making recommendations on the budget of its peers (sometimes on a line-by-line basis) and being bound by the recommendations of its peers. The process was followed until the funds had been completely distributed, and all the programs were in agreement with the distribution. In the early 1980s this process was no longer possible, and the network pursued and obtained the establishment of the Council on Domestic Violence and Sexual Assault, an administrative council in state government responsible for, among other duties, the allocation of funds. The network opened its first office in Juneau in late 1983 and hired its first paid staff person—a coordinator. The network was especially active in legislative advocacy in the 1980s, helping to acquire legislative allocations for films, public service announcements (PSAs), and educational projects and promoting the passage of marital rape and hearsay bills as well as legislation on civil compromise, confidentiality, and the termination of parental rights for sex offenders. During this time, the network developed training materials and conducted training sessions throughout the state. While continuing its legislative advocacy work, the primary emphasis of the network has now become systems advocacy. Systems advocacy involves ensuring that the laws that are already on the books are enforced. Such enforcement is pursued through the network's training of personnel in the criminal justice system and by "just plain getting after them."

Arkansas Coalition Against Violence to Women and Children (ACAVWC)
7509 Cantrell Road, Suite 213
Little Rock, AR 72207
(501) 663-4668
(800) 332-4443

The Arkansas Coalition Against Violence to Women and Children (ACAVWC) began in 1982 as a community-based, grass-roots organization to address the concerns and needs of battered women and children, sexual assault survivors, and families and friends of abused women and children. It is a nonprofit organization, made up of area shelters, safe houses, hotlines, and task forces, and represents both the rural and urban areas of Arkansas. There are currently eight crisis centers throughout the state. ACAVWC offers technical assistance and training to help victims acquire the information and survival skills necessary to take control of their lives, and it serves as a voice that works for legislative and public policy change.

Colorado Coalition Against Sexual Assault (CCASA)
P.O. Box 18663
Denver, CO 80218
(303) 861-7033

Created in 1984, the nonprofit Colorado Coalition Against Sexual Assault (CCASA) serves as a political and funds-generating advocate for sexual assault service providers in Colorado, thereby benefiting sexual assault victims. To that end, CCASA led efforts resulting in successful passage of state legislation criminalizing marital rape in 1988, and it successfully lobbied for legislation that extended the civil statute of limitations for sexual assault from one to six years. CCASA has also developed several publications and conducted related training programs throughout the state. CCASA has a membership of approximately 60, comprised of rape crisis centers, victim service agencies and advocates, district attorneys' offices, law enforcement agencies, healthcare providers, and individuals.

Publications: In 1992 CCASA published the *Colorado Sexual Assault Forensic Examination Protocol*, produced a video on the same, and began statewide training on the procedures. It has also published a training manual and a trainer's guide for hotline workers and a brochure for sexual assault victims on sexually transmitted diseases (STDs) and AIDS.

Connecticut Sexual Assault Crisis Services (CONNSACS)
763 Burnside Avenue
East Hartford, CT 06108
(203) 282-9881

Established in 1978, the Connecticut Sexual Assault Crisis Services (CONNSACS) was incorporated in 1982. Comprised of 12 centers throughout Connecticut, its stated purpose is to end sexual violence through victim assistance, community education, and legislative action. Between 1992 and 1993, in conjuction with other women's organizations, CONNSACS initiated and worked to pass five important legislative bills addressing violence toward women. It obtained more than $1 million in state and federal funding to support rape crisis programs in Connecticut, and it conducted 910 community education and professional in-services to more than 28,700 individuals, including law enforcement personnel.

CONTACT Delaware
In New Castle County:
P.O. Box 9525
Wilmington, DE 19809
(302) 761-9800 administrative
(302) 761-9100 crisis line
(302) 761-9700 TDD

In Kent and Sussex Counties:
P.O. Box 61
Milford, DE 19963
(302) 422-2078
(800) 262-9800
FAX (302) 422-2078

CONTACT Delaware is a volunteer agency that provides three essential 24-hour services to the Delaware community: the CONTACT Crisis Helpline, the Deaf CONTACT Helpline, and the Rape Crisis CONTACT Helpline. The services use volunteers who have undergone an intensive 50-hour training program. It also employs apprentices who take shifts on the helpline. Deaf CONTACT offers a 24-hour telephone counseling/crisis helpline and link-up service for the deaf and hearing impaired. CONTACT Crisis Helpline is a 24-hour telephone counseling/crisis helpline. Rape Crisis CONTACT services include 24-hour telephone counseling; accompaniment to the hospital, police station, and court; follow-up support; support groups for survivors; and information on and referral to other sources of help. All services are free, confidential, and available to anyone.

Illinois Coalition Against Sexual Assault (ICASA)
123 South 7th Street, Suite 500
Springfield, IL 62701-1302
(217) 753-4117
FAX (217) 753-8229

The Illinois Coalition Against Sexual Assault (ICASA) is a nonprofit corporation of 28 organizations that provide comprehensive, community-based services to victims of sexual assault. It began in 1977 through the efforts of 30 women who wanted to create a network of local rape crisis services. It was incorporated in 1979. Since its beginning with 12 member programs, ICASA has grown to become one of the most respected coalitions in the country, boasting a staff that includes two lawyers and a paralegal. The legal staff is currently working on research with law enforcement authorities to develop a book of recommended protocol for police procedure in sexual assault investigations. The staff conducts training sessions with law enforcement and healthcare personnel on pertinent legal issues and serves as a legal resource for member crisis centers. The coalition has been active in developing and securing more effective laws for the prosecution of sexual offenders. Because of the efforts of ICASA and other interested organizations, the Illinois Criminal Sexual Assault Act was passed in 1984.

Publications: ICASA publishes a number of educational brochures, an extensive manual for rape crisis workers, a compilation of sexual violence facts and statistics (*Sexual Violence Facts and Statistics*), and an excellent bibliography of materials on sexual violence (*Sexual Violence: A Bibliography*) (the latter two are reviewed in chapter 7).

Indiana Coalition Against Sexual Assault (INCASA)
c/o the Julian Center
2511 East 46th Street, Suite I
Indianapolis, IN 46205
(317) 568-4001
FAX (317) 545-1974

In April 1986 Sex Offense Services of South Bend brought together 30 individuals to address the needs of rape victims in Indiana. The networking created by that meeting led to the formation and incorporation in 1987 of the Indiana Coalition Against Sexual Assault (INCASA). INCASA currently has approximately 50 member centers and organizations, 30 of which provide services to victims of sexual assault. While INCASA offers support and technical assistance to sexual assault programs throughout the state and actively promotes the expansion of those services in Indiana, its primary activities are serving as an advocate for public and private sector policies affecting victims of sexual assault and striving to increase public and professional awareness of sexual assault through workshops, conferences, and training. INCASA is currently involved in the development of a statewide protocol for treatment of sexual assault victims in the emergency room. Members receive reduced conference rates, legislative updates, a newsletter, and access to regional resource centers.

Publication: INCASA publishes a quarterly newsletter entitled *IN-CASA News.*

Iowa Coalition Against Sexual Assault (IowaCASA)
Lucas State Office Building, 1st Floor
Des Moines, Iowa 50319
(515) 242-5096
FAX (515) 242-6119

The Iowa Coalition Against Sexual Assault (IowaCASA) has sought to be a collective voice for the needs and concerns of sexual assault survivors since its founding in November 1981. Currently, IowaCASA's two primary functions are the promotion of public and professional education about sexual assault and advocacy for sexual assault survivors with both the legislature and other state organizations. Additionally, it provides support and services to 28 anti–sexual assault centers throughout the state, facilitates sexual assault intervention and prevention training for various groups and agencies, and maintains a resource library of films, videos, books, brochures, and articles that are accessible to both professionals and the public.

Publication: IowaCASA publishes a one-page brochure (available free of charge to members), which provides a wealth of information, including IowaCASA's vision, goals, and services, a comprehensive definition of sexual assault and relevant statistics, a summary of Iowa's sexual abuse laws, an abbreviated listing of "survivor's rights," a summary of crime victims' legal rights under Iowa law, and a listing by city of the anti–sexual assault centers in Iowa (of the listed centers, 93 percent accept collect calls and/or have "800" numbers, and all are accessible 24 hours a day).

Kentucky Coalition Against Rape and Sexual Assault
231 South 5th Street, Suite 300
Louisville, KY 40202
(502) 625-5088
FAX (502) 625-5299

The Kentucky Coalition Against Rape and Sexual Assault was organized in the late 1970s. It represents a broad-based group of individuals and organizations who are interested in legislative efforts addressing the issue of rape and sexual assault. In each session of the Kentucky General Assembly, beginning with the

1984 session, the coalition has been successful in the passage of legislation to benefit rape victims. It has a mailing list of over 400 individuals and organizations statewide and has established a powerful network promoting information sharing and legislative advocacy.

**Louisiana Foundation Against
Sexual Assault, Inc. (LaFASA)**
P.O. Box 1450
Independence, LA 70443
(504) 878-3849
FAX (504) 878-3808

In Louisiana rape crisis programs began in the early 1970s, and they have continued to develop. There are now ten centers in the state. In 1982 the existing programs united to form the Louisiana Foundation Against Sexual Assault, Inc. (LaFASA). Membership in the organization has continued to expand, and in 1989 LaFASA joined the National Coalition Against Sexual Assault (NCASA). LaFASA was run primarily by a volunteer board of directors until 1 July 1993, when an executive director was appointed. In striving to serve as the voice of sexual assault victims in Louisiana, LaFASA's activities have included providing victim advocacy, making efforts to improve public awareness about sexual violence, supporting legislation related to the protection of sexual assault victims, and providing a forum for networking among professionals whose work brings them in contact with victims of sexual assault.

Publication: LaFASA has published *At Any Moment,* a 20-page booklet providing a directory of statewide sexual assault service programs. It also discusses Louisiana laws on sex offenses.

Maine Coalition Against Rape (MCAR)
P.O. Box 5326
Augusta, ME 04332
(207) 759-9985

The Maine Coalition Against Rape (MCAR) began in October 1982 as a joining of several groups. In early 1982 a group calling itself the Rape Crisis Intervention Coalition gathered to discuss allocation of a Public Health grant of $15,000 for rape crisis services. At that time there were two crisis centers in the state of Maine, both in major cities, along with one hospital-based team in a third city. By the end of 1982 the Rape Crisis Intervention Coalition had been joined by two other groups from two counties that were interested in establishing rape crisis centers, and collectively they became known as the Maine Coalition of Rape. The coalition quickly became politically active; in 1983 it initiated legislation to eliminate spousal exemption in the sexual assaults statute, as well as legislation for funding for rape crisis services in the state. Both bills ultimately passed, and the latter resulted in $100,000 used to create rape crisis services in eight locations in Maine. In 1990 the group changed its name to Maine Coalition Against Rape to more accurately reflect its mission. MCAR currently consists of representatives of the ten rape crisis centers in Maine, other interested individuals, an executive chair, and a legislative chair (both of whom are directors of rape crisis centers). MCAR does not have an office or paid staff, but utilizes the services of volunteers and staff of rape crisis centers. MCAR provides educational conferences, promotes legislative change, secures funding for rape crisis centers, and provides technical assistance and support to rape crisis centers.

Massachusetts Coalition of Rape Crisis Services
100 Grove Street
Worcester, MA 01605
(508) 791-9546

The Massachusetts Coalition of Rape Crisis Services, incorporated in 1981, has in its membership the 20 rape crisis centers in Massachusetts. The coalition coordinates statewide education efforts to increase public awareness of sexual violence, advocates politically for the rights and needs of sexual assault survivors and service centers, and seeks to empower member groups through technical assistance and resource sharing. Currently operating with a volunteer staff and no central office, the coalition's primary activities are focused on building the capacity of the coalition by hiring staff and acquiring an office, increasing state support of rape crisis centers, and supporting member centers.

Sexual Assault Information Network
of Michigan (SAIN)
P.O. Box 1011
Midland, MI 48641-1011
(517) 832-0662
FAX (517) 835-3681

The Sexual Assault Information Network of Michigan (SAIN) is composed of 54 centers and programs, of which 21 groups were charter members. SAIN was founded in 1986 as a nonprofit corporation to provide assistance to sexual assault victims and rape crisis centers through referrals and information services, educational publications, and training. SAIN distributes sexual assault evidence collection kits to hospitals and serves as an advocate for programs and survivors in Michigan. SAIN provides a statewide clearinghouse for sharing and accessing information resources and expertise.

Publications: In addition to its quarterly newsletter, *The SAIN Voice*, SAIN offers a number of books (including *Resource Directory of Sexual Assault Services in Michigan* and *Challenging Professional Sexual Exploitation: A Handbook for Survivors*), pamphlets, buttons, and stickers for sale, as well as an audiotape of public service announcements on date rape, two separate posters, and a 1994 chart summarizing Michigan's sexual assault laws.

Minnesota Coalition Against Sexual Assault (MCASA)
2344 Nicollet Avenue, South, #170A
Minneapolis, MN 55404
(612) 872-7734
(800) 964-8847

The rape crisis movement in Minnesota began in 1971, when a small group of women began a program in a storefront in Minneapolis. Three years later, in 1974, the commissioner of corrections received a mandate from the state legislature to develop a community-based program to assist victims of sexual assault. The program was established in 1975 and was shortly followed by the establishment of additional community-based programs throughout the state. Approximately three years later, the Minnesota Coalition of Sexual Assault Services (MCSAS) was created primarily to provide networking of information and resources among the different groups. This purpose later expanded to include education of both the public and the legislature, and the all-volunteer MCSAS was incorporated as a nonprofit corporation in 1982. Until it received funding from the state in 1989, MCSAS was unable to hire staff and open an office. The following year, its name was changed to the Minnesota Coalition Against Sexual Assault (MCASA). Serving as an umbrella organization, it currently provides information and support services to approximately 40 rape crisis programs in Minnesota. Its mission statement includes a pledge to "confront those systems, issues, and laws that perpetuate the crime of sexual assault" and to "work to eliminate sexism, racism, homophobia, classism, the oppression of persons with handicaps, religious oppression, and ageism—the roots of sexual violence." Such efforts have included press conferences protesting a university's handling of a sexual assault case involving its basketball team and a professional football team's hiring of a convicted rapist, testimony to the Minnesota Supreme Court on the examination requirements for and the treatment of sexual assault victims, and participation on numerous government task forces. MCASA has several active committees, including Legislative, Women of Color, and Building Alliances committees, and it maintains a resource library.

Publication: MCASA publishes *The MCASA Quarterly Newsletter.*

Mississippi Coalition Against Sexual Assault (MCASA)
c/o Anne R. Sims
Mississippi State Department of Health
P.O. Box 1700
Jackson, MS 39215-1700
(601) 960-7470

The Mississippi Coalition Against Sexual Assault (MCASA) was incorporated in mid-1988. Its membership consists of the seven rape crisis centers currently serving the 84 counties of Mississippi. MCASA includes representatives of sexual assault victims and/or rape crisis projects, volunteers trained to work with sexual assault victims, healthcare, social service and public safety professionals, and concerned citizens. MCASA's primary mission is one of education—fostering a greater public awareness of the nature and trauma of rape and sexual assault, distributing information on rape prevention to the public, and training victim advocates. MCASA also assists in the formation of local support groups and victim service centers. Membership is open to anyone for a low yearly fee. MCASA has monthly membership meetings, produces a monthly information packet and pertinent mailings for members, and maintains a statewide library of resource materials.

Publication: MCASA publishes a 16-page booklet entitled *At Any Moment.* The booklet lists rape crisis programs and discusses Mississippi laws on sexual offenses.

Nebraska Domestic Violence Sexual Assault Coalition
315 South 9th Street, Suite 18
Lincoln, NE 68508-2253
(402) 476-6256

Founded in 1978 by the only five domestic violence/sexual assault programs in Nebraska at that time, the Nebraska Domestic
Violence Sexual Assault Coalition was able to nearly triple the
number of Nebraska programs in existence over the following
three years. It now is made up of 24 centers, 88 percent of which
work with sexual assault survivors and whose programs are
funded through a combination of state, federal, and local funds.
There are currently no state appropriations for sexual assault services; all funding for such services comes out of appropriations
for domestic violence. The coalition is actively involved in efforts
to change this situation and has hopes of effecting such change
by 1996. In keeping with its mission to work for social change by
challenging personal, cultural, and institutional systems that op-
press women and perpetuate violence toward women, the coalition recently provided training on domestic violence to district
court judges, court personnel, county and trial attorneys, and law
enforcement personnel. Representatives also participated in a
series of seminars for K–12 teachers on racial and gender bias
and its connection to violence against women and children. The
coalition provides technical assistance to its centers, acts as a referral and information agency, and maintains a resource library
of films, videos, and written materials.

Publication: The coalition publishes a topical newsletter, *Nebraska
Domestic Violence Sexual Assault Coalition,* quarterly.

New Mexico Coalition of Sexual Assault Programs, Inc.
4004 Carlisle, NE, Suite P
Albuquerque, NM 87107
(505) 883-8020
FAX (505) 883-7530

In 1978 New Mexico's legislature created the Sexual Crimes
Prosecution and Treatment Act, which mandated that the state
provide services to professionals in the medical, mental health,
law enforcement, and social services fields to assist them in serving victims of sexual abuse. The act outlined the necessity of ongoing training for those professionals and provided for a
payment of up to $150 per client, per year, for partial payment of

all victims' medical examinations following an assault or the discovery of abuse. (This dollar amount was in effect until 1 July 1994, at which time it was increased to $300.) As a result of this act, the Division of Mental Health created the Sex Crimes Prosecution and Treatment Program to provide training and to coordinate sexual assault services throughout the state. This coordination was accomplished by designating and training a sexual abuse program coordinator at all Division of Mental Health–funded community health centers. In 1984 the Division of Mental Health decided to contract out the services, and the New Mexico Coaliton of Sexual Assault Programs, Inc., was created as a private nonprofit organization to assume the responsibilities of the Sex Crimes Prosecution and Treatment Program. The coalition provides statewide training on a variety of sexual abuse topics to any group of 15 or more, provides sexual assault billing verification, gathers statistical data on sexual assault in New Mexico, maintains a resource library, and produces and distributes rape evidence kits. The child sexual abuse examination protocol packet distributed by the coalition contains a coloring book (*When Kids Need Help*, by E. L. Wedeen) for the child to read (or have read to her or him) prior to the examination. (The coloring book is reviewed in chapter 7.) As a project of the Children's Trust Fund, the coalition developed and implemented a child abuse prevention project utilizing traditional storytelling performances, specific to the Navajo Nation, in reservation schools. In July 1993 the coalition received another grant through the Children's Trust Fund to create and implement a high school sexual abuse prevention program in schools throughout rural New Mexico. The coalition's total annual budget in 1991 was $135,000.

Publications: In addition to *When Kids Need Help,* the coalition publishes sexual abuse information brochures.

New York State Coalition Against Sexual Assault
The Women's Building
79 Central Avenue
Albany, NY 12206
(518) 434-1580
FAX (518) 432-4864

The New York State Coalition Against Sexual Assault was founded in 1988. One of the largest coalitions in the country, it is made up of 72 crisis and service centers and is divided into three regions. While the coalition does not render direct services to victims, it does serve as the linking organization, providing coordination between centers and individuals statewide in a movement to end sexual assault. The coalition's work includes public policy advocacy, networking, coordination and technical assistance for rape crisis centers, public education, general information services, and referrals.

North Dakota Council on Abused Women's Services (NDCAWS)
418 East Rosser, #320
Bismarck, ND 58501
(701) 255-6240
(800) 474-2911 (statewide hotline)

Services for victims of sexual assault and services for victims of domestic violence are gradually being merged organizationally in North Dakota. The North Dakota Council on Abused Women's Services (NDCAWS) is a manifestation of such a merger. NDCAWS was formed in 1975 as an informal group of five programs that had organized to provide shelter and services to battered women. The group was incorporated as a nonprofit organization in 1980, and it hired a director with federal funds in 1981. Six years later, the North Dakota Coalition Against Sexual Assault (NDCASA) was incorporated as a nonprofit organization. In July of 1991 NDCAWS and NDCASA merged, retaining the name of the North Dakota Council on Abused Women's Services. NDCAWS currently has in its membership 19 different programs, most of which provide services to victims of sexual assault. It also houses Nurturing Network (a network for parenting education), the Campus Violence Project, and the Criminal Justice Monitoring Project.

NDCAWS has been active in every state legislative session since 1979 and has played a significant role in the passage of key pieces of legislation relating to domestic violence and sexual assault. Because much of the population of North Dakota is widely dispersed geographically, networking opportunities for support programs are vital. Thus, NDCAWS and program representatives meet for approximately two days every other month to review legislative developments and information on grants, as well as for a general exchange of ideas and information. NDCAWS maintains a 24-hour, statewide, toll-free hotline.

Publications: NDCAWS publications include *Cassandra*, a quarterly newsletter; *Dr., Can You Help Me?*, a pamphlet on sexual assault; and *Everybody Gets Mad Sometimes*, a pamphlet on domestic violence for children.

Ohio Coalition on Sexual Assault (OCOSA)
4041 North High Street, Suite 408
Columbus, OH 43214
(614) 268-3322
FAX (614) 268-0881

The Ohio Coalition on Sexual Assault (OCOSA) provides statewide education, support, and advocacy on issues of sexual assault to service providers, survivors of sexual assault, and members of the general community. There are currently 39 rape crisis and service centers in OCOSA, which maintains an extensive resource list of books, videos, and related materials, and provides a call-in service for legal updates on legislation as well as specifics of laws regarding sexual assault. OCOSA also functions as a speakers bureau in the areas of sexual assault and related topics. OCOSA assists in the development of crisis centers in Ohio (providing training manuals for such development), and it assists centers in networking with other professionals who can provide assistance and advice.

Publications: OCOSA publishes two major publications— *Guidelines for Providing Culturally Diverse Services* and *A Directory of Services in Ohio*—as well as numerous flyers on sexual assault.

Oklahoma Coalition Against Domestic Violence and Sexual Assault (OCDVSA)
2200 Classen Boulevard, Suite 1300
Oklahoma City, OK 73106
(405) 557-1210
FAX (405) 557-1296

The Oklahoma Coalition Against Domestic Violence and Sexual Assault (OCDVSA), established in 1981, is funded by state and federal funds, membership dues, and private foundation contributions. There are 24 centers throughout Oklahoma that offer services to sexual assault victims and their families and friends. OCDVSA provides statewide awareness and educational campaigns to end violence against women, children, and men. It also maintains a resource library of videos, books, periodicals, and law reviews, provides speakers on violence against women and children's issues, and provides technical assistance for member programs, professionals, and individuals. OCDVSA developed a funding formula for state and federal funding distribution among the various centers. This formula provides for an equitable distribution of money and removes any need for competition among the centers for governmental funds. OCDVSA also developed, along with staff of the State Department of Mental Health, the standards for certification of domestic and sexual violence centers in Oklahoma. These standards for certification frequently are used as models for other states, since less than 50 percent of the states have such requirements.

Publication: OCDVSA publishes a bimonthly periodical entitled *Free To Be Safe.*

**Oregon Coalition Against Domestic
and Sexual Violence (OCADSV)**
2336 Southeast Belmont Street
Portland, OR 97214
(503) 239-4486
FAX (503) 233-9373

The Oregon Coalition Against Domestic and Sexual Violence (OCADSV) was organized in 1976 to provide assistance to domestic violence and sexual assault victim programs and to combat violence by addressing the social conditions and attitudes that cause it. In addition to networking with and providing training for member programs, OCADSV is actively involved in a number of innovative educational, community, and political projects. Its Legal Access Project, supervised by a project coordinator on staff, utilizes law students to provide assistance to domestic violence victims. The ongoing Legal Project, supervised by OCADSV's staff attorney, analyzes current legal issues and problems and pursues appropriate solutions. A recent issue raised was the implementation of Caller ID in parts of Oregon—a service OCADSV vehemently opposed because of the inherent dangers the service poses to battered women and their advocates. While OCADSV was not successful in preventing the implementation of Caller ID, their efforts did result in the phone company agreeing to create several protective measures for victims of violence, crisis agencies, and advocates. The three-year Resource Development Project created a 60-member council to explore all possible sources of stable funding for domestic and sexual violence programs, to create statewide development strategies, and to work with selected programs to increase their fund-raising ability in their communities. The Oregon Democracy Project aligned the OCADSV with the Lesbian Community Project, the Oregon Alliance for Progressive Policy, and the Coalition for Human Dignity to address the rise of organized bigotry in the state. OCADSV currently has over 30 member programs and has seen rapid growth in the last decade; approximately one-third of the programs are less than eight years old. OCADSV anticipates increasing its paid staff from seven to eleven by the end of 1995.

Publication: OCADSV publishes *Network News,* a quarterly newsletter.

Pennsylvania Coalition Against Rape (PCAR)
910 North 2nd Street
Harrisburg, PA 17102-3119
(717) 232-6745
(800) 692-7445 (in PA)
FAX (717) 232-6771

Rape crisis centers began to be created in a few counties in Pennsylvania in the early 1970s as independently operating and locally funded entities. It quickly became apparent that a broader and more unified effort was needed in order to effectively advocate for victims of sexual assault with legal and social service agencies, as well as to acquire needed state funding. In response to this need, the Pennsylvania Coalition Against Rape (PCAR) was created in 1976. Since its inception, PCAR has been extremely active and effective in the political arena in Pennsylvania. It was instrumental in the passage of a rape shield law as well as a spousal sexual assault law. PCAR worked to pass the first absolute confidential communication privilege in the nation. This privilege guarantees that information shared with a trained sexual assault counselor at a rape crisis center will remain private. PCAR continues to serve as a legislative watchdog and to advocate for sexual assault services and victims, while offering numerous training and educational programs to professionals and the public throughout the state. PCAR maintains a clearinghouse of educational materials including videos, books, and articles, and offers technical assistance to rape crisis programs in and out of the state as well as to other coalitions. Approximately 45 rape crisis centers belong to PCAR, representing about two-thirds of the centers in Pennsylvania.

**South Dakota Coalition Against Domestic Violence
and Sexual Assault (SDCADVSA)**
3221 Highway 281 South
Aberdeen, SD 57401
(605) 225-5122

The South Dakota Coalition Against Domestic Violence and
Sexual Assault (SDCADVSA) began with a meeting of five people in 1975 and has since grown to include 21 centers in the state,
representing both rural and urban areas, that offer domestic
abuse and sexual assault services. Its stated goal is the elimination of physical and sexual abuse of women and children. As a result of its belief that hierarchy is the root of violence against
women, SDCADVSA is committed to maintaining and nurturing
grass-roots programs, organizations, and communities. It strives
to ensure grass-roots leadership and involvement in all matters,
particularly policy making and governance. Its programs support and involve battered women of all racial, ethnic, religious,
and economic groups, ages, and life-styles.

Publications: SDCADVSA publishes a membership brochure,
which includes the "Bill of Rights for Women Who Have Been
Battered or Raped." This comprehensive and sensitive document
offers an excellent archetype for other coalitions' and shelters'
use in developing similar documents. SDCADVSA also publishes *Coalesce,* a quarterly newsletter.

Tennessee Coalition Against Sexual Assault (TCASA)
c/o Rape and Sexual Abuse Center
56 Lindsley Avenue
Nashville, TN 37210
(615) 259-9055

The early records of the Tennessee Coalition Against Sexual
Assault (TCASA) were destroyed in a fire in 1988, but oral history indicates that it was begun sometime in the early to middle
1980s. Current membership consists of the five rape crisis centers
in Tennessee, one rape crisis center in Virginia on the Tennessee
border, and numerous individuals. TCASA is operated by means
of staff time provided by different rape crisis centers for TCASA
work, and it is headquartered at the rape crisis center of its current chair. Nonetheless, TCASA has been active on the political
front, striving to educate legislators and the public regarding the
issues of sexual violence, monitoring legislation on a state and

national level, and supporting legislation that has a positive effect in the area of sexual assault. It seeks to assist in the development of new rape crisis centers and offers support to those already in existence.

Publication: TCASA publishes *TCASA News,* a quarterly newsletter.

Texas Association Against Sexual Assault (TAASA)
P.O. Box 684813
Austin, TX 78768
(512) 445-1049

In April 1982 approximately 40 sexual assault activists gathered together in Galveston to form an organization to lessen the isolation of, and facilitate communication between, the rape crisis centers scattered throughout the state. Another articulated purpose of the organization was to facilitate the formation of a society free from sexual violence through education and legislative reform. A president was elected, and the Texas Association Against Sexual Assault (TAASA) was under way. The following year was extremely productive for TAASA; it was incorporated, a board of directors was established, and a code of ethics for members was written. The first political success of the new organization also occurred that year, when TAASA's lobbyist and legislative task force was able to get state funding for rape crisis centers appropriated by the state legislature. Other political victories in the same year involved changing the content and vocabulary of laws pertaining to rape, among which was a lengthening of the statute of limitations, and changing the term *rape* to *sexual assault.* The first Sexual Assault Awareness Week was created in 1984 and was expanded to a month in 1991. Since 1982 TAASA has sponsored a statewide conference each year, featuring nationally known experts as keynote speakers. It obtained 501(c)3 (tax-exempt) status in 1993. While it is currently operating on a volunteer basis and has no permanent office, TAASA hopes to rectify both by mid-1995.

Publication: TAASA publishes *TAASA Connections,* a quarterly newsletter.

Virginians Aligned Against Sexual Assault (VAASA)
P.O. Box 409
Ivy, VA 22945
(804) 979-9002

In 1980 Virginians Aligned Against Sexual Assault (VAASA) was created by the existing rape crisis centers in an attempt to increase their individual efforts and to act as their collective voice. In the years that have followed, the nonprofit VAASA has significantly expanded its membership and staffing: In 1980 VAASA was staffed solely by volunteers; in 1984 it had a part-time paid staff and 11 member programs; by 1994 VAASA had four full-time positions plus an attorney on staff and had 22 centers and 1 satellite center in its membership. It is currently trying to acquire funding for 12 proposed new centers to cover the 22 percent of the counties in the state that do not have sexual assault centers. VAASA is actively involved in monitoring public policy on a state and national level in the areas of sexual assault and child sexual abuse. It seeks to further the public's awareness and understanding of sexual assault; to serve as a resource for the concerns, needs, and rights of sexual assault victims and their families; to provide technical assistance and training to the sexual assault crisis centers in the state; and to provide standards of certification for those centers in order to ensure quality services are provided to communities. VAASA compiles statewide statistics on sexual assault and maintains a resource library containing over 550 films, videos, books, cassettes, reports, and over 1,100 articles on sexual assault issues.

Publications: VAASA publishes a quarterly newsletter as well as volunteer manuals and volunteer trainers' manuals.

Washington Coalition of Sexual Assault Programs (WCSAP)
110 East 5th Avenue, #214
Olympia, WA 98501
(206) 754-7583

The nonprofit Washington Coalition of Sexual Assault Programs (WCSAP) was created in 1979 by representatives of 10 sexual assault crisis centers. In the ensuing years the membership has grown to include over 40 sexual assault crisis programs and approximately 100 supporting members. WCSAP serves as an active legislative watchdog and lobbyist and functions as a clearinghouse for information on current legislation. It sponsors numerous workshops, training sessions, and conferences for its members and professionals in related fields, and it organizes on a yearly basis Sexual Assault Awareness Week, a statewide public education campaign. WCSAP maintains a resource library of videos, audiocassettes, books, and articles for its members' usage and maintains a referral list of state and national resources.

Publications: WCSAP publishes the *Quarterly Connection* and the *Library Lowdown* (quarterly newsletters), an assortment of books and training curricula, and a legislative update.

Wisconsin Coalition Against Sexual Assault (WCASA)
1400 East Washington Avenue, Suite 148
Madison, WI 53703
(608) 257-1516

The Wisconsin Coalition Against Sexual Assault (WCASA) was created as a nonprofit organization in 1985 by the Dane County Rape Crisis Center, with the help of a federal block grant. In the decade that followed, it grew to include over 180 members. There are currently 24 comprehensive sexual assault programs attempting to serve 71 counties in Wisconsin; all are members of WCASA, which continues to be funded in part by a federal rape-prevention block grant, membership dues, and contributions. It is governed by a volunteer board of directors (comprised primarily of sexual assault centers from around the state) and maintains a paid staff of four: a director, a policy development specialist, an education and training specialist, and a membership coordinator. Much of WCASA's activities at this time focus on politics and education. The policy development specialist both monitors and seeks to initiate relevant legislation, is currently developing a legal manual for sexual assault advocates, and is working with the Department of Justice and State Funding Task Force to develop funding for anti–sexual assault programs. The education and training specialist maintains WCASA's Resource Center, prepares educational materials for both public education and professional trainings, and edits the WCASA journal. The membership coordinator seeks to facilitate membership networking within WCASA, maintains membership records, and edits the newsletter.

Publications: WCASA publishes *Connections*, a topic-oriented quarterly journal that brings together writings of various experts around the country, and *WCASA News*, a quarterly newsletter that focuses on the activities and concerns of sexual assault programs in Wisconsin.

Reference Materials 7

The following is a list of print and nonprint resources compiled with the intention of providing the reader with additional sources for researching the topic of rape and related issues. It should be noted that the material available to the public is more than abundant and that this list highlights only some of the most informative and useful works.

Print Resources

Benedict, Helen. *Recovery: How To Survive Sexual Assault for Women, Men, Teenagers, and Their Friends and Families.* New York: Doubleday, 1985. 293 pp. Index. ISBN 0-385-19206-1.

Helen Benedict has created an extensively researched work, designed to assist in the recovery of practically anyone affected by a sexual assault. Starting with a broad definition of rape as "any sexual act that is forced upon you," she addresses the immediate, short- and long-term reactions to an assault likely to be experienced by female and male teenager, adult, and elderly victims, including homosexuals of both sexes. With each victim section Benedict includes two detailed subsections: How To Help Yourself and How Others Can Help. In addition to its self-help function, the book provides a listing of rape crisis programs in the United States and Canada, as well as information on victims' assistance programs, shelters for battered women, counseling for violent men, and gay and lesbian services. Although the book is dated in terms of its resource information and its presentation of stereotypes with regard to the medical field and legal system (Benedict embraces stereotypes of mistreatment despite the extensive training and specialization of present-day professionals in the field), it is an excellent source of practical information for anyone victimized by a sexual assault.

Bohmer, Carol, and Andrea Parrot. *Sexual Assault on Campus: The Problem and the Solution.* New York: Lexington Books, 1993. 280 pp. Index and appendixes. ISBN 0-02-903715-8.

A recent and timely handbook for understanding and reducing sexual assault in the college environment, *Sexual Assault on Campus* is geared toward everyone concerned with rape on campus—administrators, students, campus security police, residence hall directors, rape crisis counselors, lawyers, rape victims, and victims' families and friends. While collecting evidence of the fact that sexual assault is a problem on college campuses, the authors examined the written campus codes of approximately 50 colleges throughout the United States. They interviewed college administrators, victims who did or did not report the assault, and parents and lawyers of victims who considered filing or did file a lawsuit. By doing so, Carol Bohmer and Andrea Parrot were able to trace the ramifications of sexual assault for both the victim and the assailant. The authors paid particular attention to cases that had gone to court and what those cases revealed about the handling of campus rape cases by college administrations. The authors identify mishandling and proper handling of campus rape cases, and they demonstrate that the way in which sexual assault is dealt with by college officials often varies greatly from the manner and standards utilized by the criminal justice system. Bohmer and Parrot illustrate that the manner in which college administrators handle rape complaints is likely to have a significant effect on the future reporting of rape cases by students and offer specific steps administrations can take to help prevent sexual assault or to handle cases that do occur. These steps mandate education and training of administrators, faculty, staff, and students and the establishment of written policies and protocol.

Following extensive discussion of the above, the book provides a "summary of recommendations to create a campus free of acquaintance rape" in clear, outline format. The book concludes with seven appendixes containing information regarding specific legislation, grant guidelines from the Secretary of Education for campus sexual offense education, a checklist guide for administrators regarding sexual assault, and copies of brochures regarding legal options and procedures for assisting a friend who has been sexually assaulted; an extensive list of references; and an index.

Bradway, Becky. *Sexual Violence: A Bibliography*. Springfield, IL: Illinois Coalition Against Sexual Assault, 1993. 250 pp.

This excellent bibliography is published by and available from the Illinois Coalition Against Sexual Assault (ICASA), one of the premier coalitions in the country. Becky Bradway, the communications coordinator of ICASA, organized and catalogued the extensive work. Divided into 17 subject areas with a total of 3,000 citations, the bibliography lists book, article, booklet, film, and video resources as recent as 1993. Sections include Acquaintance Rape, Adult Survivors of Child Sexual Abuse, Legal Aspects of Sexual Violence, Medical Aspects of Sexual Violence, Political and Social Issues pertaining to Sexual Violence, Prevention of Sexual Violence, Special Populations and Sexual Violence, Sex Offenders, Sexual Harassment, and Treatment Methods for Victims of Sexual Violence. Each category is divided further into clear subcategories. For example, the section on Acquaintance Rape is divided into 13 headings, ranging from "Adolescents" to "Criminal Justice System" to "Public Perceptions." An invaluable tool for researchers and professionals in the field, the book is available directly from ICASA, as are copies of the bibliography of separate topics. ICASA also publishes *Sexual Violence Facts and Statistics* (reviewed below), and the brochure *Acquaintance Rape: When the Rapist Is Someone You Know*.

————. *Sexual Violence Facts and Statistics*. Springfield, IL: Illinois Coalition Against Sexual Assault, 1993. 80 pp.

Like its sister volume, *Sexual Violence: A Bibliography* (reviewed above), *Sexual Violence Facts and Statistics* provides a wealth of information in a concise format. Divided into 12 chapters of fact sheets, the book covers such topics as acquaintance rape, AIDS and sexual assault, child sexual abuse, self-defense, sex offenders, and sexual harassment. Each chapter is clearly divided into major subtopics such as Introduction, Statistics, Impact on the Victim, and Special Issues, which are in turn divided into appropriate sections. In the chapter on child sexual abuse, for example, the Introduction is further divided into "Definition," "Incest," "Adult Survivors," and "How Statistics Are Collected," which is further divided into "Governmental Statistics" and "Studies and Surveys." In each division facts are clearly presented in paragraph format; almost all of the information presented is footnoted to specific references. Unlike other publications that present "facts" with little or no supporting citation, each chapter of *Sexual Violence Facts and Statistics* concludes with a complete listing of the cited references. An invaluable tool for researchers and professionals in the field, the book is available directly from ICASA, as are copies of the fact sheets of seperate topics. ICASA also publishes *Sexual Violence: A Bibliography*, and the brochure *Acquaintance Rape: When the Rapist Is Someone You Know.*

Brownmiller, Susan. *Against Our Will: Men, Women, and Rape.* New York: Simon & Schuster, 1975. 472 pp. Index. ISBN 0-553-34516-8.

Four years in the making, this book is a classic in the field of feminist literature; a tour de force considered by many to be the landmark feminist statement that focused the public's attention on rape. While some readers may be offset by Susan Brownmiller's controversial statements and thesis (". . . rape is the quintessential act by which a male demonstrates to a female that she is conquered—vanquished—by his superior power and strength. . ."; ". . . [rape] is nothing more or less than a conscious process of intimidation by which *all men* keep *all women* in a state of fear") (italics in original), the book provides an extensive review of the act and societal view of rape through history. Brownmiller's discussion of rape in World War I, World War II, Bangladesh, and Vietnam, as well as her analysis of slavery in the antebellum South, are particularly thorough.

Chappell, Duncan, Robley Geis, and Gilbert Geis, eds. *Forcible Rape: The Crime, the Victim, and the Offender.* New York: Columbia University Press, 1977. 393 pp. Bibliography and index.

The editors have brought together 16 different treatises, plus a comprehensive introduction and bibliography, that cover a broad spectrum of concerns regarding forcible rape—social issues and philosophy, behavioral science studies, and legal trends. Much of the information is extremely dated, in some cases in excess of 20 years. Many of the social problems that are presented in the essays (ignorant/untrained/biased police, a dearth of trained counselors, hospitals being unwilling/unable to handle rape victims, rape victims being savaged on the witness stand, etc.) as being the rule, rather than the exception, are no longer of such epidemic proportions in contemporary society. The majority of statistics presented have been supplanted in recent years by far more accurate and current ones. There is, however, material of historical value contained in the book that may not be found in later works. The introduction contains an excellent summary and critique of early feminist works, while the chapter entitled "Race, Rape, and the Death Penalty" provides important historical data extending from 1909 to 1969.

Educational Series for Teens. Alexandria, VA: Office on Women, 1989. 24–48 pp. (varies by booklet).

The *Educational Series for Teens* is a series of six booklets covering a variety of areas of sexual assualt: stranger rape, incest, acquaintance rape, gang rape, rape of males, and post-rape reactions and procedures. The first five booklets follow the same format, varying the initial story as appropriate to the topic. Each booklet covers basic information regarding the nature and prevalence of sexual assault, common post-rape reactions of victims, friends, and family, and a listing of sexual assault crisis centers in Virginia. Each booklet is illustrated with unobtrusive ink drawings. The most extensive of the booklets is *Tonya's Story: After a Sexual Assault.* This booklet adds to the standard format and utilizes with great effect a fictional diary account of post-rape events as seen and experienced by the victim. In addition to the diary account, the booklet details the medical and legal procedures a sexual assault victim may experience, from the initial report through a trial. The booklets are sold by the set for $6, and are available from the Office on Women (Office on Women, 110 North Royal Street, #201, Alexandria, VA 22314).

Estrich, Susan. ***Real Rape: How the Legal System Victimizes Women Who Say No.*** Cambridge, MA: Harvard University Press, 1987. 160 pp. Indexes. ISBN 0-674-74943-X.

Susan Estrich, a professor of criminal law at Harvard University Law School and herself a rape victim, contends that the legal system has not considered or dealt with "simple" rape as real rape. She defines "simple" rape as being rape committed by a known assailant, in which there is no use of a weapon or obvious effort of physical force, as opposed to aggravated assault. (Estrich acknowledges that the victim, while realizing that she had intercourse as a result of physical force, may not recognize the forced sex as rape.) Estrich asserts that there has been extreme reluctance on the part of district attorneys to prosecute—and juries to convict—a man who commits "simple" rape. She maintains that the trend in the judicial system has been to shift responsibility from the accused to the victim, thereby victimizing the victim a second time in cases of "simple" rape. Estrich builds her case by presenting studies conducted during the 1970s and 1980s and law cases and commentaries from the nineteenth century to 1985. She effectively demonstrates that historically judges and juries have held it to be the victim's responsibility to physically resist to her utmost ability, and that any response short of that nullified the act as "rape." While the laws requiring physical resistance are no longer in force, there is no doubt that the mentality that gave rise to such laws is still very much in effect. *Real Rape* is an eloquent argument and call to change such social bias. The book has excellent commentaries and footnote format, as well as a fine case index and general index.

Fairstein, Linda. *Sexual Violence: Our War against Rape.* New York: William Morrow, 1993. 288 pp. ISBN 0-688-06715-8.

Linda Fairstein has been an assistant district attorney in New York County since 1972 and has served as the director of the Sex Crimes Prosecution Unit for that county since 1976. She has written what is probably the most optimistic view of rape prosecution to date, basing her view on her personal work experience of the past two decades. Fairstein acknowledges that the commonly held beliefs of the horrors of rape prosecution were founded in fact; that the legal system did victimize rape victims a second time, particularly in the areas of corroboration, victim history and interrogation, and evidence of "earnest resistance." She, however, maintains that the legal system has changed as a result of legislative reform and that the needed legal reforms are in place; what is needed now is for peoples' attitudes to change. While it may be argued that her position is far too simplistic, the book will help generate such change. *Sexual Violence* is an articulate call for rape victims to report the crime and continue through the criminal justice system to prosecute the criminal. The book may be overly optimistic; though Fairstein does briefly acknowledge in the introduction that "progress . . . has been uneven across the country," she focuses on the changes that have legally (if not practically) occurred and the implementation of those changes in *her office only*. She also briefly acknowledges the presence of magazine pieces that ". . . still echo the myths about the criminal justice system," but she attributes such stories to well-meaning others who are not "professional investigators or prosecutors." Even if the book does not reflect how things actually are in the majority of jurisdictions, it does model how the legal system can, and should, work.

Fay, Jennifer J., et al. *"He Told Me Not To Tell": A Parent's Guide for Talking to Children about Sexual Assault.* King County, WA: King County Sexual Assault Resource Center, [1979], 1991. 32 pp. ISBN 0-941953-14-9.

Originally published in 1979 and revised in 1991 by staff members at King County Sexual Assault Resource Center (KCSARC), this surprisingly comprehensive booklet has won national acclaim. Through the liberal use of first-person accounts and comments, simple and clear charts, "question-and-answer" sections, and specific subject discussions, the work gently, but directly, guides parents through a myriad of pertinent concerns and subjects. It identifies and debunks common myths and stereotypes of child sexual abuse, addresses the inherent difficulties many parents have of talking with their child about sexual abuse and offers specific suggestions of how to go about doing so, identifies common methods by which children are victimized, and points out the reasons why children are so vulnerable to abuse and means to counter that vulnerability. The booklet concludes with a discussion of indicators of sexual abuse and response suggestions. *"He Told Me Not To Tell"* is an extremely valuable manual for parents and caregivers of young children. KCSARC also publishes *No es un juego* by Jorge Chacon (ISBN 0-941953-12-2), a sexual abuse prevention booklet for parents that adapts some of *"He Told Me Not To Tell"* in Spanish.

Fay, Jennifer J., and Billie Jo Flerchinger. *Top Secret: Sexual Assault Information for Teenagers Only.* King County, WA: King County Sexual Assault Resource Center, 1982. 32 pp. ISBN 0-941953-10-6.

This booklet was written by staff members of the King County Sexual Assault Resource Center (KCSARC), with assistance by other staff, advocates, and area teenagers. It succeeds in conveying a tremendous amount of pertinent information in 32 pages through a colorful and interesting format. While the use of varied type and type size, handwriting, cartoons, poster-style pages, stories, playlets, and advice columns threaten at times to overpower the reader, they do permit instant conveyance of important information at a glance. Topics such as stranger rape, offender profiles and motivations, acquaintance rape, incest, sexual exploitation, and post-assault guidelines and options are covered precisely and accurately in a manner that speaks directly to teenagers with no trace of condescension. *Top Secret* is a unique booklet that meets an important need. KCSARC also publishes *"He Told Me Not To Tell": A Parent's Guide for Talking to Children about Sexual Assault*.

Finkelhor, David, and Kersti Yllo. *License To Rape: Sexual Abuse of Wives*. New York: Holt, Rinehart & Winston, 1985. 258 pp. Index. ISBN 0-03-059474-X.

David Finkelhor and Kersti Yllo wrote this book with the expressed desire of "raising awareness about the seriousness of marital rape, and detailing the ways in which the problem is ignored or minimized." Their work is based primarily on two studies: (1) a child sexual abuse questionnaire (that contained questions about sexual assault in a cohabiting or marriage relationship) administered in the Boston area to 323–326 women who had a child between the ages of 6 and 14 living with them, and (2) interviews with 50 women who were referred by family planning agencies and shelters, who were self-referrals, or who responded to an ad in *Ms.* magazine. The survey revealed significant demographics of the Boston-area victims. Case histories and authors' commentaries drawn from the interviews do much to illustrate the seriousness and social dynamics of marital rape. The primary weakness of the book lies in the authors' zeal to impress the reader with the magnitude and severity of the problem. They were admittedly biased in the interview process on at least three occasions, and on several occasions they do not hesitate to "interpret" the statements of the subjects when those statements appear to be in conflict with their beliefs and research desires. Such apparent research bias may serve to weaken the validity of the studies for some readers.

Funk, Rus Ervin. *Stopping Rape: A Challenge for Men.* Philadelphia: New Society Publishers, 1993. 178 pp. Bibliography. ISBN 0-86571-268-9.

Rus Ervin Funk is one of the first male authors to directly address rape as a male problem and "response-ability." Written in first person and a conversational tone, the book is primarily directed to men who want to work to end men's violence, with a secondary audience of women who want to know what men can do to stop rape and other forms of sexual violence. Funk encourages and seeks to enable men to raise their awareness of and sensitivity around sexual violence, to confront rape behavior and sexism, and to talk with other men about rape, sexual violence, and sexism. Unfortunately, the broad generalizations that Funk readily indulges in ("[rape] says a lot about [men] in terms of 'being a man'..."; "... prison, ... the military, and ... fraternities ... were developed and are maintained to sustain a social structure of male supremacy"; "for most men, violence and sex have become intertwined") may serve to offend and alienate many male readers who do not already share his views, rather than win converts. The book provides many powerful questions for males to use in self-examination, as well as excellent suggestions on such subjects as establishing and maintaining men's groups, responding to sexual assault survivors, designing and making effective presentations, and specific exercises for consciousness- raising workshops.

Groth, A. Nicholas, with Jean Birnbaum. *Men Who Rape: The Psychology of the Offender.* New York: Plenum Publishing, 1979, 1984 (seventh printing). 227 pp. Index. ISBN 0-306-40268-8.

A. Nicholas Groth is currently the executive director of Forensic Mental Health Associates in Orlando, Florida. He is the founder and former director of the Sex Offender Program at the Connecticut Correctional Institute in Somers (1978–1986). Groth is the former chief psychologist at the Massachusetts Center for the Diagnosis and Treatment of Sexually Dangerous Persons in Bridgewater (1966–1976), where Jean Birnbaum worked with him as a member of the psychology staff. Groth is a nationally recognized consultant for numerous state law enforcement agencies and the FBI. This book is based on 15 years of extensive clinical research involving over 500 sexual offenders, and it is considered a classic in its field. It provides a means for understanding the development and motivation of the rapist and further presents clinical guidelines for identifying, assessing, and treating the sexual offender. Addressing the myths, realities, psychodynamics, clinical aspects, and patterns of rape, the book is very readable and extremely informative. Its nontechnical style is supplemented with extensive use of direct quotes from offenders, an inclusion that affords the reader a frightening opportunity to view rape from the perspective of the perpetrator. This is a landmark book of significant value to professionals whose work brings them in contact with offenders and/or victims.

Guernsey, JoAnn Bren. *The Facts about Rape.* New York: Crestwood House, 1990. 47 pp. Glossary and index. Series. ISBN 0-89686-533-9.

This book is part of a Facts About series published by Crestwood House, a subsidiary of Macmillan Publishing Company. It covers a broad spectrum of information in its 47 pages, including discussion of the standard myths, statistics, and emotional effects of rape, as well as advice on preventing, surviving, reporting, prosecuting, and recovering from an attack. JoAnn Bren Guernsey has written a book that is extremely accessible to her target audience (teenage females) in particular, but it is not limited to that audience. The use of effective photographs of young women dealing with the circumstances prior to or following an attack, coupled with descriptions of the experiences of teenage rape victims and a very gentle "author's voice," allow her to address the subject in a manner that is very readable and informative. Particularly effective is her integration of statistical information in a nonempirical format. Ironically, the author's gentle and accessible approach to the subject is the greatest weakness of the book. The recounting of rape victims' experiences is very generalized or implied, thereby losing much of the impact and horror of the event for all but readers who have already experienced rape. Other readers may be put off by Guernsey's (unsubstantiated) blaming the entertainment industry (film, television, video, pornography, and contemporary rock music) for a rise in attacks against women. While citing the lyrics (songs unspecified) of two identified bands, Guernsey surprisingly passes over rap artists whose lyrics are clearly misogynistic and advocate violence against women, saying only that "several rap artists sound very antifemale. . . ." Nonetheless, the book fills a crucial gap as a reference text for teenagers and others.

McCombie, Sharon L., ed. *Rape Crisis Intervention Handbook: A Guide for Victim Care.* New York: Plenum Publishing, 1980. 252 pp. ISBN 0-306-40401-X.

Sharon L. McCombie is the director of the Rape Crisis Intervention Program at Beth Israel Hospital in Boston, Massachusetts. She has compiled this handbook as a training resource for professionals who interact with rape victims and their families, basing it on clinical experience with over 600 victims of sexual assault, as well as on studies by counseling, legal, medical, and law enforcement professionals. In addition to offering an overview of crisis theory, the book covers the response process from the initial report of an attack through aftercare counseling, offering guidelines for crisis counseling of victims and their families, medical treatment, police investigation, and judicial preparation and process. The book further addresses the emotional and psychological ramifications rape has on the service provider, with a special section focusing on male professionals who interact with rape victims. The book is a valuable resource for all rape crisis professionals. It also serves to broaden their knowledge of other related professional areas.

McEvoy, Alan W., and Jeff B. Brookings. *If She Is Raped: A Book for Husbands, Fathers and Male Friends.* Homes Beach, FL: Learning Publications, 1984. 131 pp. Appendixes. ISBN 0-918452-71-6.

The title's specification of "husbands, fathers and male friends" is both misleading and sexist; the information contained in the book is pertinent to, and valuable for, all individuals affected by a loved one's rape, regardless of sex or relationship. The book attempts to assist secondary victims in understanding what the victim is likely to experience following the rape and to provide methods and strategies by which they can assist (and not hinder) the rape victim's recovery. It provides valuable information on personally coping with the rape of a loved one in a positive and constructive manner by identifying common reactions and suggesting appropriate ways in which to deal with them. Though the statistics and courtroom tactics cited are necessarily dated, the value of the book lies in its excellent guidelines for communication and dealing with the victim immediately following the assault and over the long term. Specific sections address rape trauma syndrome, post-rape sex, and the possible ramifications of acquaintance and interracial rape. Three appendixes contain illustrative case studies, a dated national listing of rape crisis centers, and a limited bibliography of suggested readings.

Novacek, Jill, Robert Raskin, David Bahlinger, Linda Firth, and Suzan Rybicki. *Rape: Tulsa Women Speak Out.* Tulsa, OK: Tulsa Institute of Behavioral Sciences, 1993. 149 pp.

In June of 1992 the *New York Times* printed an article that declared Tulsa, Oklahoma, to be the United States' "most typical" city, as a result of a study conducted for *American Demographics* magazine. That description makes the information contained in *Rape: Tulsa Women Speak Out* all the more chilling. In the fall of 1992 the Tulsa Institute of Behavioral Sciences administered a survey of 980 adult women living in Tulsa. The survey contained three tracks: (1) women who had never been raped, (2) women who had been raped and had reported it to the police, and (3) women who had been raped and had not reported it to the police. All respondents were further questioned about how rape in the community affected their lives, about their knowledge and opinions on rape, and about their opinions on what they thought could be done to eliminate rape. The results are published in *Rape: Tulsa Women Speak Out.* The book covers a very wide range of specifics, including rape prevalence, victim demographics, victim relationship to the assailant, attack logistics, victim behavior during and after the assault (resistance, seeking medical treatment, reporting to the police, etc.), and the impact of the assault on the victim. The results of the study do much to debunk common societal myths about rape frequency and reporting, offender identity, and "who gets raped." (The "average" woman in the study was white, in her thirties, employed full time, married or living with a significant other, had at least one child, had attended at least some college, and had a family income of over $50,000. One in three of the respondents had been raped, 80 percent of them by someone they knew. Over 80 percent of the victims did not report the assault to the police, and only 20 percent had a medical/forensic examination.) The book is well organized and lavishly illustrated with charts and graphs. It is available directly from the Tulsa Institute of Behavioral Sciences. (Tulsa Institute of Behavioral Sciences, 1620 East 12th Street, Tulsa, OK 74120, (918) 586-4220.)

Novacek, Jill, Robert Raskin, Suzan Rybicki, David Bahlinger, and Linda Firth. *Anatomy of Rape: Tulsa Reported Rapes July*

1990–December 1991. Tulsa, OK: Tulsa Institute of Behavioral Sciences, 1993. 81 pp.

Anatomy of Rape is the culmination of a study conducted of 608 complete Tulsa Police Department files on rapes reported within an 18-month time period. The study was conducted by the Tulsa Institute of Behavioral Sciences with the intent of producing information and resultant procedures to assist police departments in monitoring rape in their jurisdictions and to assist women (through education) in protecting themselves from sexual assault. The study examined a number of specifics, including victim and assailant demographics and relationships, attack logistics, victim and assailant behavior during the assault, victim behavior after the assault, and the final police dispositions of reported rapes. Of particular interest is the study's examination of reported rapes that did not end in arrest and the role the rape victim frequently plays in that outcome. The book is well organized and profusely illustrated with charts and graphs. *Anatomy of Rape* provides an extensive look at sexual assault from the perspective of the police sex crimes unit of a major metropolitan area. Its sister publication, *Rape: Tulsa Women Speak Out* (reviewed below), provides a frightening look at the subject from the victim's perspective. Together, the books provide what may be the most comprehensive view of rape figures and behavior in contemporary America currently available. Both are available directly from the Tulsa Institute of Behavioral Sciences.

Roden, Marybeth, and Gail Abarbanal. *How It Happens: Understanding Sexual Abuse and Date Rape.* Santa Monica, CA: Rape Treatment Center, Santa Monica Hospital Medical Center, [1987], 1993. 37 pp.

How It Happens is a very well-written and concise manual, aimed primarily at a teenage audience. The booklet contains a great deal of valuable information that accurately identifies the nature and numerous forms of sexual abuse, sexual assault, and rape. The text utilizes realistic case examples and conveys information without preaching or condescending to its intended audience. Common myths and questions regarding rape are discussed in an intelligent and clear manner, and positive approaches to avoiding victimization are offered. *How It Happens* is realistic in its approach; it goes beyond the standard warnings to avoid alcohol and drugs, recognizes that some young people are likely to drink or use drugs regardless of any warnings, and offers solid suggestions on how to help prevent acquaintance rape in situations involving alcohol or drugs. One special section details common victim feelings and reactions after being raped, with the acknowledgment that not every victim reacts the same way. Another section identifies positive steps to take if the reader is raped, along with a clear rationale for each suggestion. Still another section provides very specific information and positive suggestions for helping a friend who has been sexually assaulted. An excellent layout format is used throughout the book, utilizing a varied, multicolored structure—colored highlighting, italics, boldface, and colored boxes of key information. Both authors have published several impressive articles and chapters that appear in other works. *How It Happens* is available at a very low cost directly from the Rape Treatment Center (see p. 134).

Rosenberg, Jean. *Fuel on the Fire: An Inquiry into "Pornography" and Sexual Aggression in a Free Society.* Orwell, VT: The Safer Society Press, 1989. 87 pp. Appendixes.

With *Fuel on the Fire,* Jean Rosenberg has created a well-crafted, solidly researched, and objective examination of the relationship of (what is loosely termed by society as) "pornography" and sexual violence. (Rather than *pornography,* she prefers to use the term, and offers six categories of, *sexual media.*) Rosenberg reviews major theories of feminists and findings of social science researchers, and adds to them the gathered findings and opinions of 20 major sex offender treatment specialists. The result is a very concise and readable work that does not offer simplistic, cut-and-dried answers. Rosenberg acknowledges that the subject area of pornography is by definition a gray area and realistically seeks to present the strongest indications of its effect, rather than seizing on any one finding or hypothesis as "proof." The title of the book refers to the general consensus of researchers and treatment providers: pornography does not in and of itself cause sexual violence, but it may serve to influence those individuals who are predisposed to sexual violence. In other words, pornography may stimulate existing interests and inclinations, thus "adding fuel to the fire."

Smith, Susan E. *Fear or Freedom: A Woman's Options in Social Survival and Physical Defense.* Racine, WI: Mother Courage Press, 1986. 212 pp. ISBN 0-941300-03-X.

The tone and intent of this book is made clear with its opening quotation from Susan B. Anthony: "Woman must not depend on the protection of man but must be taught to defend herself." *Fear or Freedom* is a powerful self-defense manual containing the usual assortment of tips and techniques of physical resistance, but it is also an excellent social and psychological study of the dynamics of sexual assault. Susan E. Smith, herself a martial artist and founder of the White Lotus system of self-defense, has written a book designed to counteract "victim mentality." The book has been divided into seven chapters, each well footnoted and with additional references. In the first chapter, Smith elaborates on her personal philosophy of self-defense as a positive means of personal growth. She seeks to empower women by focusing on their inherent strengths and abilities, options, and self-worth. She urges women to "claim (their) rights as a human being." Self-defense is considered a matter of attitude, not simply an "external set of reactions." In the second chapter, Smith addresses 17 common myths about rape and self-defense and responds from a feminist perspective, supported by numerous cited studies. The third chapter highlights the results of an informal four-part survey Smith conducted, focusing on known assailant and stranger attacks, successful resistance options and dynamics, and the dynamics of the assault itself. In this excellent chapter, Smith identifies factors that work to the advantage of the assailant. She then shows how such dynamics can actually be used to the victim's advantage in many cases. The fourth chapter is on attack deterrents. It covers a broad spectrum of social behavior that can eliminate a threat before it becomes a physical reality, and it offers excellent guidelines for communication in professional and social situations. A section on home security is extensive and replete with clear illustrations of simple security modifications. The fifth chapter explores degrees of threat and degrees of resistance, charting the levels and progressions of each. The sixth chapter is devoted to self-defense techniques, covering target areas, physical weapons, strategies, and specific techniques. The physical techniques presented are basic, effective, and clearly illustrated for learning and practice. The final chapter deals with last-resort techniques—techniques that are designed to incapacitate the assailant. The author accomplishes her goal; Smith shows positive steps a woman can take to make herself less vulnerable to attack and to empower herself to avoid or deal with an assault.

Stringer, Gayle M., and Deanna Rants-Rodriguez. *So What's It to Me? Sexual Assault Information for Guys.* Renton, WA: King County Sexual Assault Resource Center, 1989. 35 pp. ISBN 0-94195305-X.

The intention of *So What's It to Me?* is to provide teenage males with information on sexual assault and to challenge those males to examine their beliefs, values, and actions relating to both sexual assault and harassment. Unlike similar works, the booklet addresses its male readers as both potential perpetrators and victims, in a manner that is straightforward and realistic with no trace of condescension. The first two-thirds of *So What's It to Me?* covers the effects of social conditioning on adopted behavior, nonsexist communication alternatives and the need for effective communication with others, the nature of sexual harassment and assault, and facts regarding sexual assault. The last third speaks directly to cases of males being sexually assaulted by other males and explores possible actions prior to and following such an assault. The scenarios presented are realistic and identifiable; heterosexual teenage males will recognize that they are potential victims too. While the authors have made use of the same type of varied type, handwriting, cartoons, poster-style pages, stories, and quizzes found in another King County Sexual Assault Resource Center (KCSARC) publication for teenagers, *Top Secret* (see above), they have greatly improved upon the earlier model. The booklet is sufficiently eye-catching and effective in its conveyance of information, without danger of visual overload. *So What's It to Me?* answers its title question in a very impressive manner.

Sussman, Lee, and Sally Bordwell. *The Rapist File: Interviews with Convicted Rapists.* New York: Chelsea House, 1981. 215 pp. Appendix. ISBN 0-87754-094-2.

Lee Sussman and Sally Bordwell, a Chicago area journalist and photographer-journalist respectively, interviewed 25 convicted rapists in an attempt to gain a more accurate picture of the rapists as human beings than that afforded by societal stereotype. They sought to gain understanding of the "workings of a rapist's mind" to be able to offer "fresh insights into the phenomenon of rape." Sussman and Bordwell interviewed rapists in three states from five prison facilities, including a prison in the swamps of Louisiana and a minimum-security facility in rural Illinois. From the 25 interviews, the authors chose 15 for inclusion in the book. There are a number of factors that prevent *The Rapist File* from being considered a "valid" study. The authors have no background in psychology. Names and prisoner numbers of convicted rapists were acquired by soliciting other prisoners to supply the information for money. The interviewed rapists were paid for their interview. (The authors report that the primary concerns of the rapists were confidentiality and how much they would be paid.) The interviews took place once, and they lasted between 30 and 60 minutes (the average interview was 45 minutes long). Only the "most interesting" stories were selected for the book. There was no indication by the authors of any follow-up on, or verification of, the rapists' stories. In fact, one of the interviewed rapists speculated that much of what is said by rapists about their crimes is a glorification of the actual events—a product of their own imagination. But while the book cannot be taken as a presentation of facts about rapists, it does have considerable value. Even with the recognition that much of the detail offered by the rapists may be macho fantasy, *The Rapist File* still speaks with their voice. It is a chilling voice, and does, in fact, offer a glimpse into the mind-set of the most predatory of criminals.

Tomaselli, Sylvana, and Roy Porter, eds. *Rape*. New York: Basil Blackwell, 1986. 292 pp. Index. ISBN 0-631-13748-3.

The authors have brought together the writings of 12 different academicians representing the disciplines of anthropology, art, biology, history, law, philosophy, and psychology in an attempt to examine and review rape "in the broadest perspective." The book is written with the intention of spurring other academicians to examine the nature and history of rape in their respective disciplines and, by doing so, to afford greater insight into the cause and (future) eradication of rape in contemporary society. The work of several of the authors serves to dispel commonly held opinions regarding the representation and meaning of rape in Greek myths and visual arts, while other writings challenge the notion of rape as a constant, rather than a variable, in society's history. Unfortunately, the book is written in "academese" for academicians and will be difficult reading for the lay reader.

Vachss, Alice. *Sex Crimes: Ten Years on the Front Lines Prosecuting Rapists and Confronting Their Collaborators*. New York: Random House. 1993. 284 pp. ISBN 0-679-42435-0.

Alice Vachss' book is a biographical summation of the decade she worked in the Queens County (New York) District Attorney's Office, specializing in sex crimes. She served as the head of the Special Victims Bureau from early 1985 to late 1991, when she was fired "in a political feud." The book is angry and aptly titled;

Vachss views the prosecution of rapists to be a war with two clearly delineated sides—hers and the rapists'. Anyone who does not completely align themselves with her views and objectives, who she feels is not making the ultimate effort to put rapists away in prison "for the count" (be they judges, prosecuting or defense attorneys, police officers, social workers, or jury members who acquit the defendant), runs the risk of being characterized a "rape collaborator." Vachss has no hesitancy in voicing her anger and bitterness. She declares that rapists are not sick, but are evil; that attorneys who find "common cause" with rapists are "simply worms"; that the only "viable treatment" for rapists is removal from the rest of society for long periods of time (possibly life). Vachss concludes her biography with a call for numerous legal reforms, beginning with a national declaration of war on rape. While some readers may be offended by Vachss' personal glorification and vilification of her "enemies," others may be heartened by her combative, black-and-white stance on rape and rapists. Readers who are able to view the book objectively will gain fascinating insight into some of the personal dynamics that can exist in the preparation and occurrence of a rape trial.

Warner, Carmen Germaine. *Rape and Sexual Assault: Management and Intervention.* Germantown, MD: Aspen, 1980. 364 pp. Index. ISBN 0-89443-172-2.

Carmen Germaine Warner has collected essays from 18 experts in a wide variety of fields, each covering a separate, practical aspect of dealing with sexual assault. The result is a comprehensive volume of use to anyone involved in victim management and therapeutic intervention. Some specific chapters cover the initial police response and investigation (with guidelines for dealing with male and female adults and minors); emergency room medical examination procedures for the adult female victim; examination procedures for the adult male victim; examination procedures for the female child; examination procedures for the heterosexual and homosexual accused rapist; rape and older women; intervention and management in cases of incest; the role of the victim advocate; basic legal process in rape cases, from the initial report through sentencing options; and models for community education and rape prevention, among other topics. The separation of rape victims and offenders into categories, rather than lumping their needs together, demonstrates the uniqueness and value of this book. The book is clearly organized and very readable, making the information accessible to the lay reader and professional alike.

Wedeen, Eve Loren. *When Kids Need Help.* Albuquerque, NM: New Mexico Coalition of Sexual Assault Programs. 1993. 14 pp.

Written and illustrated by Eve Loren Wedeen, *When Kids Need Help* is a coloring book that is included in the Child Sexual Abuse Protocol Packet distributed by the New Mexico Coalition of Sexual Assault Programs, Inc. (discussed in chapter 6). The protocol packet instructs the bearer to give the coloring book to the child to read before the examination (or to the accompanying, nonoffending adult if the child cannot read). The book immediately and continually validates the child's feelings, and it seeks to reassure the child of her or his safety, privacy, and rights. In a simple and straightforward manner, it strives to prepare the child for the immediate examination by describing the procedure in general terms and for possible future events such as numerous interviews or temporary housing at a shelter. The child is allowed to establish, through the medium of the coloring book, the vocabulary that will be used by the healthcare provider to describe parts of the body in the examination. While the illustrations are not polished or commercially slick, they do portray a number of ethnicities of both sexes in a variety of significant roles (parents, children, healthcare providers, police, etc.) and provide enough variety to allow the child to pleasurably pass time in the waiting room. A red crayon in a mechanical pencil is attached to the book; healthcare centers and/or advocates would do well to provide additional crayons. Copies of *When Kids Need Help* are available directly from the coalition, and the author has generously given her permission for anyone to copy the book in its entirety, provided acknowledgment is made of the author and the coalition.

Wong, Debbie, and Scott Wittet. *Be Aware. Be Safe.* Renton, WA: King County Sexual Assault Resource Center, 1987. 34 pp. Glossary. ISBN 0-941953-08-4.

This unique booklet is designed specifically for Southeast Asian teenagers, ages 12 to 19. Parts of the booklet were adapted from another King County Sexual Assault Resource Center (KCSARC) publication, *Top Secret: Sexual Assault Information for Teenagers Only* by Jennifer Fay and Billie Jo Flerchinger (reviewed above). Through the use of realistic stories of sexual assault, text, quizzes, and exercises, the booklet conveys important information about the nature, source, ramifications, and prevention of sexual assault in a manner that is culturally relevant for the reader. The book is in English, but it concludes with a glossary of important terms listed in Vietnamese, Khmer, Lao, Chinese, and English.

Wong, Debbie, and Scott Wittet, et al. *Helping Your Child To Be Safe.* Renton, WA: King County Sexual Assault Resource Center, 1987. 40 pp. Glossary. ISBN 0-941953-04-1 (Cambodian/Lao), 0-941953-07-6 (Chinese/Vietnamese).

This important booklet is designed for Southeast Asian parents of children ages 2 to 19. It takes much of the information contained in *Be Aware. Be Safe.* (reviewed above) and presents it, along with additional information, from a parent's perspective. In addition to addressing the nature, source, and ramifications of sexual assault, the booklet identifies specific ways parents can help protect their children, signs of sexual abuse, and actions they should take if abuse is suspected. *Helping Your Child To Be Safe* acknowledges the difficulties parents may experience in talking with their children about sexual abuse and addresses those reservations in a sensitive, constructive manner. The booklet is available in two editions; booklet #7A is written in English, Cambodian, and Lao; while booklet #7B is in English, Vietnamese, and Chinese. Both editions are extensively illustrated and contain a glossary that defines six key terms.

Films and Videos

Be Aware. Be Safe.
Type: 1/2″ video
Length: 18 minutes
Date: 1988
Cost: Purchase $100 (complete training package—
             video and activity guide)
Source: King County Sexual Assault Resource Center
             P.O. Box 300
             Renton, WA 98057
             (206) 226-5062

The video of *Be Aware. Be Safe.* is part of a training package of the same name designed specifically for Southeast Asian teenagers. While the video is in English, it features a cast of volunteer actors composed almost entirely of Southeast Asians. The video is designed to be used in conjunction with the presenter's guidebook, and it has several stopping points for group discussion. The goal of the film is to present information about sexual assault and its nature and prevention, in the context of Asian cultural values. The video presents scenarios of three types of assaults: (1) an attempted abduction by someone slightly known to the victim, (2) an assault by an acquaintance at a party, and (3) incest by the victim's uncle. While the accompanying presenter's guide does an excellent job of targeting and addressing the cultural-specific concerns of a particularly vulnerable segment of American society, the video has several weaknesses that may limit its effectiveness among its intended audience of 12- to 19-year-olds. While the central characters are generally well portrayed, the extras and supporting cast in the party and incest sections are clearly not actors, and they tend to disrupt the viewer's suspension of disbelief with their performances. The abduction vignette moves swiftly and effectively, but the party vignette suffers greatly from a lack of judicious editing. While the booklet *Be Aware. Be Safe.* (see Print Resources) portrays a dating situation in which the victim is raped, the video version has much less impact. The party is extremely conservative: at least two adult chaperones and many young children are present, and there is no indication of alcohol or drugs being used. The victim steps out the back door to get some air with her acquaintance. The young man attempts to kiss her neck twice, she tells him "no" firmly, pushes him away, and runs back inside. The young man remains outside the house while the victim tells a girlfriend inside of the assault. The incest vignette builds tension well, but lacks believability and closure in its resolution. The video establishes that the victim is abused by her uncle numerous times before her mother begins to realize that something is wrong. The victim is shown to begin to tell her mother ("Uncle Hang said he would punish me. . . ."), but the film then jumps to the mother telling the victim that it was right to have told her. The action jumps again to the mother alluding to the abuse to the father ("She told me everything about what Hang did to her."), and urging that he see a counselor to help him feel better. The vignette ends there. While the booklet describes the legal and familial ramifications of the attack and the assailant is given the option of counseling or jail, the video does not address post-attack realities at all. Despite its weaknesses, the video does contain valuable suggestions for rape prevention, and the accompanying guide provides excellent information, suggestions, and activities for educators addressing the targeted ethnic group. The same video, with slight modifications in narration, is included in *Helping Your Child To Be Safe: A Training Package for Southeast Asian Parents.*

Beyond Rape: Seeking an End to Sexual Assault

Type:	1/2″, 3/4″ video (product # WC01 VHS)
Length:	30 minutes
Date:	1983
Cost:	Purchase $59
Source:	MTI Film & Video
	420 Academy Drive
	Northbrook, IL 60062
	(800) 777-2400

Beyond Rape is designed to educate and raise the awareness of the viewer about the realities of sexual assault and abuse. Through the use of narration, rape and child sexual abuse survivor group discussion, and interviews, the film is successful in addressing a surprising amount of information, cultural theories, and societal myths. While technically marketed for various rape treatment, response, and prevention agencies, the film will best serve as a powerful introduction of the subject to audience groups not already involved professionally in the area of sexual violence, such as students, educators, women's groups, and the like. Technically the film appears somewhat dated, but the relevancy of the content easily overcomes any shifting of style. Unfortunately, there are times when the film works against itself in its manner of presentation. The narration is occasionally upstaged by the ongoing sound of the group sessions (which are extremely powerful in their own right) and by what is being visually presented, particularly in the section showing advertisements and record and magazine covers that glamourize sexual violence. The film opens and closes with an extremely powerful performance of the song "Fight Back," by Holly Near. *Beyond Rape* calls upon the viewer to accept a personal responsibility for sexual violence existing in society and to actively combat it.

Blackbird Fly

Type:	1/2″, 3/4″ video (product # 6543M VHS)
Length:	27 minutes
Date:	1990
Cost:	Purchase $375; rental $75

Source: MTI Film & Video
420 Academy Drive
Northbrook, IL 60062
(800) 777-2400

Blackbird Fly is a brief treatment of child sexual abuse, targeted to intermediate through high school students, guidance departments, parent/teacher organizations, and social service agencies. Based on the short story "Time To Care" by Ashley Tyler and Holle Robertson, the film was written and directed by Tyler and produced by Tyler and Robertson. The story focuses on the plight of Carin (Rain Pryor), a sweet, talented, and intelligent teenager from a middle-class family, whose widowed father (Garrett Morris) routinely abuses her sexually. Through the assistance and support of an adult friend (Whoopi Goldberg), Carin is able to confront her father and break the cycle of abuse. The film concludes with Carin's father seeking help from a professional counselor (Esther Rolle). Despite powerful performances from a stellar cast, the film's effectiveness in convincing a sexually abused adolescent to come forward is questionable. Several problems in the plot serve to seriously undermine the film's noble intentions. The protagonist is portrayed as personally recognizing, publically acknowledging, and physically breaking a pattern of incest that has existed most of her life, all in a matter of minutes. In real life, such actions can take many years to accomplish. The father's sudden recognition of himself as a child abuser and his immediate repentance is rather incredulous, despite Garrett Morris' considerable acting finesse. There is no indication given of any legal ramifications of the actions of the father (especially pertinent as the victim, as well as the target audience of seventh- to twelfth-graders, appears to be a minor). There is never any indication of any present or future action by the police or court system. Sadly, the conclusion of the film could well serve to disturb and frighten current abuse victims into remaining silent: the father shows up to get counseling at the very children's facility where Carin has sought help, thereby violating any sense of sanctuary for victims. Though a very timely and laudable effort, the film has sacrificed too much in its brevity, and it could ultimately do more harm than good by its simplistic presentation and pat answers. A brief discussion guide includes a synopsis, the film's objectives, questions for before and after viewing discussion, and a listing of child abuse hotlines, agencies, and organizations.

Campus Rape

Type:	1/2″ video
Length:	20 minutes
Date:	1990
Cost:	Purchase $50
Source:	Rape Treatment Center
	Santa Monica Hospital Medical Center
	1250 16th Street
	Santa Monica, CA 90404
	(213) 319-4000

This documentary-style video features Susan Dey and Corbin Bernsen as narrators, with a brief appearance and comments by Kelly McGillis (herself a rape victim). The video addresses the causes and impact of campus rape, using interviews with two victims of stranger rape and two victims of acquaintance rape, as well as family members and friends directly affected by the rape. *Campus Rape* does not rely on Hollywood flash; there is no soundtrack, the interviews of victims take place in a simple room, and the narration is outside on a college campus. It addresses key issues of communication, attitudes, and stereotypes regarding rape, and it presents a few means for preventing stranger and acquaintance rape in a college environment. Simple, compact, and effective, the video will be of particular value when used in college orientation sessions. The accompanying ten-page discussion guide is equally clear and concise.

Child Sexual Abuse: A Solution

Type:	1/2″ video, audio filmstrip
Length:	11–15 minutes
Date:	1985
Cost:	Purchase $249 (video or filmstrip)
Source:	James Stanfield Company, Inc.
	P.O. Box 41058
	Santa Barbara, CA 93140
	(805) 897-1185
	FAX (805) 897-1187

Child Sexual Abuse: A Solution consists of a six-part prevention program targeted at parents (one videotape), teachers (two videotapes), and children in grades K–2, 2–4, and 5–6 (one videotape each). The program consists of filmstrip slides with narration and music; the videos are simply the filmstrips on tape. The slides used are clear, well edited, and relevant to and supportive of the narration. The soundtrack is supportive without being intrusive, and the narration is clear and concise. The programs for grades K–2 and 2–4 utilize a well-illustrated, cartoon fantasy story called "Chester the Cat: A Most Unusual Tale" to effectively address the issue of unwanted touching in a very nonthreatening way. The viewer watches Chester become empowered through the realization that his body is his own and that he has the right to decide who touches it. Chester reiterates that message several times directly to the viewer, both verbally and in writing. The video for K–2 is divided into two parts to allow parents to discuss the first part with their children. The second part introduces Chester's "human friends," who tell of their experiences with unwanted touching. The incidents range from teasing by a peer to attempted abuse by a babysitter and a mother's boyfriend. The response behavior modeled (and reiterated throughout the film) is saying "no" in an "important voice," leaving if possible, and telling someone about the incident. The film emphasizes that if the child cannot say "no," or is tricked into abusive behavior, it is not the child's fault. The video for grades 2–4 is basically the same as the one for K–2, but with no break following the illustrated story, a couple of different scenarios, and older children in the slides. The video for grades 5–6 does not use Chester; is narrated by children; identifies the nature and prevalence of sexual abuse; acknowledges and validates the difficulty children have in talking about abuse; offers additional scenarios of abuse; acknowledges and addresses the possibility that the abused child will not be believed initially; and provides the elaborated response model of saying "no" (in a "firm" voice), leaving if possible, telling someone, and continuing to tell others if not initially believed. The program for parents states the realities of the prevalence and nature of child sexual abuse and abusers and effectively dispels common myths. It identifies specific ways in which parents can both help children protect themselves from abuse and maintain communication with their child if abuse does occur. The film identifies common symptoms of child abuse, and presents a model (developed by Cordelia Anderson and the Illusion Theatre Company—see chapters 4 and 6) for dealing with an abused child. The two videos for teachers cover the same information as the video for parents, with additional attention paid to the ethical and legal responsibilities of teachers for reporting suspected child abuse. The videos attempt to address common concerns of teachers, such as possible parental reactions to teaching about sexual abuse, legal ramifications of reporting and not reporting, and the possible ramifications of an unfounded report. The program is not without its flaws. The modeled behavior of the victim and the portrayed reaction of the offender does not deal with the reality that simply saying "no" does not always stop the assault. As a result, the program could create a false sense of security. With the exception of one female babysitter presented in the film for grades K–2, all the offenders portrayed are male. While statistics do indeed indicate that an overwhelming percentage of child molesters are male, it is also believed by professionals in the field that the actual percentage of female offenders is much higher than statistics suggest. Women are most often in the traditional role of caretakers and as such are in a much better position to molest children under perceived "legitimate" circumstances (such as bathing) than are men. Again, the picture painted could lead to a false sense of security. The legal ramifications of the crime of child sexual abuse is addressed on a limited basis in the videos for teachers and omitted entirely from the other videos. Important questions regarding the potential reaction of both children and parents to the presentation of information about child sexual abuse are answered in a brief and relatively simplistic manner. While the program as a whole is commendable, these several shortcomings may reduce its effectiveness. Potential buyers would do well to preview the program to determine if it meets their needs.

Child Sexual Abuse: What Your Children Should Know (series)

Type: 1/2″, 3/4″ video, 16mm film
Length: 30–90 minutes
Date: 1983
Cost: Purchase $150–$340 (video); rental $25–$45 (video)
Source: Indiana University
            Audio-Visual Center
            Bloomington, IN 47405
            (812) 335-8087

The *Child Sexual Abuse* series consists of four programs geared toward a specific audience: parents, grades K–3, grades 4–7, and senior high students. Hosted by Mike Farrell, the series draws on the knowledge and ability of experts to address each specific audience about the nature and prevention of child sexual abuse. The program for parents (though it is valuable for any adult who deals with children) makes use of a panel discussion format (featuring Cordelia Anderson, formerly of the Illusion Theatre—see chapters 4 and 6) to address the nature and prevalence of the problem, the reasons why child sexual abuse is such a "hidden" crime, symptoms and patterns indicative of abuse, as well as steps the viewer can take to prevent it. The program is clear and direct and, through a studio audience, responds to a number of questions likely to be asked by a viewer (including identification of the line between exploitation and legitimate touching). The programs for grades K–3 and 4–7 feature a filmed classroom discussion led by Mary Ellen Stone of the King County Sexual Assault Resource Center (KCSARC) (see chapter 6). Stone identifies positive and negative types of touching, validates the sovereignty of each individual's body, identifies warning signs of impending sexual abuse, and utilizes "what if?" questions and storytelling to help identify appropriate responses for children to make in an abuse situation. The format of both programs provides an excellent opportunity for parents watching to pause the video and discuss the questions raised with their own children. Both programs do a fine job of presenting the subject matter in a serious but nonthreatening manner that is appropriate to each age group. The program for senior high students utilizes a seminar-like discussion led by Billie Jo Flerchinger, formerly of KCSARC. Flerchinger helps the students identify the nature of sexual assault, contributing factors and warning signs of a potential sexual assault situation, and means to minimize risk of assault. Despite its production date, the series remains timely and effective.

Date Rape: Violence between Friends
Type: 1/2″, 3/4″ video (product #87-909-954)
Length: 20 minutes
Date: 1991
Cost: Purchase $66
Source: SRA (a division of Macmillan/McGraw-Hill)
             P.O. Box 543
             Blacklick, OH 43004-0543
             (800) 843-8855

This brief video uses testimony from two college-age female survivors of date rape, along with comments from the director of a rape crisis intervention program, to illustrate and address the dynamics, ramifications, and possible means of preventing date rape. The video attempts to touch on a little bit of everything, and at times paints with too large a brush. Statistics are presented ("one out of three women are raped," "one out of four college women surveyed were raped," "one out of four college men surveyed had attempted to force sex to the point that the victim cried or fought back") without any specific studies identified. Three major myths about rape are identified ("women want to be raped," "men rape because they cannot control their desires," and "women commonly make false accusations") and are attributed to societal conditioning of children ("boys are taught to be tough, with macho sports players as their heros," "girls are taught to be polite and passive, and to please men"). Television, films, and advertising are charged with reinforcing such conditioning. Sound advice is presented on ways to prevent a date rape from evolving, as well as what to do if a rape does occur. The film's combination of staged photos with live interviews is somewhat distracting; the live interviews are generally very effective and unforced. A teacher's guide supplies discussion questions, a review quiz, and an annotated bibliography.

Dating, Sex, and Trouble
Type:	1/2″ video (product # 2336-03)
Length:	25 minutes
Date:	1990
Cost:	Purchase $169; rental $75 (per week)
Source:	Sunburst Communications, Inc.
	39 Washington Avenue
	P.O. Box 40
	Pleasantville, NY 10570-2838
	(914) 769-5030
	(800) 431-1934

Sunburst Communications specializes in educational videos for grades K–12. *Dating, Sex, and Trouble* is part of their Sex Education series, and it is targeted at teenagers. Narrated by a young teenage couple, the video utilizes interviews with three teenage date rape victims and the comments of a male psychologist, a female counselor, and several male and female teenagers. The video defines date rape as an act of violence that uses sex as a disguise, identifies numerous factors that can contribute to its occurrence (peer pressure, societal myths and stereotypes, alcohol, etc.), and touches on the ramifications of rape. It provides several suggestions on how to prevent a sexual assault from developing and what to do if one does occur. Unfortunately, the film suffers from a lack of immediacy and reality for its intended audience, and it is unlikely to have any real impact on the majority of contemporary teenagers. Both the victims and potential offenders speak of a hypothetical future or a relatively removed past. The film does not capitalize on the notion of appearances being deceiving; the characters all look like stereotypes of the girl/boy next door. There is too little shown that the intended audience can identify with; the couples in the video look like they are going to a church youth group and do not even hold hands. This distance from reality extends to the script itself; there is no information conveyed on what the victim should *not* do following an assault (douche, wash, change clothes, etc.). While it is stated that rape is a felony crime, the only actual case that the video reports is the conviction of a rapist for statutory rape. The potential legal ramifications of rape—arrest, conviction, and prison—are only mentioned and not portrayed. Despite a fine job by the two young narrators, the film's lack of impact will allow the subject matter to be too easily forgotten by its audience. The accompanying teacher's guide contains six very general learning objectives, discussion questions, suggested activities, a dated reading list, and the script of the video.

"Friends" Raping Friends: Strategies for Prevention

Type:	1/2″ video (product #96400VS)
Length:	36 minutes
Date:	1991
Cost:	Purchase $189; rental $40 (per week)
Source:	Human Relations Media
	175 Tompkins Avenue
	Pleasantville, NY 10570
	(800) 431-2050
	FAX (914) 747-0839

The stated objective of *"Friends" Raping Friends* is to educate the viewer on how to prevent date rape. To that end the video attempts to examine the social conditioning and dynamics that promote date rape, and it suggests warning signs and preventative measures women can observe.

The format used is a television interview show, with a facilitator interviewing a date rape expert. Dramatizations of sexual assaults, monologues of actors portraying the victim and attacker, and group interviews with male and female students on campus seek to supply additional insight and emotional impact. While the interview with the expert does provide much good information, the dramatizations, monologues, and group interviews are largely ineffective and may serve to distance some viewers. The dramatizations are shot in black and white to increase their "edge," but through editing and portrayal they fail to capture a realistic feel of an actual attack's violence. The monologues of the "victims" are generally believable; the point-of-view monologues of the "rapists" contain too many obvious clichés, thereby lessening the male viewer's ability to relate. Some of the comments of the students may serve to offend the viewers; speaking of a friend who was raped after she had passed out, one student said "you feel sorry for her, but it's also her fault—she shouldn't have been drinking." While acknowledging the man's responsibility in a date rape situation, the video's main emphasis is on what the woman can do to prevent rape. The film is suggested for grades 8 through college, but the teacher's guide contains review and discussion questions, as well as research and related activities suggestions that may be too advanced for the younger viewers. The excellent works listed in the bibliography of the guide are definitely for upper-level readers.

No Means No: Understanding Acquaintance Rape

Type:	1/2″ video (product #93100VS)
Length:	32 minutes
Date:	1991
Cost:	Purchase $189; rental $40 (per week)
Source:	Human Relations Media
	175 Tompkins Avenue
	Pleasantville, NY 10570
	(800) 431-2050
	FAX (914) 747-0839

This award-winning video is quite deserving of the "five-star" rating it received from the *Video Rating Guide for Libraries*. Though Human Relations Media is gearing the video toward grades 9 through 12, its content and manner of presentation make it very appropriate for adults of all ages as well. Through the use of discussion groups of young female and male adults, rape survivors' reflections, and comments of professionals working in the arena, a clear and realistic picture of many of the facets of date/acquaintance rape is presented. The social and legal aspects of acquaintance rape are addressed in a straightforward manner. The difficulties and dangers presented by and inherent in ambiguous communication on a date are discussed by young college students of both sexes. A district attorney frankly acknowledges the difficulties of prosecuting acquaintance rape, while a defense attorney expresses the belief that rape charges are "a tremendous tool for a vendetta." The rape survivors discuss the psychological impact of rape, including the ramifications of reporting or not reporting the rape. The most powerful (and often chilling) aspect of the video is its incorporation of a mock rape trial, based on an actual acquaintance rape that was never brought to trial. The judge, defense and prosecuting attorneys, and court officials are real, as is the jury selected from the jurors pool of Jefferson Parrish, Louisiana. No aspect of the trial was staged or rehearsed. Viewers hear portions of the witness examination and the prosecutor's summation, as well as the jury's deliberations. The spontaneous—and often quite heated—discussion of the actual jurors has tremendous impact; the opinions of the jurors range from one extreme to the other. One juror goes so far as to state his belief that after a certain point the woman ". . . doesn't have the right to say 'no.' If she went too far, she's lost that right." Such flashes of personal honesty as exhibited by the jurors and the survivors do much to remove the issues addressed in *No Means No* from the theoretical and ground them in current reality. The accompanying 23-page teacher's guide contains adequate learning objectives and review questions, but the 21 discussion questions are so obvious and leading that they are ineffective. The guide also contains a brief bibliography that lists several magazine articles from the early 1990s.

Self Defense Seminar

Type: 1/2″ video
Length: 45 minutes
Date: 1993
Cost: Free, but $4.75 to cover shipping and materials
Source: S. K. Productions
P.O. Box 290206
Wethersfield, CT 06129-0206

This video is a rough condensation of a ten-hour self-defense seminar conducted for mothers and daughters by Master Sang H. Kim. The camera was hand-held, the editing is uneven, and the picture and audio quality are fair to poor much of the time. The tape, however, provides an excellent introduction to general options available to women for preventing and resisting physical assault. Topics touched on in the tape include assault prevention and personal awareness, effective escape techniques, use of environmental weapons, and personal empowerment. Master Kim is very personable; he presents the material in a manner that is nonintimidating and reassuring to the viewer/participant. While not an instructional video, the tape is a very effective resource for rape discussion groups, seminars, and programs. S. K. Productions is making the film available to interested groups free as a public service.

Teenage Sex: Resisting the Pressure

Type:	1/2″ video (product # 239303)
Length:	29 minutes
Date:	1992
Cost:	Purchase $189; rental $75 (per week)
Source:	Sunburst Communications, Inc.
	39 Washington Avenue
	P.O. Box 40
	Pleasantville, NY 10570-2838
	(914) 769-5030
	(800) 431-1934

Teenagers are in an extremely high-risk group for becoming victims of rape. While *Teenage Sex* does not specifically address date or acquaintance rape, it does contain much valuable information that can aid young women and men in avoiding or diffusing situations that could lead to rape. Targeted at adolescents in grades 7–12, this well-made video is divided into two parts: "Setting Limits" and "Being Assertive." Both sections make use of narrating male and female "teen magazine columnists," along with vignettes of teenagers in pressure situations, to impart information. The first section emphasizes the need for teens to examine their feelings about sexual activity, and to establish clear limits of behavior, prior to finding themselves in a sexual situation. Emphasis is placed on the individual's personal rights to determine their own behavior, while highlighting the dangers of waiting until sex is imminent to decide what they want. The editorial bias is clearly toward abstinence, but the manner is not so didactic as to offend sexually active viewers. Various suggestions are offered to help the viewers determine what is right for themselves. The second section is a mini-course in assertiveness training. It presents basic assertiveness techniques in the context of believable scenarios and demonstrates the manner of and need for effective communication. The application of these techniques can do much to prevent individuals from being manipulated into unwanted sex. The video very effectively addresses and debunks frequently heard lines and myths used to pressure individuals into sex. The accompanying teacher's guide contains excellent discussion questions, suggested activities, and guidelines for role-playing, as well as an annotated bibliography and the video script.

A Time To Tell: Teen Sexual Abuse

Type:	1/2″, 3/4″ video (product #68629 VHS)
Length:	18 minutes
Date:	1990
Cost:	Purchase $295; rental $75
Source:	MTI Film & Video
	420 Academy Drive
	Northbrook, IL 60062
	(800) 777-2400

Produced by Disney Educational Productions, *A Time To Tell* is designed to promote and facilitate discussion among teenage groups regarding date rape and incest. The video features young actors in a support group setting, and it traces the development of an attempted date rape through narration and flashbacks. The date rape portion of the film is effective in depicting the dynamics that can lead to (and accordingly warn of) such an attack. The second portion of the film, dealing with incest, is much less effective. Unlike the date rape portion, there is no depiction of an actual assault or portrayal of the dynamics that create an ongoing incestuous relationship. Lip service is paid to the abuser's method of manipulation, but without significant impact. The film encourages victims to speak of their experiences and seek counseling. The brief discussion guide provides good questions for group discussions prior to and following viewing the video.

War Zone

Type:	1/2″ video
Length:	13 minutes
Date:	1992
Cost:	Contact source
Source:	Film Fatale
	121 St. Marks Place, Suite 9
	New York, NY 10009
	(212) 260-5774

War Zone is an attempt by filmmaker Maggie Hadleigh-West to document sexual harassment and aggression on the streets of New York City. For seven and one-half hours in the summer of 1991, Hadleigh-West walked the streets of her neighborhood with a Super 8 camera in hand, followed and filmed by a cameraman. As she encountered 112 incidents of what she terms "street abuse," she immediately began filming the perpetrator with her camera. The cameraman following captured the entire exchange. The film blends black-and-white footage from both cameras with a soundtrack consisting of street sounds, narration by Hadleigh-West, vocal sound effects, and aggressive remarks read by third parties. Hadleigh-West eloquently describes the loss of power women experience as a result of street abuse, and effectively addresses the ramifications of that abuse. Several viewings of the film are necessary to gain the full value and impact of it; there is an overload of information and stimuli coming at the viewer simultaneously. Much of the narration directly speaks to the relationship between sexual harassment and sexual violence, but it is unfortunately lost amidst the rapid barrage of filmed encounters and sound effects. *War Zone* is an angry film. Hadleigh-West speaks of her filming as "an act of retaliation," and refers to her camera as "an unexpected tool for revenge." Such prevailing subjectivity weakens the overall impact of the work and opens the door for criticism of it as a valid documentary. Her ten definitions of street abuse range from verbal and physical threats to "unintentional degradation through ignorance." The soundtrack does not permit the viewer to hear the perpetrator's comments, and Hadleigh-West included leers or stares alone in her criterion for filming. The most violent action shown in the film—a male "giving the finger"—is shown repeatedly, and it was clearly directed initially toward the cameraman following Hadleigh-West. When Hadleigh-West began filming the man, she fell subject to the obscene gesture as well. Despite its technical obstacles and lack of objectivity, *War Zone* does an excellent job of raising questions for self-examination of behavior, specifically that of men as aggressors and of women as conditioned recipients of aggression. A sequel is planned for release in late 1995, and will feature Hadleigh-West interviewing men who have leered or made comments to her immediately after the fact.

Whatever It Takes
Type: 1/2″ video
Length: 25 minutes

Date: 1994
Cost: Purchase $29.95 (wholesale rates available)
Source: Super Winning Attitude Team
               P.O. Box 23095
               Albuquerque, NM 87192-1095
               (505) 293-3295
               FAX (505) 293-5731

Within the context of a finite scope, *Whatever It Takes* is one of the stronger self-defense for women videotapes currently on the market. The nature of the scenarios is rather limited; the attacks portrayed are primarily the types that would occur in a stranger or battering-spouse assault. The intent of the video is to present and teach simple physical techniques that are designed to allow a woman to effect an escape from an assailant, and it is largely successful in doing so. The format of the instruction is consistent and clear. The instructor explains the attack scenario in detail: the theory behind the defensive techniques, the application of the techniques, and the follow-up response. The instructor frequently suggests mental associations (such as raising a hand in class or reaching forward to turn off a yard sprinkler that is on) to assist in learning the techniques. The instructor demonstrates the techniques and has a model student walk through them. The video then shows the model student executing the techniques at full speed, followed by a stop-action presentation that breaks down the elements of the defense. The ten scenarios portray the victim being grabbed, quickly responding with a short series of simple techniques, and running away. In 80 percent of the scenarios, the techniques presented are effective and easy to learn. The ninth scenario (being choked in a standing position from the front) is impractical and probably ineffective, and the tenth scenario (being charged from the front with the intent to tackle) requires sufficient warning of the assault and a matador-like response that would only be developed with lots of practice. The video makes good use of simple camera angles in teaching and demonstrating the techniques. The soundtrack and screen editing manipulations are unnecessarily intrusive. One of the strongest points of *Whatever It Takes* is its avoidance of a common error among self-defense materials—using a woman who is clearly a proficient martial artist and who is much more physically able than "Jane Doe." The result of using such a model is that viewers are intimidated by the dissimilarity of the actor's and their own physical capabilities and assume accordingly that they are unable to defend themselves. The student model used in *Whatever It*

Takes is a 45-year-old bookkeeper, who is clearly not a martial artist. Her demonstrated ability to learn and use the techniques validates the film's content. The end of the video acknowledges that there are many different ways to attack and defend, and that those portrayed are only a few specific defenses against specific attacks. Follow-up videos will address defenses against binding grabs and defenses from the ground.

Index